M000024135

# Eclipse 4 Plug-in Development by Example Beginner's Guide

How to develop, build, test, package, and release Eclipse plug-ins with features for Eclipse 3.x and Eclipse 4.x

**Dr Alex Blewitt**

[PACKT] open source*
PUBLISHING    community experience distilled

BIRMINGHAM - MUMBAI

# Eclipse 4 Plug-in Development by Example Beginner's Guide

Copyright © 2013 Packt Publishing

All rights reserved. No part of this book may be reproduced, stored in a retrieval system, or transmitted in any form or by any means, without the prior written permission of the publisher, except in the case of brief quotations embedded in critical articles or reviews.

Every effort has been made in the preparation of this book to ensure the accuracy of the information presented. However, the information contained in this book is sold without warranty, either express or implied. Neither the author, nor Packt Publishing, and its dealers and distributors will be held liable for any damages caused or alleged to be caused directly or indirectly by this book.

Packt Publishing has endeavored to provide trademark information about all of the companies and products mentioned in this book by the appropriate use of capitals. However, Packt Publishing cannot guarantee the accuracy of this information.

First published: June 2013

Production Reference: 1140613

Published by Packt Publishing Ltd.
Livery Place
35 Livery Street
Birmingham B3 2PB, UK.

ISBN 978-1-78216-032-8

www.packtpub.com

Cover Image by Asher Wishkerman (wishkerman@hotmail.com)

# Credits

**Author**

Dr Alex Blewitt

**Reviewers**

Ann Ford

Thomas Fletcher

Jeff MAURY

**Acquisition Editor**

Kartikey Pandey

**Lead Technical Editor**

Dayan Hyames

**Technical Editors**

Prasad Dalvi

Mausam Kothari

Worrell Lewis

Pushpak Poddar

Amit Ramadas

**Project Coordinator**

Arshad Sopariwala

**Proofreaders**

Linda Morris

Lindsey Thomas

**Indexers**

Hemangini Bari

Tejal R. Soni

**Production Coordinator**

Arvindkumar Gupta

**Cover Work**

Arvindkumar Gupta

# About the Author

**Dr Alex Blewitt** has been developing Java applications since Version 1.0 was released in 1996, and has been using the Eclipse platform since its first release as part of the IBM WebSphere Studio product suite. He even migrated some plugins from Visual Age for Java to WebSphere Studio/Eclipse as part of his PhD on Automated Verification of Design Patterns. He got involved in the open source community as a tester when Eclipse 2.1 was being released for Mac OS X, and then subsequently as an editor for EclipseZone, including being a finalist for Eclipse Ambassador in 2007.

More recently, Alex has been writing for InfoQ, covering generic Java and specifically, Eclipse and OSGi subjects. He keynoted the 2011 OSGi Community Event on the past, present, and future of OSGi. The coverage of both new releases of the Eclipse platform and its projects, as well as video interviews with some of the Eclipse project leads can be found via the InfoQ home page, for which he was nominated and won the Eclipse Top Contributor 2012 award.

Alex currently works for an investment bank in London. He also has a number of apps on the Apple AppStore through Bandlem Limited. When he's not working on technology, and if the weather is nice, he likes to go flying from the nearby Cranfield airport.

Alex writes regularly at his blog, `http://alblue.bandlem.com`, as well as tweets regularly from Twitter and App.Net as `@alblue`.

# Acknowledgement

I'd like to thank my wife Amy for supporting me during the development of this book, (particularly the late nights and weekends that were spent completing it), and indeed throughout our decade plus marriage. I'd also like to thank my parents, Derek and Ann, for installing a sense of independence and self-belief which has taken me many places in my lifetime. I hope that I can encourage a similar level of confidence and self-belief in my children, Sam and Holly.

Special thanks are due to Ann Ford, who provided detailed feedback about every chapter and the exercises therein. Without her diligence and attention, this book would contain many more errors than I would like. Any remaining errors are my own. My thanks also go to the other reviewers of earlier draft chapters: Thomas Fletcher and Jeff Maury, for their comments and suggestions.

During the later stages of the book, I was also fortunate enough to receive some good feedback and advice from Paul Webster and Lars Vogel, both of whom are heavily involved in the Eclipse 4 platform. Their comments on the chapter on Eclipse 4 have measurably improved the content.

Finally, I'd like to thank OD, DJ, and JC for their support in making this book possible.

# About the Reviewers

**Ann Ford** is an experienced Eclipse plugin developer who has contributed significant portions of the Eclipse Technology Accessibility Tools Framework incubator project as a former committer. Having over 30 years of programming experience with IBM, she has worked on tools and components of OS/2, DB2, and the IBM JDK, with extensive experience in issues of usability, accessibility, and translation. Currently, she specializes in the design and development of GUIs for desktop applications and tools using Java Swing, Eclipse SWT, and JFace, with an eye towards mobile applications in the future.

**Thomas Fletcher** has worked in the field of real-time and embedded software development for more than 10 years and is a frequent presenter at industry conferences. He is a Technical Subject Matter Expert and Thought Leader on Embedded System Architecture and Design, Real-time Performance Analysis, Power Management, and High Availability.

Prior to Crank Software, Thomas directed QNX Software Systems' Tools Development Team. He was the Lead Architect for Multimedia, Team Leader of Core OS, and regularly engaged with sales and marketing as a result of his ability to bridge technology and customer needs.

Thomas is an active participant within the Eclipse Community. He was a committer with the C/C++ Development Tools (CDT) project and represented QNX on the Eclipse Architecture and the Multicore Association review boards.

Thomas holds a degree in Master of Computer Engineering from Carleton University, focusing on instrumentation and performance analysis of embedded systems, and a degree in Bachelor of Electrical Engineering from the University of Victoria.

**Jeff MAURY** is currently working as the technical lead for the Java team at SYSPERTEC, a French ISV offering mainframe integration tools.

Prior to SYSPERTEC, he co-founded in 1996 a French ISV called SCORT, precursor of the application server concept and offering J2EE-based integration tools.

He started his career in 1988 at MARBEN, a French integration company specialized in telecommunication protocols. At MARBEN, he started as a software developer and finished as X.400 team technical lead and Internet division strategist.

I would like to dedicate my work to Jean-Pierre ANSART, my mentor, and thank my wife Julia for her patience and my three sons Robinson, Paul, and Ugo.

# www.PacktPub.com

## Support files, eBooks, discount offers and more

You might want to visit www.PacktPub.com for support files and downloads related to your book.

Did you know that Packt offers eBook versions of every book published, with PDF and ePub files available? You can upgrade to the eBook version at www.PacktPub.com and as a print book customer, you are entitled to a discount on the eBook copy. Get in touch with us at service@packtpub.com for more details.

At www.PacktPub.com, you can also read a collection of free technical articles, sign up for a range of free newsletters and receive exclusive discounts and offers on Packt books and eBooks.

http://PacktLib.PacktPub.com

Do you need instant solutions to your IT questions? PacktLib is Packt's online digital book library. Here, you can access, read and search across Packt's entire library of books.

## Why Subscribe?

- Fully searchable across every book published by Packt
- Copy and paste, print and bookmark content
- On demand and accessible via web browser

## Free Access for Packt account holders

If you have an account with Packt at www.PacktPub.com, you can use this to access PacktLib today and view nine entirely free books. Simply use your login credentials for immediate access.

# Table of Contents

Preface                                                                      1

Chapter 1: Creating Your First Plug-in                                       7
   Getting started                                                           7
   Time for action – setting up the Eclipse SDK environment                  8
   Creating your first plug-in                                              11
   Time for action – creating a plug-in                                     11
   Running plug-ins                                                         15
   Time for action – launching Eclipse from within Eclipse                  15
   Debugging a plug-in                                                      18
   Time for action – debugging a plug-in                                    18
   Time for action – updating code in debugger                              22
   Debugging with step filters                                              23
   Time for action – setting up step filtering                              23
   Using different breakpoint types                                         25
   Time for action – breaking at method entry and exit                      25
   Using conditional breakpoints                                            26
   Time for action – setting a conditional breakpoint                       26
   Using exceptional breakpoints                                            28
   Time for action – catching exceptions                                    28
   Time for action – using watch variables and expressions                  31
   Summary                                                                  34

Chapter 2: Creating Views with SWT                                          35
   Creating views and widgets                                               35
   Time for action – creating a view                                        36
   Time for action – drawing a custom view                                  38
   Time for action – drawing a second hand                                  41

Time for action – animating the second hand     42
Time for action – running on the UI thread     43
Time for action – creating a reusable widget     45
Time for action – using layouts     47
Managing resources     50
Time for action – getting colorful     51
Time for action – finding the leak     52
Time for action – plugging the leak     54
Interacting with the user     56
Time for action – getting in focus     57
Time for action – responding to input     58
Using other SWT widgets     60
Time for action – adding items to the tray     60
Time for action – responding to the user     62
Time for action – modal and other effects     64
Time for action – groups and tab folders     66
Summary     73

**Chapter 3: Creating JFace Viewers**     **75**
Why JFace?     75
Creating TreeViewers     76
Time for action – creating a TreeViewer     76
Time for action – using Images in JFace     81
Time for action – styling label providers     84
Sorting and filtering     86
Time for action – sorting items in a viewer     87
Time for action – filtering items in a viewer     89
Interaction and properties     91
Time for action – adding a double-click listener     92
Time for action – showing properties     95
Tabular data     100
Time for action – viewing time zones in tables     100
Time for action – syncing selection     104
Summary     107

**Chapter 4: Interacting with the User**     **109**
Creating actions, commands, and handlers     109
Time for action – adding context menus     110
Time for action – creating commands and handlers     111
Time for action – binding commands to keys     114

Time for action – changing contexts                                         115
Time for action – enabling and disabling the menu's items                   118
Time for action – reusing expressions                                       120
Time for action – contributing commands to pop-up menus                     121
Jobs and progress                                                           124
Time for action – running operations in the background                      125
Time for action – reporting progress                                        127
Time for action – dealing with cancellation                                 128
Time for action – using subtasks and subprogress monitors                   129
Time for action – using null progress monitors and submonitors              131
Time for action – setting job properties                                    133
Reporting errors                                                            137
Time for action – showing errors                                            137
Summary                                                                     141

**Chapter 5: Storing Preferences and Settings**                             **143**
Storing preferences                                                         143
Time for action – persisting a value                                        144
Time for action – creating a preference page                                145
Time for action – creating warning and error messages                       147
Time for action – choosing from a list                                      148
Time for action – using a grid                                              150
Time for action – placing the preferences page                              151
Time for action – using other field editors                                 153
Time for action – adding keywords                                           154
Time for action: using IEclipsePreferences                                  156
Using IMemento and DialogSettings                                           157
Time for action – adding a memento for the Time Zone View                   158
Time for action – using DialogSettings                                      159
Summary                                                                     161

**Chapter 6: Working with Resources**                                       **163**
Using the workspace and resources                                           163
Time for action – creating an editor                                        164
Time for action – writing the markup parser                                 166
Time for action – building the builder                                      168
Time for action – iterating through resources                               170
Time for action – creating resources                                        173
Time for action – implementing incremental builds                           174

Time for action – handling deletion                                      175
Using natures                                                            178
Time for action – creating a nature                                      178
Using markers                                                            182
Time for action – error markers if the file is empty                     182
Time for action – registering a marker type                             184
Summary                                                                  186

**Chapter 7: Understanding the Eclipse 4 Model**                         187
Working with the Eclipse 4 model                                         188
Time for action – installing E4 tooling                                  188
Time for action – creating an E4 application                             190
Time for action – creating a part                                        195
Time for action – styling the UI with CSS                                200
Using services and contexts                                              206
Time for action – adding logging                                         206
Time for action – getting the window                                     208
Time for action – obtaining the selection                                209
Time for action – dealing with events                                    212
Time for action – calculating values on demand                           215
Time for action – using preferences                                      217
Time for action – interacting with the UI                                219
Using Commands, Handlers, and MenuItems                                  221
Time for action – wiring a menu to a command with a handler              221
Time for action – passing command parameters                             224
Time for action – creating a direct menu and keybindings                 226
Time for action – creating a pop-up menu and a view menu                 229
Creating custom injectable classes                                       232
Time for action – creating a simple service                              232
Time for action – injecting subtypes                                     233
Summary                                                                  235

**Chapter 8: Creating Features, Update Sites, Applications, and Products** 237
Grouping plug-ins with features                                          237
Time for action – creating a feature                                     238
Time for action – exporting a feature                                    240
Time for action – installing a feature                                   242
Time for action – categorizing the update site                           244
Time for action – depending on other features                            249
Time for action – branding features                                      250

| | |
|---|---|
| Building applications and products | 254 |
| Time for action – creating a headless application | 254 |
| Time for action – creating a product | 259 |
| Summary | 263 |
| **Chapter 9: Automated Testing of Plug-ins** | **265** |
| Using JUnit for automated testing | 265 |
| Time for action – writing a simple JUnit test case | 266 |
| Time for action – writing a plug-in test | 267 |
| Using SWTBot for user interface testing | 268 |
| Time for action – writing an SWTBot test | 268 |
| Time for action – working with menus | 271 |
| Working with SWTBot | 273 |
| Time for action – hiding the welcome screen | 273 |
| Time for action – avoiding SWTBot runtime errors | 274 |
| Working with views | 274 |
| Time for action – showing views | 275 |
| Time for action – interrogating views | 276 |
| Interacting with the UI | 277 |
| Time for action – getting values from the UI | 277 |
| Time for action – waiting for a condition | 278 |
| Summary | 281 |
| **Chapter 10: Automated Builds with Tycho** | **283** |
| Using Maven to build Eclipse plug-ins with Tycho | 283 |
| Time for action – installing Maven | 284 |
| Time for action – building with Tycho | 286 |
| Building features and update sites with Tycho | 289 |
| Time for action – creating a parent project | 289 |
| Time for action – building a feature | 292 |
| Time for action – building an update site | 293 |
| Time for action – building a product | 295 |
| Testing and releasing | 300 |
| Time for action – running automated tests | 300 |
| Time for action – changing the version numbers | 303 |
| Signing update sites | 305 |
| Time for action – creating a self-signed certificate | 305 |
| Time for action – signing the plug-ins | 307 |
| Time for action – serving an update site | 309 |
| Summary | 310 |

## Appendix: Pop Quiz Answers                                          311
Chapter 1, Creating Your First Plug-in                                 311
Chapter 2, Creating Views with SWT                                     312
Chapter 3, Creating JFace Viewers                                      314
Chapter 4, Interacting with the User                                   315
Chapter 5, Storing Preferences and Settings                            317
Chapter 6, Working with Resources                                      317
Chapter 7, Understanding the Eclipse 4 Model                           318
Chapter 8, Creating Features, Update Sites, Applications, and Products  320
Chapter 9, Automated Testing of Plug-ins                               320
Chapter 10, Automated Builds with Tycho                                321

## Index                                                               323

# Preface

This book provides a general introduction to developing plug-ins for the Eclipse platform. No prior experience, other than Java, is necessary to be able to follow the examples presented in this book. By the end of the book, you should be able to create an Eclipse plug-in from scratch, as well as be able to create an automated build of those plug-ins.

## What this book covers

*Chapter 1, Creating Your First Plug-in*, provides an overview of how to download Eclipse, set it up for plug-in development, create a sample plug-in, launch, and debug it.

*Chapter 2, Creating Views with SWT*, provides an overview of how to build views with SWT, along with other custom SWT components such as system trays and resource management.

*Chapter 3, Creating JFace Viewers*, discusses creating views with JFace using `TableViewers` and `TreeViewers`, along with integration with the properties view and user interaction.

*Chapter 4, Interacting with the User*, discusses using commands, handlers, and menus to interact with the user, as well as the `Jobs` and `Progress` APIs.

*Chapter 5, Storing Preferences and Settings*, tells how to store preference information persistently, as well as displaying it via the preferences pages.

*Chapter 6, Working with Resources*, teaches how to load and create `Resources` in the workbench, as well as how to create a builder and nature for automated processing.

*Chapter 7, Understanding the Eclipse 4 Model*, discusses the key differences between the Eclipse 3.x and Eclipse 4.x models, as well as how to migrate existing content to the new model.

*Chapter 8, Creating Features, Update Sites, Applications, and Products*, tells how to take the plug-ins created so far in this book, aggregate them into features, publish to update sites, and how applications and products are used to create standalone entities.

*Chapter 9, Automated Testing of Plug-ins*, teaches how to write automated tests that exercise Eclipse plug-ins, including both UI and non-UI components.

*Chapter 10, Automated builds with Tycho*, details how to build Eclipse plug-ins, features, update sites, applications, and products automatically with Maven Tycho.

# What you need for this book

To run the exercises for this book, you will need a computer with an up-to-date operating system (running Windows, Linux, or Mac OS X). Java also needs to be installed; JDK 1.7 is the current released version although the instructions should work for a newer version of Java as well.

This book has been tested with the Eclipse SDK (Classic/Standard) for Juno (4.2) and Kepler (4.3). Newer versions of Eclipse may also work. Care should be taken while installing Eclipse for RCP and RAP developers, as this will cause the applications created in *Chapter 7, Understanding the Eclipse 4 Model* and *Chapter 8, Creating Features, Update Sites, Applications, and Products*.

The first chapter explains how to get started with Eclipse, including how to obtain and install both Eclipse and Java.

# Who this book is for

This book is aimed at Java developers who are interested in learning how to create plug-ins, products, and applications for the Eclipse platform. The book starts with how to install and use Eclipse to build and debug plug-ins, covers different types of user interfaces, and finishes with how to create update sites and build and test plug-ins automatically.

This book will also be useful to those who already have some experience in building Eclipse plug-ins and want to know how to create automated builds using Maven Tycho, which has become the de-facto standard for building Eclipse plug-ins.

Finally, those Eclipse developers who are familiar with the Eclipse 3.x model but are interested in learning about the changes that the Eclipse 4.x model brings will find the information presented in *Chapter 7, Understanding the Eclipse 4 Model* a useful summary of what opportunities the new model provides.

☞ E4: In this book, both the Eclipse 3.x and Eclipse 4.x models are covered. The Eclipse 4 platform contains a backwards-compatible runtime for the Eclipse 3.x APIs. Where the Eclipse 3.x APIs differ from the Eclipse 4.x APIs, the icon ☞ E4 will be used to call out a difference. A full explanation of the Eclipse 4 concepts will be covered in *Chapter 7, Understanding the Eclipse 4 Model*; so the E4 notes can be skipped on the first reading if necessary.

If you are developing an Eclipse IDE-based plug-in, you should consider using the Eclipse 3.x APIs, as these will work in both older Eclipse instances, as well as newer ones. If you are developing an Eclipse RCP-based application and do not need to support older versions, consider building an Eclipse 4-based application. Future versions of the Eclipse platform (4.4/Luna and afterwards) will make it possible to use some of the Eclipse 4 APIs in the IDE.

# Conventions

In this book, you will find several headings appear frequently.

To give clear instructions of how to complete a procedure or task, we use:

## Time for action – heading

1. Action 1
2. Action 2
3. Action 3

Instructions often need some extra explanation so that they make sense, so they are followed with:

## What just happened?

This heading explains the working of tasks or instructions that you have just completed.

You will also find some other learning aids in the book, including:

## Pop quiz – heading

These are short multiple-choice questions intended to help you test your own understanding.

## Have a go hero – heading

These practical challenges give you ideas for experimenting with what you have learned.

You will also find a number of styles of text that distinguish between different kinds of information. Here are some examples of these styles, and an explanation of their meaning.

Code words in text are shown as follows: "You may notice that we used the Unix command rm to remove the Drush directory rather than the DOS del command."

A block of code is set as follows:

```
# * Fine Tuning
#
key_buffer = 16M
key_buffer_size = 32M
max_allowed_packet = 16M
thread_stack = 512K
thread_cache_size = 8
max_connections = 300
```

When we wish to draw your attention to a particular part of a code block, the relevant lines or items are set in bold:

```
# * Fine Tuning
#
key_buffer = 16M
key_buffer_size = 32M
max_allowed_packet = 16M
thread_stack = 512K
thread_cache_size = 8
max_connections = 300
```

Any command-line input or output is written as follows:

```
cd /ProgramData/Propeople

rm -r Drush

git clone --branch master http://git.drupal.org/project/drush.git
```

**New terms** and **important words** are shown in bold. Words that you see on the screen, in menus or dialog boxes for example, appear in the text like this: "On the **Select Destination Location** screen, click on **Next** to accept the default destination".

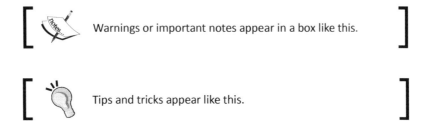

Warnings or important notes appear in a box like this.

Tips and tricks appear like this.

# Reader feedback

Feedback from our readers is always welcome. Let us know what you think about this book—what you liked or may have disliked. Reader feedback is important for us to develop titles that you really get the most out of.

To send us general feedback, simply send an e-mail to feedback@packtpub.com, and mention the book title through the subject of your message.

If there is a topic that you have expertise in and you are interested in either writing or contributing to a book, see our author guide on www.packtpub.com/authors.

# Customer support

Now that you are the proud owner of a Packt book, we have a number of things to help you to get the most from your purchase.

## Downloading the example code

You can download the example code files for all Packt books you have purchased from your account at http://www.packtpub.com. If you purchased this book elsewhere, you can visit http://www.packtpub.com/support and register to have the files e-mailed directly to you.

The code samples from this book are also available from the GitHub repository at http://github.com/alblue/com.packtpub.e4. There are ten branches, each corresponding to the state of the book's examples at the end of each chapter.

# Errata

Although we have taken every care to ensure the accuracy of our content, mistakes do happen. If you find a mistake in one of our books—maybe a mistake in the text or the code—we would be grateful if you would report this to us. By doing so, you can save other readers from frustration and help us improve subsequent versions of this book. If you find any errata, please report them by visiting http://www.packtpub.com/submit-errata, selecting your book, clicking on the **errata submission form** link, and entering the details of your errata. Once your errata are verified, your submission will be accepted and the errata will be uploaded to our website, or added to any list of existing errata, under the Errata section of that title.

See also the book's GitHub repository at http://github.com/alblue/com.packtpub. e4. If any code samples need to be updated, they will be updated there.

# Piracy

Piracy of copyright material on the Internet is an ongoing problem across all media. At Packt, we take the protection of our copyright and licenses very seriously. If you come across any illegal copies of our works, in any form, on the Internet, please provide us with the location address or website name immediately so that we can pursue a remedy.

Please contact us at copyright@packtpub.com with a link to the suspected pirated material.

We appreciate your help in protecting our authors, and our ability to bring you valuable content.

# Questions

You can contact us at questions@packtpub.com if you are having a problem with any aspect of the book, and we will do our best to address it.

# 1
# Creating Your First Plug-in

*Eclipse is a highly modular application, consisting of hundreds of plug-ins, and can be extended by installing additional plug-ins. Plug-ins are developed and debugged with the Plug-in Development Environment (PDE).*

In this chapter, we shall:

- ◆ Set up an Eclipse environment for performing plug-in development
- ◆ Create a plug-in with the new plug-in wizard
- ◆ Launch a new Eclipse instance with the plug-in enabled
- ◆ Debug the Eclipse plug-in

## Getting started

Developing plug-ins requires an Eclipse development environment. This book has been developed and tested on Juno (Eclipse 4.2) Kepler (4.3). Use the most recent version available.

Eclipse plug-ins are generally written in Java. Although it's possible to use other JVM-based languages (such as Groovy or Scala), this book will use the Java language.

There are several different packages of Eclipse available from the downloads page, each of which contains a different combination of plug-ins. This book has been tested with:

- ◆ Eclipse SDK from `http://download.eclipse.org/eclipse/downloads/`
- ◆ Eclipse Classic and Eclipse Standard from `http://www.eclipse.org/downloads/`

These contain the necessary **Plug-in Development Environment** (**PDE**) feature as well as the source code, the help documentation, and other useful features. (The RCP and RAP package should not be used, as it will cause problems with exercises in the *Chapter 7, Understanding the Eclipse 4 Model*.)

It is also possible to install the Eclipse PDE feature into an existing Eclipse instance. To do this, go to the **Help** menu and select **Install New Software**, followed by choosing the **General Purpose Tools** category from the update site. The Eclipse Plug-in Development Environment feature contains everything needed to create a new plug-in.

## Time for action – setting up the Eclipse SDK environment

Eclipse is a Java-based application, which needs Java installed. Eclipse is distributed as a compressed archive and doesn't require an explicit installation step.

1. To obtain Java, go to `http://java.com` and follow the instructions to download and install Java. Note that Java comes in two flavors; a 32-bit install and a 64-bit install. If the running OS is a 32-bit, install the 32-bit JDK; alternatively, if the running OS is 64-bit, install the 64-bit JDK.

2. Running `java -version` should give output like so:

   ```
   java version "1.7.0_09"

   Java(TM) SE Runtime Environment (build 1.7.0_09-b05)

   Java HotSpot(TM) 64-Bit Server VM (build 23.5-b02, mixed mode)
   ```

3. Go to `http://www.eclipse.org/downloads/` and select the **Eclipse Classic** or **Eclipse Standard** distribution.

4. Download the one which matches the installed JDK. Running `java -version` should report either:

   ❑ If it's a 32-bit JDK:

   ```
   Java HotSpot(TM) Client VM
   ```

   ❑ If it's a 64-bit JDK:

   ```
   Java HotSpot(TM) 64-Bit Server VM
   ```

 On Linux, Eclipse requires GTK2 to be installed. Most Linux distributions have a window manager based on GNOME that provides GTK2.x.

5. To install Eclipse, download and extract the contents to a suitable location. Eclipse is shipped as an archive, and needs no administrator privileges. Do not run it from a networked drive as this will cause performance problems.

Note that Eclipse needs to write to the folder from which it is extracted, so it's normal that the contents are writable afterwards. Generally, installing into `/Applications` or `C:\Program Files`, while being logged in with administrator account, is not recommended.

**6.** Run Eclipse by double-clicking on the Eclipse icon, or by running `eclipse.exe` (Windows), `eclipse` (Linux), or `Eclipse.app` (OS X).

**7.** Upon startup, the splash screen should be shown:

**8.** Choose a workspace, which is the location in which projects are be stored, and click on **OK**:

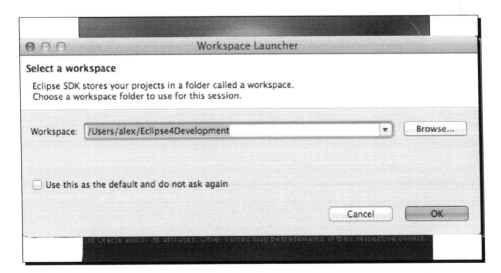

**9.** Close the welcome screen by clicking on the cross icon ⌧ in the tab next to the **Welcome** text. The welcome screen can be re-opened by navigating to **Help | Welcome**:

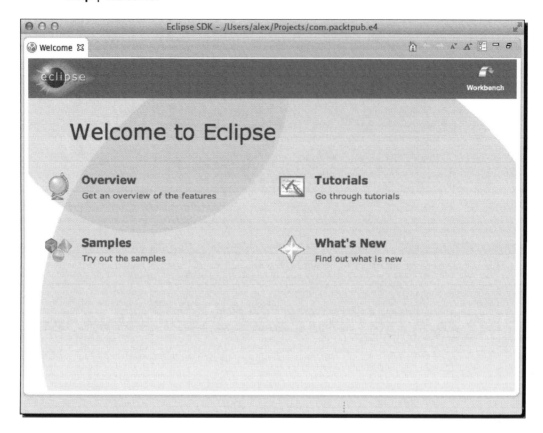

## *What just happened?*

Eclipse needs Java to run, and so the first step involved in installing Eclipse is ensuring that an up-to-date Java installation is available. By default, Eclipse will find a copy of Java installed on the path or from one of the standard locations. It is also possible to specify a different Java version by using the -vm command-line argument.

If the splash screen doesn't show up, the Eclipse version may be incompatible with the JDK (for example, a 64-bit JDK with a 32-bit Eclipse, or vice-versa). Common error messages shown at the launcher may include `Unable to find companion launcher` or a cryptic message about being unable to find an `SWT` library.

On Windows, there is an additional `eclipsec.exe` launcher, which allows log messages printed to the console to be seen. This is sometimes useful if Eclipse fails to load and no other message is displayed. Other operating systems can use the `eclipse` command. Both `eclipse.exe` and `eclipse` support the `-consolelog` argument, which can display more diagnostic information about problems while launching Eclipse.

The Eclipse workspace is a directory used for two purposes: as the default project location, and to hold the `.metadata` directory containing Eclipse settings, preferences, and other runtime information. The Eclipse runtime log is stored in the `.metadata/.log` file.

The workspace chooser dialog has an option to set the chosen value as the default workspace. It can be changed within Eclipse by navigating to **File | Switch Workspace**. It can also be overridden by specifying a different workspace location with the `-data` command-line argument.

Finally, the welcome screen is useful for first-time users, but is worth closing (rather than minimizing) once Eclipse has started.

# Creating your first plug-in

In this task, Eclipse's plug-in wizard will be used to create a plug-in.

## Time for action – creating a plug-in

In the Plug-in Development Environment (PDE), every plug-in has its own individual project. A plug-in project is typically created with the **New Project** wizard, although it is possible to upgrade an existing Java project to a plug-in project by adding the PDE nature and the required files (by navigating to **Configure | Convert to plug-in project**).

**1.** To create a Hello World plugin, navigate to **File | New | Project**:

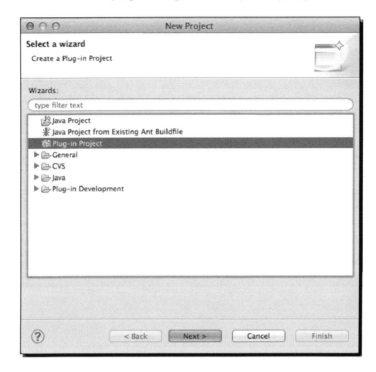

**2.** The project types shown may be different from this list, but should include **Plug-in Project** with Eclipse Classic. If nothing is shown under the **File | New menu**, navigate to **Window | Open Perspective | Other | Plug-in Development** first; the entries should then be seen under the **File | New** menu.

**3.** Choose **Plug-in Project** and click on **Next**. Fill in the dialog as follows:

- **Project name:** com.packtpub.e4.hello.ui
- Select the checkbox for **Use default location**
- Select the checkbox for **Create a Java project**
- **Target Eclipse Version:** 3.5 or greater

**4.** Click on **Next** again, and fill in the plug-in properties:

- **ID:** com.packtpub.e4.hello.ui
- **Version:** 1.0.0.qualifier
- **Name:** Hello
- **Vendor:** PacktPub

- ❑ **Execution Environment**: Use the default (for example: JavaSE-1.6 or JavaSE-1.7)
- ❑ Select the checkbox for **Generate an Activator**
- ❑ **Activator**: com.packtpub.e4.hello.ui.Activator
- ❑ Select the checkbox for **This plug-in will make contributions to the UI**
- ❑ **Rich client application**: No

**5.** Click on **Next** and a set of templates will be provided:

- ❑ Select the checkbox for **Create a plug-in using one of the templates**
- ❑ Choose the **Hello World Command** template

**6.** Click on **Next** to customize the sample, including:

- ❑ The Java package name, which defaults to the project's name
- ❑ The handler class name, which is the code that gets invoked for the action
- ❑ The message box text, which is the message supplied

**7.** Finally, click on **Finish** and the project will be generated.

**8.** If a dialog asks, click on **Yes** to show the plug-in development perspective.

## What just happened?

Creating a plug-in project is the first step towards creating a plug-in for Eclipse. The **New Plug-in Project** wizard was used with one of the sample templates to create a project.

Plug-ins are typically named in reverse domain name format, so these examples will be prefixed with com.packtpub.e4. This helps to distinguish between many plug-ins; the stock Eclipse SDK comes with more than 440 individual plug-ins, for example, the Eclipse-developed ones start with org.eclipse.

> Conventionally, plug-ins which create additions to (or require) the use of the UI have .ui. in the name. This helps to distinguish from those that don't, which can often be used headlessly. Of the 440+ plug-ins that make up the Eclipse SDK, 120 of those are UI related and the rest are headless.

The project contains a number of files which are automatically generated, based on the content filled in the wizard. The key files in an Eclipse plug-in are:

- ◆ META-INF/MANIFEST.MF: The OSGi manifest describes the plug-in's dependencies, version, and name. Double-clicking it will open a custom editor, which shows the information entered in the wizards; or it can be opened in a standard text editor.

The Manifest follows standard Java conventions; continuations are represented by a new line followed by a single space character, and the file must end with a new line. (For example, the maximum line length is 72 characters, although many ignore this.)

- `plugin.xml`: The `plugin.xml` file declares what extensions this plug-in provides to the Eclipse runtime. Not all plug-ins need a `plugin.xml` file; headless (non-UI) plug-ins often don't need to have one. Extension points will be covered in more detail later, but the sample project creates an extension for the commands, handlers, bindings, and menus extension points. (If the older Hello World template was chosen, present on 3.7 and older, only the `actionSets` extension will be used.)

  Text labels for the commands, actions, or menus are represented declaratively in the `plugin.xml` file, rather than programmatically; this allows Eclipse to show the menu before needing to load or execute any code.

> This is one of the reasons Eclipse starts so quickly; by not needing to load or execute classes, it can scale by showing what's needed at the time, and then load the class on demand when the user invokes the action. Java Swing's Actions provides labels and tool tips programmatically, which can result in a slower initialization of the user interface.

- `build.properties`: This file is used by PDE at development time and at build time. Generally it can be ignored, but if resources are added that need to be made available to the plug-in (such as images, properties files, HTML content, and so on), an entry must be added here as otherwise it won't be found. Generally, the easiest way to do this is by going to the **Build** tab of the `build.properties` file, which will give a tree-like view of the project's contents.

This file is an archaic hangover from the days of Ant builds, and is generally useless when using more up-to-date builds such as Maven Tycho, which will be covered in *Chapter 10, Automated Builds with Tycho*.

## Pop quiz – Eclipse workspaces and plug-ins

Q1. What is an Eclipse workspace?

Q2. What is the naming convention for Eclipse plug-in projects?

Q3. What are the names of the three key files in an Eclipse plug-in?

# Running plug-ins

To test an Eclipse plug-in, Eclipse is used to run or debug a new Eclipse instance with the plug-in installed.

## Time for action – launching Eclipse from within Eclipse

Eclipse can launch a new Eclipse application by clicking on the Run button, or via the **Run** menu.

1. Select the plug-in project in the workspace.

2. Click on the Run button 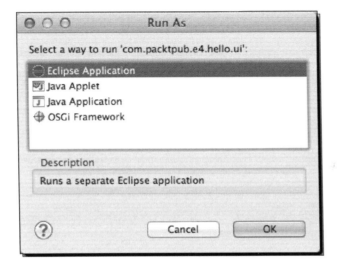 to launch the project. The first time this happens, a dialog will be shown; subsequent launches will remember the previous type:

3. Choose the **Eclipse Application** type and click on **OK**, and a new Eclipse instance will be launched.

4. Close the welcome page in the launched application, if shown.

5. Click on the Hello World icon in the menu bar, or navigate to **Sample Menu | Sample Command**, and the dialog box created via the wizard will be shown:

**6.** Quit the test Eclipse instance by closing the window, or via the usual keyboard shortcuts or menus (*Cmd + Q* on OS X, *Alt + F4* on Windows).

# What just happened?

When clicking Run 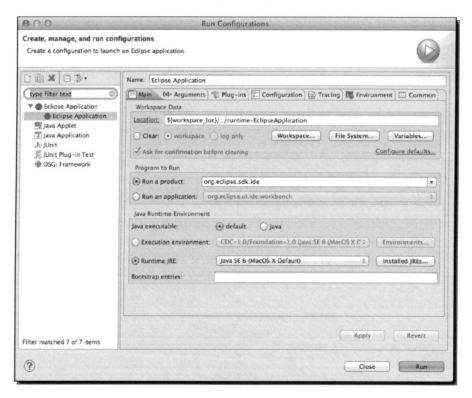 in the toolbar (or via the **Run | Run As | Eclipse Application** menu) a launch configuration is created, which includes any plug-ins open in the workspace. A second copy of Eclipse—with its own temporary workspace—will enable the plug-in to be tested and verified so that it works as expected.

The Run operation is intelligent, in that it launches an application based on what is selected in the workspace. If a plug-in is selected, it will offer the opportunity to run as an Eclipse application; if a Java project with a class with a `main` method, it will run it as a standard Java application; and if it has tests then it will offer to run the test launcher instead.

However, the Run operation can also be counter-intuitive; if clicked a second time, and in a different project context, something other than the expected launch might be run.

A list of the available launch configurations can be seen by going to the Run menu, or by going to the drop-down list to the right of the Run icon. The **Run | Run Configurations** menu shows all the available types, including any previously run:

By default, the runtime workspace is kept between runs. The launch configuration for an Eclipse application has options that can be customized; in the previous screenshot, the **Workspace Data** section in the **Main** tab shows where the runtime workspace is stored, and an option is shown that allows the workspace to be cleared (with or without confirmation) between runs.

Launch configurations can be deleted by clicking on the red Delete icon ☒ on the top-left, and new launch configurations can be created by clicking on the New icon. Each launch configuration has a type:

- ◆ **Eclipse Application**
- ◆ **Java Applet**
- ◆ **Java Application**
- ◆ **JUnit**
- ◆ **JUnit Plug-in Test**
- ◆ **OSGi Framework**

The launch configuration can be thought of as a precanned script, which can launch different types of programs. Additional tabs are used to customize the launch, such as the environment variables, system properties, or command-line arguments. The type of the launch configuration specifies what parameters are required, and how the launch is executed.

When a program is launched with the Run icon, changes to the project's source code do not take effect. However, as we'll see in the next section, if it's launched with the Debug icon, changes can take effect.

If the test Eclipse is hanging or otherwise unresponsive, in the host Eclipse instance the **Console** view (shown with the **Window** | **View** | **Show View** | **Other** | **General** | **Console** menu) can be used to stop (▣) the test Eclipse instance.

## Pop quiz – launching Eclipse

Q1. What are the two ways of terminating a launched Eclipse instance?

Q2. What are launch configurations?

Q3. How do you create and delete launch configurations?

## Have a go hero – modifying the plug-in

Now that you've got the Eclipse plug-in running, try the following:

◆ Change the message of the label and title of the dialog box to something else

◆ Invoke the action by using the keyboard shortcut (defined in `plugin.xml`)

◆ Change the tool tip of the action to a different message

◆ Switch the action icon to a different graphic (note that if you use a different filename, remember to update `build.properties`).

# Debugging a plug-in

Since it's rare that everything works first time, it's often necessary to develop iteratively, adding progressively more functionality each time. Secondly, sometimes it's necessary to find out what's going on under the covers when trying to fix a bug, particularly if it's hard to track down exceptions such as `NullPointerException`.

Fortunately, Eclipse comes with excellent debugging support, which can be used for debugging both standalone Java applications as well as Eclipse plug-ins.

## Time for action – debugging a plug-in

Debugging an Eclipse plug-in is almost the same as running an Eclipse plug-in, except that breakpoints can be used, and the state of the program can be updated, variables, and minor changes to the code can be done. Rather than debugging plug-ins individually, the entire Eclipse launch configuration is started in debug mode. That way, all the plug-ins can be debugged at the same time.

Although run mode is slightly faster, the added flexibility of being able to make changes makes debug mode much more attractive to use as a default.

Start the test Eclipse, by navigating to the **Debug | Debug As | Eclipse Application** menu, or by clicking on Debug (🔯) in the toolbar.

***1.*** Click on the Hello World icon 🔘 in the test Eclipse to display the dialog, as before, and click on **OK** to dismiss it.

**2.** In the host Eclipse, open the `SampleHandler` class and go to the `execute()` method.

**3.** Add a breakpoint by double-clicking in the vertical ruler (the gray/blue bar on the left of the editor), or by pressing *Ctrl + Shift + B* (or *Cmd + Shift + B* on OS X). A blue dot 🔵 representing the breakpoint will appear in the ruler:

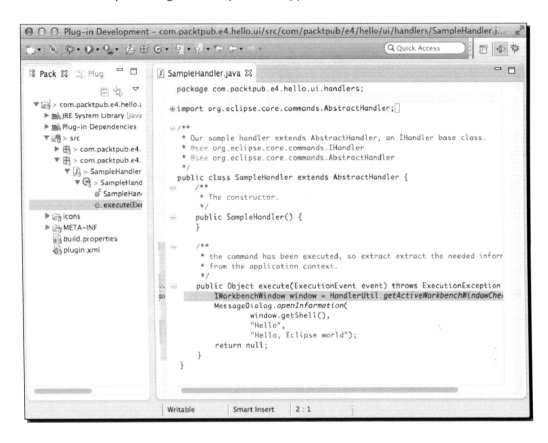

**4.** Click on the Hello World icon  in the test Eclipse to display the dialog, and the debugger will pause the thread at the breakpoint in the host Eclipse:

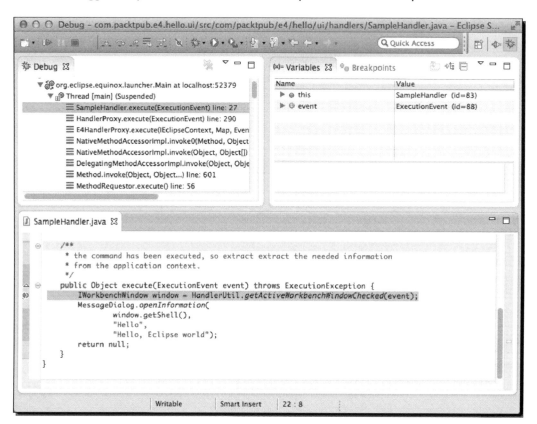

> The debugger perspective will open whenever a breakpoint is triggered and the program will be paused. While it is paused, the test Eclipse is unresponsive. Any clicks on the test Eclipse application will be ignored, and it will show a busy cursor.

**5.** On the top-right, variables that are active in the line of code are shown. In this case, it's just the implicit variables (via `this`), any local variables (none, yet) as well as the parameter (in this case, `event`).

**6.** Click on Step Over 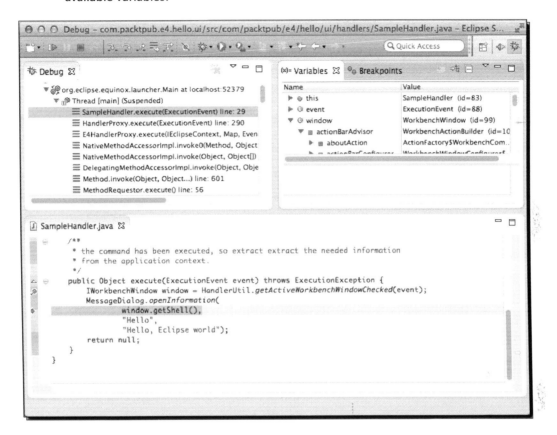 or press *F6*, and window will be added to the list of available variables:

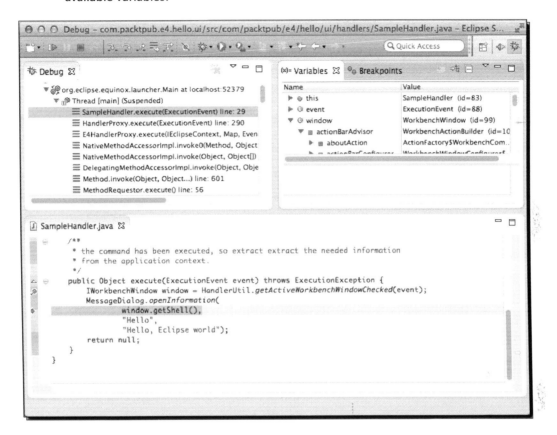

**7.** When ready to continue, click on Resume or press *F8* to keep running.

## What just happened?

The built-in Eclipse debugger was used to launch Eclipse in debug mode. By triggering an action which led to a breakpoint, the debugger was revealed allowing the local variables to be introspected.

When in the debugger, there are several options available for stepping through the code:

◆ Step Over – allows stepping over line-by-line in the method

◆ Step Into – follow the method calls recursively as execution unfolds

There is also a **Run | Step into Selection** menu item that does not have a toolbar icon. It can be invoked with *Ctrl + F5* (*Alt + F5* on OS X), and is used to step into a specific expression.

♦ Step Return — jump to the end of a method

♦ Drop to Frame — return to a stack frame in the thread to re-run an operation

## Time for action – updating code in debugger

When an Eclipse instance is launched in run mode, changes made to the source code aren't reflected in the running instance. However, debug mode allows changes made to the source to be reflected in the running test Eclipse instance.

*1.* Launch the test Eclipse in debug mode by clicking on the Debug icon.

*2.* Click on the Hello World icon in the test Eclipse to display the dialog, as before, and click on **OK** to dismiss it. It may be necessary to remove or resume the breakpoint in the host Eclipse instance to allow execution to continue.

*3.* In the host Eclipse, open the `SampleHandler` class and go to the `execute()` method.

*4.* Change the title of the dialog to `Hello again, Eclipse world` and save the file. Provided that **Project | Build Automatically** is enabled, the change will be recompiled.

*5.* Click on the Hello World icon in the test Eclipse instance again. The new message should be shown.

## *What just happened?*

By default, Eclipse ships with **Project | Build Automatically** enabled. Whenever changes are made to Java files, they are recompiled along with their dependencies if necessary.

When a Java program is launched in run mode, it will load classes in on-demand and then keep using that definition until the JVM shuts down. Even if the classes are changed, the JVM won't notice that they have been updated, and so no differences will be seen in the running application.

However, when a Java program is launched in debug mode, whenever changes to classes are made, it will update the running JVM with the new code if possible. The limits to what can be replaced are controlled by the JVM through the JVMTI and whether, for example, the virtual machine's `canUnrestrictedlyRedefineClasses()` call returns `true`. Generally, updating an existing method and adding a new method or field will work, but changes to interfaces and super classes may not be. (Refer to http://en.wikipedia.org/wiki/Java_Virtual_Machine_Tools_Interface for more information.)

The ex-Sun Hotspot JVM cannot replace classes if methods are added or interfaces are updated. Some JVMs have additional capabilities which can substitute more code on demand. With the merging of JRockit and Hotspot over time, more may be replaceable at runtime than before; for everything else, there's JRebel.

Other JVMs, such as IBM's, can deal with a wider range of replacements.

Note that there are some changes which won't be picked up; for example, new extensions added to the `plugin.xml` file. In order to see these changes, it is possible to start and stop the plug-in through the command-line OSGi console, or restart Eclipse inside or outside the host Eclipse to see the change.

# Debugging with step filters

When debugging using Step Into, the code will frequently go into Java internals, such as the implementation of Java collections classes or other internal JVM classes. These don't usually add value, but fortunately Eclipse has a way of ignoring uninteresting classes.

## Time for action – setting up step filtering

Step filtering allows for uninteresting packages and classes to be ignored during step debugging.

1.  Run the test Eclipse application in debug mode.

2.  Ensure a breakpoint is set at the start of the `SampleHandler` class's `execute()` method.

3.  Click on the Hello World icon, and the debugger should open at the first line as before.

4.  Click on Step Into 🔲 five or six times. At each point, the code will jump into the next method in the expression; first through various methods in `HandlerUtil` and then into `ExecutionEvent`.

5.  Click on Resume 🔲 to continue.

6.  Open **Preferences**, and then navigate to **Java | Debug | Step Filtering**.

7.  Check the **Use Step Filters** option.

**8.** Click on **Add Package** and enter `org.eclipse.ui`, followed by clicking on **OK**.

**9.** Click on the Hello World icon again.

**10.** Click on Step Into  as before. This time, the debugger goes straight to `getApplicationContext()` in the `Execution Event` class.

**11.** Click on the Resume icon to continue.

**12.** To make debugging more efficient by skipping accessors, go back into the **Step Filters** preference and select the **Filter Simple Getters** from the **Step Filters** preference's page.

**13.** Click on the Hello World icon again.

**14.** Click on Step Into as before.

**15.** Instead of going into the `getApplicationContext()` method, execution will drop through to the `ExpressionContext` class's `getVariable()` method instead.

## What just happened?

The **Step Filters** preferences allows uninteresting packages to be skipped, at least from the point of debugging. Typically, JVM internal classes (such as those beginning with `sun` or `sunw`) are not helpful when debugging and can easily be ignored. This also avoids debugging through the class loader, as it loads classes on demand.

Typically, it makes sense to enable all the default packages in the Step Filters dialog, as it's pretty rare to need to debug any of the JVM libraries (internal or public interfaces). This means when stepping through the code, if a common method such as `List.toString()` is called, debugging won't step through the internal implementation.

It also makes sense to filter out simple setters and getters (those that just set a variable, or those that just return a variable). If the method is more complex (like the `getVariable()` method discussed previously), it will still stop in the debugger.

Constructors and static initializers can also be specifically filtered.

# Using different breakpoint types

Although it's possible to place a breakpoint anywhere in a method, a special breakpoint type exists, which can fire on method entry, exit, or both. Breakpoints can also be customized to only fire in certain situations or when certain conditions are met.

## Time for action – breaking at method entry and exit

Method breakpoints allow the user to see when a method is entered or exited.

1. Open the `SampleHandler` class, and go to the `execute()` method.

2. Double-click in the vertical ruler at the method signature, or select **Toggle Method Breakpoint** from the method in one of the **Outline**, **Package Explorer**, or **Members** views.

3. The breakpoint should be shown on the line `public Object execute(...)` `throws ExecutionException {`.

4. Open the breakpoint properties by right-clicking on the breakpoint or via the **Breakpoints** view, which is shown in the debug perspective. Set the breakpoint to trigger at the method entry and method exit.

5. Click the Hello World icon again.

6. When the debugger stops at the method entry, click on the Resume icon.

7. When the debugger stops at the method exit, click on the Resume icon.

## What just happened?

The breakpoint triggers at the time the method enters and subsequently when the method's `return` statement is reached.

Note that the exit is only triggered if the method returns normally; if an exception is raised which causes the method to return, this is not treated as a normal method exit, and so the breakpoint won't fire.

Other than the breakpoint type, there's not a significant difference between creating a breakpoint on method entry and creating one on the first statement of the method. Both give the ability to introspect the parameters and do further debugging prior to any statements in the method itself are called.

The method exit breakpoint, on the other hand, will only trigger once the `return` statement is about to leave the method. Thus, any expression in the method's return value will have been evaluated prior to the exit breakpoint firing. Compare and contrast this to the line breakpoint, which will wait to evaluate the argument of the `return` statement.

Note that Eclipse's Step Return icon has the same effect; this will run until the method's `return` statement is about to be executed. However, to find when a method returns, using a method exit breakpoint is far faster than stopping at a specific line and then clicking on Step Return.

# Using conditional breakpoints

Breakpoints are useful, since they can be invoked on every occasion that a line of code is triggered. However, sometimes they need to break for specific actions only, such as when a particular option is set, or when a value has been incorrectly initialized. Fortunately, this can be done with **conditional breakpoints**.

## Time for action – setting a conditional breakpoint

Normally, breakpoints fire on each invocation. It is possible to configure breakpoints such that they fire when certain conditions are met.

1.  Go to the `execute()` method of the `SampleHandler` class.

2.  Clear any existing breakpoints by double-clicking them or using **Delete all breakpoints** from the **Breakpoints** view.

3.  Add a breakpoint to the first line of the `execute()` method body.

4.  Right-click on the breakpoint and select the **Breakpoint Properties** menu. (It can also be shown by *Ctrl* + double-clicking, or *Cmd* + double-clicking on OS X on the breakpoint icon itself.)

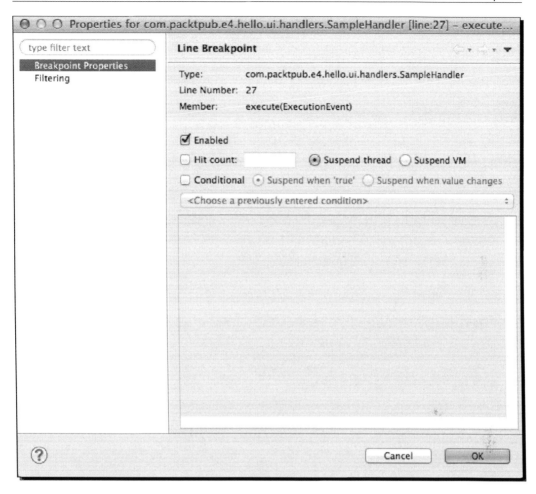

5. Set the **Hit Count** field to 3, and click on **OK**.

6. Click on the Hello World icon button three times. On the third click, the debugger will open up at that line of code.

7. Open the breakpoint properties, deselect **Hit Count** and select the **Enabled** and **Conditional** options. Put the following code into the conditional trigger field:

   ```
   ((org.eclipse.swt.widgets.Event)event.trigger).stateMask == 65536
   ```

8. Click on the Hello World icon and the breakpoint will not fire.

9. Hold down *Alt*, click on the Hello World icon, and the debugger will open. (65536 is the value of SWT.MOD3, which is the *Alt* key.)

## What just happened?

When a breakpoint is created, it is enabled by default. A breakpoint can be temporarily disabled, which has the effect of removing it from the flow of execution. Disabled breakpoints can be trivially re-enabled on a per-breakpoint basis, or from the **Breakpoints** view. Quite often it's useful to have a set of breakpoints defined in the codebase, but not necessarily have them all enabled at once.

It is also possible to temporarily disable all breakpoints using the **Skip All Breakpoints** setting, which can be changed from the corresponding item in the **Run** menu (when the debug perspective is enabled), or the corresponding icon 🔲 in the **Breakpoints** view. When this is toggled, no breakpoints will be fired.

Conditional breakpoints must use a Boolean expression, rather than a statement or a set of statements. Sometimes this is constraining; if that's the case, having a utility class with a static method allows more complex code paths (with the caveat that all interesting data must be passed in as method arguments).

# Using exceptional breakpoints

Sometimes when debugging a program, an exception occurs. Typically this isn't known about until it happens, when an exception message is printed or displayed to the user via some kind of dialog box.

## Time for action – catching exceptions

Although it's trivial to put a breakpoint in the `catch` block, this is merely the location where the failure was ultimately caught, not where it was caused. The place where it was caught can often be in a completely different plug-in from where it was raised, and depending on the amount of information encoded within the exception (particularly if it has been transliterated into a different exception type), it may hide the original source of the problem. Fortunately, Eclipse can handle such cases with a Java Exception breakpoint.

*1.* Introduce a bug into the `SampleHandler` class's `execute()` method, by adding the following just before the `MessageDialog.openInformation()` call:

```
window = null;
```

**Downloading the example code**

You can download the example code files for all Packt books you have purchased from your account at `http://www.packtpub.com`. If you purchased this book elsewhere, you can visit `http://www. packtpub.com/support` and register to have the files e-mailed directly to you.

2. Click on the Hello World icon.

3. Nothing will appear to happen in the target Eclipse, but in the **Console** view of the host Eclipse instance, the following error message should be seen:

```
Caused by: java.lang.NullPointerException
  at com.packtpub.e4.hello.ui.handlers.SampleHandler.
execute(SampleHandler.java:30)
  at org.eclipse.ui.internal.handlers.HandlerProxy.
execute(HandlerProxy.java:293)
  at org.eclipse.ui.internal.handlers.E4HandlerProxy.
execute(E4HandlerProxy.java:76)
```

4. Create a Java Exception breakpoint 🔳 in the **Breakpoints** view of the debug perspective. The exception dialog will be shown as follows:

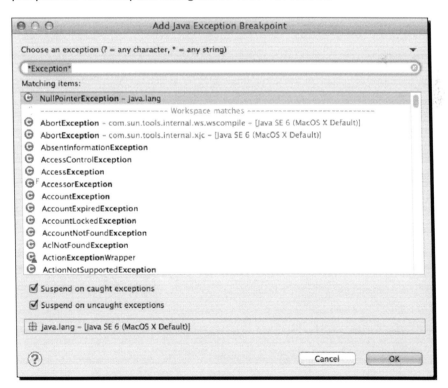

**5.** Enter `NullPointerException` into the search dialog and click on **OK**.

**6.** Click on the Hello World icon and the debugger will stop at the line the exception is thrown, instead of where it is caught:

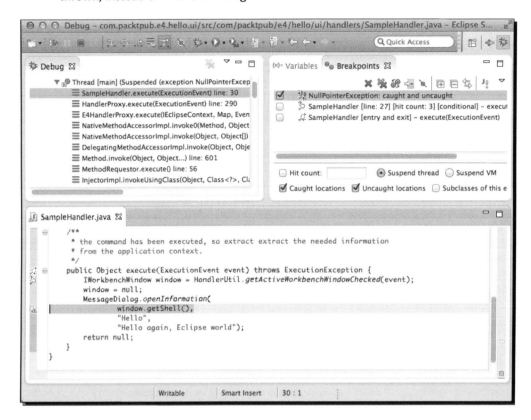

## *What just happened?*

The Java Exception breakpoint stops when an exception is thrown, not when it is caught. The dialog asks for a single exception class to catch and by default, the wizard has been prefilled with any class whose name includes `*Exception*`. However, any name (or filter) can be typed into the search box, including abbreviations such as `FNFE` for `FileNotFoundException`. Wildcard patterns can also be used, which allows searching for `Nu*Ex` or `*Unknown*`.

By default, the exception breakpoint corresponds to instances of that specific class. This is useful (and quick) for exceptions such as `NullPointerException`, but not so useful for ones with an extensive class hierarchy such as `IOException`. In this case, there is a checkbox visible in the **Breakpoint** properties window and the bottom of the **Breakpoints** view, which allows the selection of all subclasses of that exception, not just of the specific class itself.

There are also two other checkboxes, which say whether the debugger should stop when the exception is caught or uncaught. Both of these are selected by default; if both are deselected, the breakpoint effectively becomes disabled. Caught means that the exception is thrown in a corresponding `try`/`catch` block, and Uncaught means that the exception is thrown without a `try`/`catch` block (thus, bubbles up to the method's caller).

# Time for action – using watch variables and expressions

Finally, it's worth seeing what the **Variables** view can do.

1. Create a breakpoint at the start of the `execute()` method.

2. Click on the Hello World icon again.

3. Highlight the `openInformation()` call and navigate to **Run | Step Into Selection**.

4. Select the `title` in the the **Variables** view.

5. Modify where it says `Hello` in the bottom half of the **Variables** view and change it to `Goodbye`:

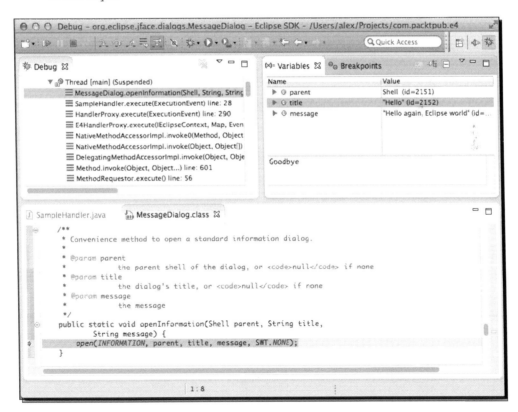

**6.** Save the value using *Ctrl + S* (or *Cmd + S* on OS X).

**7.** Click on the Resume icon and the newly updated title can be seen in the dialog.

**8.** Click on the Hello World icon again.

**9.** With the debugger stopped in the `execute()` method, highlight event in the **Variables** view.

**10.** Right-click on the value and choose **Inspect** (*Ctrl + Shift + I* or *Cmd + Shift + I* on an OS X) and the value is opened in the **Expressions** view:

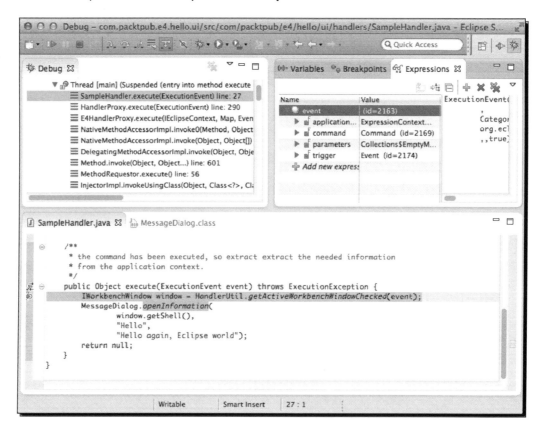

**11.** Click on the **Add new expression** option in the bottom of the **Variables** view.

**12.** Add new `java.util.Date()` and the right-hand side will show the current time.

**13.** Right-click on the new `java.util.Date()` and choose **Re-evaluate Watch Expression**. The right-hand pane shows the new value.

**14.** Step through the code line by line, and notice that the watch expression is reevaluated after each step.

**15.** Disable the watch expression by right-clicking on it and choosing **Disable**.

**16.** Step through the code line by line and the watch expression will not be updated.

## What just happened?

The Eclipse debugger has many powerful features, and the ability to inspect (and change) the state of the program is one of the more important ones.

Watch expressions, when combined with conditional breakpoints, can be used to find out when data becomes corrupted or used to show the state of a particular object's value.

Expressions can also be evaluated based on objects in the **Variables** view, and the code completion is available to select methods, with the result being shown with **Display**.

## Pop quiz – debugging

Q1. How can an Eclipse plug-in be launched in debug mode?

Q2. How can certain packages be avoided when debugging?

Q3. What are the different types of breakpoints that can be set?

Q4. How can a loop debugged that only exhibits a bug after 256 iterations?

Q5. How can a breakpoint be set on a method when its argument is null?

Q6. What does inspecting an object do?

Q7. How can the value of an expression be calculated?

## Have a go hero – working with breakpoints

Using the conditional breakpoint to stop at a certain method is fine if the data is simple, but sometimes there needs to be more than one expression. To implement additional functionality, the breakpoint can be delegated to a `breakpoint()` method in a `Utility` class. The following steps will help you to work with breakpoints:

1. Create a `Utility` class with a static method `breakpoint()`, this will return a `true` value if the breakpoint should stop and `false` otherwise:

```
public class Utility {
  public static boolean breakpoint() {
    System.out.println("Breakpoint");
    return false;
  }
}
```

2. Create a conditional breakpoint in the `execute()` method, which calls `Utility.breakpoint()`.

3. Click on the Hello World icon again and the message will be printed to the host Eclipse's **Console** view. The breakpoint will not stop.

4. Modify the `breakpoint()` method to return `true` instead of `false`. Run the action again. The debugger will stop.

5. Modify the `breakpoint()` method to take the message as an argument, along with a Boolean value that is returned to say if the breakpoint should stop.

6. Set up a conditional breakpoint with the following code:

```
Utility.breakpoint(
  ((org.eclipse.swt.widgets.Event)event.trigger).stateMask
   != 0,"Breakpoint")
```

7. Modify the `breakpoint()` method to take a varargs `Object` array, and use that in conjunction with the message to use `String.format()` for the resulting message:

```
Utility.breakpoint(  ((org.eclipse.swt.widgets.Event)event.
trigger).stateMask
   != 0,"Breakpoint" %s %h",event,
     new java.util.Date().getTime()))
```

# Summary

In this chapter, we covered how to get started with Eclipse plug-in development. From downloading the right Eclipse package (from a bewildering array of choices) to getting started with a wizard-generated plug-in, you should now have the tools to follow through with the remainder of the chapters in this book.

Specifically, we covered:

◆ The Eclipse SDK (also known as Eclipse Classic) has the necessary Plug-in Development Environment to get you started

◆ The plug-in creation wizard can be used to create a plug-in project, optionally using one of the example templates

◆ Testing an Eclipse plug-in launches a second copy of Eclipse with the plug-in installed and available for use

◆ Launching Eclipse in debug mode allows you to update code and stop execution at breakpoints defined via the editor

Now that we've learned about how to get started with Eclipse plug-ins, we're ready to look at creating plug-ins which contribute to the IDE; starting with **SWT** and **Views**, which is the topic of the next chapter.

# 2

# Creating Views with SWT

*SWT is the widget toolkit that Eclipse uses, which gives performant access to the platform's native tools in a portable manner. Unlike Swing, which is rendered with Java native drawing operations, SWT delegates the drawing to the underlying operating system.*

In this chapter, we shall:

- ◆ Create an Eclipse view with SWT widgets
- ◆ Create a custom SWT widget
- ◆ Work with resources and learn how to detect and fix resource leaks
- ◆ Handle focus operations
- ◆ Group components and resize them automatically
- ◆ Create system tray items
- ◆ Display non-rectangular windows
- ◆ Provide scrolling and tabbed navigation

## Creating views and widgets

This section introduces views and widgets and uses as its example clocks.

## Time for action – creating a view

The Eclipse UI consists of multiple views, which are the rectangular areas that display content such as the Outline, Console, or Package Explorer. In Eclipse 3.x, views are created by adding an extension point to an existing plug-in, or by using a template. A `clock.ui` plug-in will be created to host the clock widgets and views.

**1.** Open the plug-in wizard by navigating to **File | New | Other | Plug-in Project**. Enter the details as follows:

- ❑ **Project name**: `com.packtpub.e4.clock.ui`
- ❑ Select the checkbox for **Use default location**
- ❑ Select the checkbox for **Create a Java project**
- ❑ **Target Eclipse Version**: `3.5 or greater`

**2.** Click on **Next** again, and fill in the plug-in properties:

- ❑ **ID**: `com.packtpub.e4.clock.ui`
- ❑ **Version**: `1.0.0.qualifier`
- ❑ **Name**: `Clock`
- ❑ **Vendor**: `PacktPub`
- ❑ Select the checkbox for **Generate an Activator**
- ❑ **Activator**: `com.packtpub.e4.clock.ui.Activator`
- ❑ Select the checkbox for **This plug-in will make contributions to the UI**
- ❑ **Rich client application**: `No`

**3.** Click on **Next** to choose from a set of templates:

- ❑ Select the checkbox for **Create a plug-in using one of the templates**
- ❑ Choose the **Plug-in with a view** template

**4.** Click on **Next** to customize a few aspects of the sample, including:

- ❑ **Java package name**: `com.packtpub.e4.clock.ui.views`
- ❑ **View class name**: `ClockView`
- ❑ **View name**: `Clock View`
- ❑ **View category ID**: `com.packtpub.e4.clock.ui`
- ❑ **View category name**: `Timekeeping`
- ❑ **Viewer type**: `Table Viewer`

**5.** Deselect the **Add** checkboxes as these are not required.

6.   Click on **Finish** to create the project.

7.   Run the Eclipse application via the Run toolbar icon.

8.   Go to **Window | Show View | Other | Timekeeping | Clock View** to show the **Clock View**, which has a simple list view with **One**, **Two**, **Three** listed:

## What just happened?

It's not usual to create a plug-in project per view (or per action) but often plug-ins are encapsulated and provide functionality specific to that particular plug-in. In this case, clocks aren't related to the Hello World one created before, so a new plug-in was created to host them.

The plug-in wizard created an empty plug-in project, as well as two key files.

### MANIFEST.MF

The manifest contains references to dependent plug-ins and interfaces, and includes the following:

```
Bundle-SymbolicName: com.packtpub.e4.clock.ui; singleton:=true
Bundle-Version: 1.0.0.qualifier
Bundle-Activator: com.packtpub.e4.clock.ui.Activator
Require-Bundle: org.eclipse.ui, org.eclipse.core.runtime
```

Plug-ins that contribute to the user interface need to do two things:

◆   Depend on `org.eclipse.ui`

◆   Have `;singleton:=true` after the bundle symbolic name

The dependency on the `org.eclipse.ui` bundle gives access to the Standard Widget Toolkit and other key parts of the Eclipse framework.

The clause `;singleton:=true` is an OSGi directive, which means that only one version of this plug-in can be installed in Eclipse at one time. For plug-ins which add dependencies to the UI, there is a restriction that they must be singletons. (This constraint is one of the main reasons why installing a new plug-requires the IDE to restart.)

The Manifest sets up the project's classpath. Any additional plug-in dependencies need to be added to the Manifest.

### plugin.xml

The `plugin.xml` file defines a list of extensions that this plug-in provides. Extension points are how Eclipse advertises the plug-in extensions, much like a USB hub provides a generic connector that allows many other types of devices to be plugged in.

The Eclipse extension points are documented in the help system, and each has a `point` identifier, with optional children that are point-specific. In this case, the extension is defined using the `org.eclipse.ui.views` point, which expects a combination of `category` and `view` elements. In this case, it will look like:

```xml
<plugin>
    <extension point="org.eclipse.ui.views">
        <category name="Timekeeping"
          id="com.packtpub.e4.clock.ui"/>
        <view name="Clock View"
          icon="icons/sample.gif"
          category="com.packtpub.e4.clock.ui"
          class="com.packtpub.e4.clock.ui.views.ClockView"
          id="com.packtpub.e4.clock.ui.views.ClockView"/>
    </extension>
</plugin>
```

The class in this case extends the `ViewPart` abstract class, which is used for all views in Eclipse 3.x.

 ☞ E4: The Eclipse 4 model defines views in a different way, which is covered in more detail in *Chapter 7, Understanding the Eclipse 4 Model*. The Eclipse 4.x SDK includes a 3.x compatibility layer, so these examples will work in Eclipse 4.x SDKs.

The viewer component is a default table view, which will be replaced in the next section.

## Time for action – drawing a custom view

An SWT `Canvas` can be used to provide custom rendering for a view. As a starting point for drawing a clock, the `Canvas` will use `drawArc()` to create a circle.

1. Remove the content of `ClockView` leaving behind an empty implementation of the `setFocus()` and `createPartControl()` methods.

2. Run the target Eclipse instance and see that `ClockView` is now empty.

**3.** In the `createPartControl()` method, do the following:

1. Create a new `Canvas`, which is a drawable widget.

2. Add `PaintListener` to the `Canvas`.

3. Get `gc` from `PaintEvent` and call `drawArc()` to draw a circle.

The code will look like:

```
import org.eclipse.swt.*;
import org.eclipse.swt.events.*;
import org.eclipse.swt.widgets.*;
import org.eclipse.ui.part.ViewPart;
public class ClockView extends ViewPart {
  public void createPartControl(Composite parent) {
    final Canvas clock = new Canvas(parent,SWT.NONE);
    clock.addPaintListener(new PaintListener() {
      public void paintControl(PaintEvent e) {
        e.gc.drawArc(e.x,e.y,e.width-1,e.height-1,0,360);
      }
    });
  }
  public void setFocus() {
  }
}
```

**4.** Run the Eclipse instance and show the **Clock View**.

**5.** Resize the view and the clock should change size with it:

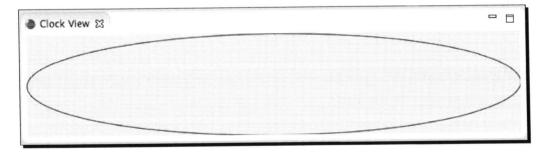

## What just happened?

In SWT, the widget used for custom drawing is `Canvas`. The view is constructed with a call to `createPartControl()`, which is invoked once when the view is shown for the first time. If the view is minimized, then maximized, this is not invoked again; however, if the view is closed and a new view is opened, then a call will be made to a new instance of `ClockView` to initialize it.

Unlike other Java GUI frameworks, a widget is not added or removed to a containing parent once created; the widget's parent is specified at construction time. Thus, instead of creating it with an empty constructor and then adding it, the parent is passed into the widget's constructor.

> There is also a `style` flag that is passed in. This is used by widgets in different ways; for example, the `Button` widget takes various flags to indicate whether it should be rendered as a push button, radio button, checkbox, toggle, or arrow. For consistency, in SWT all widgets have an `int` `style` flag, which enables up to 32 bits of different options to be configured.
>
> These are defined as constants in the `SWT` class; for example, the checkbox button style is represented as `SWT.CHECKBOX`. Options can be combined; to specify a flat button, one would *bitwise or* the values of the two fields together:
>
> ```
> new Button(parent,SWT.PUSH|SWT.FLAT)
> ```
>
> Generally, the value `SWT.NONE` can be used to represent default options.

The code adds an empty `Canvas` to the view, but how can it be drawn on? SWT does not expose a paint method on any of its widgets. Instead, `PaintListener` is called whenever the canvas needs to be repainted.

> **All in the name of performance**
>
> You may wonder why all these little things are different between the way SWT handles its widgets versus how AWT or Swing handle them. The answer is in the name of speed and delegation to native rendering and controls if at all possible. This mattered back in the early days of Java (Eclipse 1.0 was released when Java 1.3 was the most advanced runtime available) when neither the JITs nor the CPUs were as powerful as today.
>
> Secondly, the goal of SWT was to offload as much of the processing onto native components (like AWT) and let the OS do the heavy work instead of Java. By doing that, the time spent in the JVM could be minimized while allowing the OS to render the graphics in the most appropriate (and performant) way. The paint listener is one such example of how to avoid performing unnecessary drawing-related calls unless a component actually needs it.

The `paintControl()` method is invoked with a `PaintEvent` argument, which contains references to all the data needed to draw the component. To minimize method calls, the fields are publicly readable (not considered to be a good style, but certainly performant in this case). It also contains a reference to the graphics context (`GC`) which can be used to invoke drawing commands.

Finally, the event also records the region in which the paint event is to be fired. The x and y fields show the position of the top-left to start from, and the `width` and `height` fields of the event shows the drawing bounds.

In this case, the graphics context is set up with the necessary foreground color, and `drawArc()` is called between the bounds specified. Note that the arc is specified in degrees (from 0 with a 360 span) rather than radians or any other measure.

# Time for action – drawing a second hand

A clock with no hands and no numbers is just a circle.

Since arcs are drawn anticlockwise from 0 (on the right, or 3 p.m.) through 90 (12 p.m.), then 180 (9 p.m.), then 270 (6 p.m.), and finally back to 360 (3 p.m.), it is possible to calculate the arc's position for the second hand by using `(15-s)*6%360`.

1. Go to the `paintControl()` method of the `PaintListener` inside `ClockView`.

2. Add a variable `seconds` that is initialized to `new Date().getSeconds()`.

3. Get `SWT.COLOR_BLUE` via the display and store it in a local variable `blue`.

4. Set the background color of the graphics context to `blue`.

5. Draw an arc using the previous formula to draw the second hand.

   The code should look like the following:

```
public void paintControl(PaintEvent e) {
    int seconds = new Date().getSeconds();
    int arc = (15-seconds) * 6 % 360;
    Color blue = e.display.getSystemColor(SWT.COLOR_BLUE);
    e.gc.setBackground(blue);
    e.gc.fillArc(e.x,e.y,e.width-1,e.height-1,arc-1,2);
}
```

6. Start Eclipse and show the Clock View. The second hand will be shown once but won't change.

7. Resize the view then the second hand will be drawn in the new location.

# What just happened?

The code calculates the position on the arc that the second hand will need to be drawn. Since the arc degrees go anticlockwise, the seconds have to be negative. The offset of 15 represents the fact that 0 represents 15 seconds on the clock (3 p.m.). This is then multiplied by 6 (60 seconds = 360 degrees) and finally the result is calculated modulus 360, to ensure that it's up to 360 degrees. (The value can be negative; the arc calculation works in this way as well.)

Although `drawArc()` colors in the foreground color, the `fillArc()` colors in the background color. The GC maintains two colors; a foreground and a background color. Normally, an SWT `Color` object needs to have `dispose()` after use, but to simplify this example the `Display` class' `getSystemColor()` is used, whose result does not need to be disposed.

Finally, the arc is drawn from the second hand position and 2 degrees afterwards. To center it, it starts from `pos-1`, so the arc is drawn from `pos-1` to `pos+1`.

When the view is resized, a `redraw()` is issued on the `Canvas`, and so the second hand is drawn in the correct position. However, to be useful as a clock, this should be done automatically; do this while the view is active.

# Time for action – animating the second hand

The second hand is drawn with a `redraw()` on the `Canvas`, but this will need to be run periodically. If it is redrawn once per second, it can emulate a clock ticking.

Eclipse has a mechanism called **jobs** which would be just right for this task, but these will be covered in *Chapter 4, Interacting with the User*. So to begin with, a simple `Thread` class will be used to issue the redraw.

1. Open the `ClockView` class.

2. Add the following to the bottom of the `createPartControl()` method:

```
new Thread("TickTock") {
  public void run() {
  while (!clock.isDisposed()) {
    clock.redraw();
    try {
      Thread.sleep(1000);
    } catch (InterruptedException e) {
      return;
    }
  }
  }
}.start();
```

3. Re-launch the test Eclipse instance and open the Clock View.

4. Open the host Eclipse instance and look in the Console View for the errors.

## *What just happened?*

When the Clock View is created, a `Thread` is created and started, which runs once per second. Every second, in the host Eclipse instance's Console View, an exception is generated that looks like this:

```
Exception in thread "TickTock"
org.eclipse.swt.SWTException: Invalid thread access
   at org.eclipse.swt.SWT.error(SWT.java:4361)
   at org.eclipse.swt.SWT.error(SWT.java:4276)
   at org.eclipse.swt.SWT.error(SWT.java:4247)
   at org.eclipse.swt.widgets.Widget.error(Widget.java:775)
   at org.eclipse.swt.widgets.Widget.checkWidget(Widget.java:570)
   at org.eclipse.swt.widgets.Control.redraw(Control.java:2748)
   at com.packtpub.e4.clock.ui.views.ClockView$2.run(ClockView.java:41)
```

This is expected behavior in this case, but it's worth taking a dive into the SWT internals to understand why.

Many windowing systems have a UI thread which is responsible for coordinating the user interface updates with the program code. If long running operations execute on the UI thread, the program can appear to hang and become unresponsive. Many windowing systems will have an automated process, which changes the cursor into an hourglass if the UI thread for an application is blocked for more than a short period of time.

SWT mirrors this by providing a UI thread for interacting with the user interface, and ensures that updates to SWT components are done on this thread. Redraws occur on the SWT thread, as do calls to methods like `createPartControl()`.

 Technically, SWT is capable of supporting multiple OS UI threads.

In the clock update example, updates are being fired on a different thread (in this case, the `TickTock` thread) and it results in the preceding exception. So how are these updates run on the right thread?

## Time for action – running on the UI thread

To execute code on the UI thread, `Runnables` are posted to the `Display` class via two methods, `syncExec()` and `asyncExec()`. The `syncExec()` method runs the code synchronously (that is, the caller blocks until the code has been run), while the `asyncExec()` method runs the code asynchronously (that is, the caller continues while the code is run in the background).

The `Display` class is SWT's handle to a monitor (so a runtime may have more than one `Display` object, and each may have its own resolution). To get hold of an instance, call either `Display.getCurrent()` or `Display.getDefault()`. However, it's much better to get a `Display` class from an associated view or widget. In this case, the `Canvas` has an associated `Display`.

1. Go to the `TickTock` thread inside the `createPartControl()` method of the `ClockView` class.

2. Inside the `run()` method, replace the call to `clock.redraw()` with:

```
clock.getDisplay().asyncExec(new Runnable() {
  public void run() {
    if(clock != null && !clock.isDisposed())
      clock.redraw();
  }
});
```

3. Run the test Eclipse instance and show the Clock View. The second hand should now update automatically.

## What just happened?

This time, the event will execute as expected. One thread, `TickTock`, is running in the background, and every second it posts a `Runnable` to the UI thread, which then runs asynchronously. This example could have used `syncExec()`, and the difference would not have been noticeable; but in general, using `asyncExec()` is to be preferred unless there is a specific reason to need the synchronous blocking behavior.

The thread is in a while loop and is guarded with a call to `clock.isDisposed()`. Each SWT widget is non-disposed when it is initially created, and then subsequently disposed with a call to `dispose()`. Once a widget is disposed, any native operating system resources are returned and any further operations will throw an exception. In this example, the `Canvas` is disposed when the view is closed, which in turn disposes the components contained therein. As a result, when the view is closed, the `Thread` automatically ceases its loop. (The `Thread` can also be aborted by interrupting it during its 1 second sleep pauses.)

Note that the test for whether the widget is not `null` or disposed is done in the `Runnable` as well. Although the widget isn't disposed when it is added to the event queue, it might be when the event is processed some time later.

# Time for action – creating a reusable widget

Although the `ClockView` shows an animated clock, creating an independent widget will allow the clock to be reused in other places.

1. Create a new class in the `com.packtpub.e4.clock.ui` package, called `ClockWidget`, that extends `Canvas`.

2. Create a constructor that takes a `Composite parent` and an `int style` bits parameter, and passes them to the superclass:

```
public ClockWidget(Composite parent, int style) {
   super(parent, style);
}
```

3. Move the implementation of the `paintControl()` method from the `ClockView` to the `ClockWidget`. Remove the `PaintListener` references from the `ClockView` class.

4. In the `ClockWidget` constructor, register an anonymous `PaintListener` that delegates the call to the `paintControl()` method:

```
addPaintListener(new PaintListener() {
   public void paintControl(PaintEvent e) {
     ClockWidget.this.paintControl(e);
   }
});
```

5. Move the `TickTock` thread from `ClockView` to the `ClockWidget` constructor; this will allow the `ClockWidget` to operate independently. Change any references for `clock` to `ClockWidget.this`:

```
new Thread("TickTock") {
  public void run() {
    while (!ClockWidget.this.isDisposed()) {
      ClockWidget.this.getDisplay().asyncExec(
       new Runnable() {
         public void run() {
           if (!ClockWidget.this.isDisposed())
             ClockWidget.this.redraw();
         }
      });
      try {
        Thread.sleep(1000);
      } catch (InterruptedException e) {
        return;
      }
    }
  }
}.start();
```

**6.** Add a `computeSize()` method to allow the clock to have a square appearance that is the minimum of the `width` and `height`. Note that `SWT.DEFAULT` may be passed in, which has the value `-1`, so this needs to be handled explicitly:

```
public Point computeSize(int w,int h,boolean changed) {
  int size;
  if(w == SWT.DEFAULT) {
    size = h;
  } else if (h == SWT.DEFAULT) {
    size = w;
  } else {
    size = Math.min(w,h);
  }
  if(size == SWT.DEFAULT)
    size = 50;
  return new Point(size,size);
}
```

**7.** Finally, change `ClockView` to instantiate the `ClockWidget` instead of the `Canvas` in the `createPartControl()` method:

```
final ClockWidget clock = new ClockWidget(parent,SWT.NONE);
```

**8.** Run the test Eclipse instance and the clock should be shown as before.

## What just happened?

The drawing logic was moved into its own widget, and hooked up `PaintListener` to a custom method in `ClockWidget` so that it could render itself. This allows `Clock` to be used standalone in any Eclipse or SWT application.

In a real application, the clocks would not have their own thread; it would either be the case that a single `Thread` would control updates to all `Clock` instances, or they would be set up with repeating `Jobs` using the Eclipse jobs framework. `Jobs` will be covered in *Chapter 4, Interacting with the User*.

The technique of using an anonymous class to bind a specific listener type to the instance of the class is a common pattern in SWT. The convention is to use the same method name in the enclosing class; this helps to disambiguate the use. (Remember to set the listener at startup, as otherwise it can be confusing why it's not getting called.) It's also why `ClockWidget.this` is used in the delegation call; directly invoking `this.paintControl()` or `paintControl()` would have ended up in an infinite loop.

It's also possible for `ClockWidget` to implement `PaintListener` directly; in this case, `addPaintListener(this)` would be called in the constructor. Modern JITs will optimize the calls to equivalent code paths in any case; it comes down to a style decision as to whether `ClockWidget` should implement the `PaintListener` interface or not.

Finally, compute the size based on the hints. This is called by the layout manager to determine what size the widget should be. For widgets with a fixed size (say, a text string or an image) the size can vary depending on the layout. In this case, it returns a square, based on the minimal size of the supplied width and height hints, or 50, whichever is bigger. The `SWT.DEFAULT` value is `-1` which has to be dealt with specifically.

# Time for action – using layouts

Now that `ClockWidget` has been created, multiple instances can be added into `ClockView`.

1. Modify the `ClockView` class's `createPartControl()` method to create three `ClockWidget` instances:

   ```
   final ClockWidget clock1 = new ClockWidget(parent, SWT.NONE);
   final ClockWidget clock2 = new ClockWidget(parent, SWT.NONE);
   final ClockWidget clock3 = new ClockWidget(parent, SWT.NONE);
   ```

2. Run the test Eclipse instance and show the Clock View. Three clocks will be shown, counting in seconds:

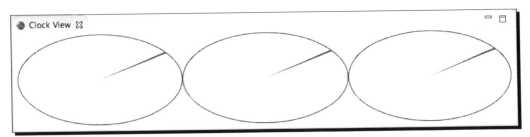

3. In the `ClockView` constructor, create a new `RowLayout` with `SWT.HORIZONTAL`, and then set it as the layout on `parent Composite`:

   ```
   public void createPartControl(Composite parent) {
       RowLayout layout = new RowLayout(SWT.HORIZONTAL);
       parent.setLayout(layout);
   ```

**4.** Run the code again now and the clocks will be in a row (horizontal):

**5.** Resize the view, the clocks will flow into different rows:

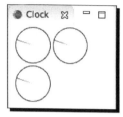

RowLayout has a number of fields that can affect how the widgets are laid out:

 ◆ center – if components are centered (vertically or horizontally)
 ◆ fill – if the entire size of the parent should be taken up
 ◆ justify – if the components should be spaced so they reach the end
 ◆ pack – if components should get their preferred size or expanded to fill space
 ◆ wrap – if the components should wrap at the end of the line

There are also options to control any pixel spacing between elements (spacing) and any margins at the edge (marginHeight and marginWidth, or which can be specified individually as marginTop, marginBottom, marginLeft, and marginRight).

**6.** Every SWT widget has an optional layout data object, which is specific to the kind of layout being used by its containing parent. In the ClockView class's createPartControl() method, add a RowData object to the first and last clocks:

```
clock1.setLayoutData(new RowData(20,20));
clock3.setLayoutData(new RowData(100,100));
```

**7.** Open the **Clock View**, and the clocks are shown in increasing order of size:

# What just happened?

A `Composite` is capable of handling multiple widgets, and the job of deciding where to put these components is done by the associated `LayoutManager`. The standard layout managers include `FillLayout`, `RowLayout`, `GridLayout`, `FormLayout`, and `CellLayout` (note that `CellLayout` is technically not SWT, but part of the Eclipse UI Workbench). The default for Eclipse Views is to use a `FillLayout`; though a manually created `Composite` has no associated layout by default.

Both `FillLayout` and `RowLayout` create a horizontal or vertical set of widgets with controlled sizes. `FillLayout` is the default for views and expands the size of the widgets to the space available. `RowLayout` will set the component's sizes to their default size as calculated by `computeSize(0,0)`.

Layout managers have different properties such as `SWT.HORIZONTAL` and `SWT.VERTICAL`, which change how elements are wrapped if the row becomes full. The documentation for each layout manager has information as to what it supports.

Layout data objects are used to specify different values for objects within `Composite`. The preceding example looked at `RowData` options.

The corresponding `FillData` class for `FillLayout` has no public fields, and therefore is of lesser use. Other layout managers, such as `GridLayout`, have more extensive customization options in the `GridData` class. Remember when changing `LayoutManager` the associated layout data objects will need to be modified accordingly.

## Pop quiz – understanding views

Q1. What is the parent class of any views that you create?

Q2. How do you register views with the Eclipse workbench?

Q3. What two arguments are passed into every SWT widget and what are they for?

Q4. What does it mean for a widget to be disposed?

Q5. How do you draw a circle on a `Canvas`?

Q6. What listener do you have to register to execute drawing operations?

Q7. What happens if you try and update an SWT object from outside a UI thread?

Q8. How do you update SWT components from a different thread?

Q9. What value is `SWT.DEFAULT` used for?

Q10. How do you specify a specific size for a widget in a `RowLayout`?

## Have a go hero – drawing hours and minute hands

Now that the Clock View is animating a second hand, do the same calculation for the hour and minute hands. Minutes will be calculated the same way as seconds; for hours, multiply the hours by 5 to map onto the same path.

Draw lines for every five minutes using the `drawLine()` function. Some simple maths will be required to calculate the start and end points of the line.

Finally, draw the text lettering for the numbers in the right locations. The `drawText()` method can be used to place a string at a particular place. Use this to print out the current time in the center of the clock, or print out the date.

# Managing resources

One of the challenges in adopting SWT is that native resources must be freed when they are no longer needed. Unlike AWT or Swing, which perform these operations automatically when an object is garbage collected, SWT needs manual resource management.

**Why does SWT need manual resource management?**

A common question asked is why SWT has this rule, when Java has had perfectly acceptable garbage collection for many years. In part, it's because SWT predated acceptable garbage collection, but it's also to try and return native resources as soon as they are no longer needed.

From a performance perspective, adding a `finalize()` method to an object also causes the garbage collector to work harder; much of the speed in today's garbage collectors are because they don't need to call methods, as they are invariably missing. It also hurts in SWT's case because the object must post its dispose request onto the UI thread, which delays its garbage collection as the object becomes reachable again.

Not all objects need to be disposed; in fact, there is an abstract class `Resource`, which is the parent of all resources that need disposal. It is this class that implements the `dispose()` method, as well as the `isDisposed()` call. Once a resource is disposed, subsequent calls to its methods will throw an exception with a **Widget is disposed** or **Graphic is disposed** message.

Further confusing matters, some instances of `Resources` should not be disposed by the caller. Generally, instances owned by other classes in accessors should not be disposed; for example, the `Color` instance returned by the `Display` class's `getSystemColor()` method is owned by the `Display` class, so shouldn't be disposed by the caller. `Resources` that are instantiated by the caller must be disposed of explicitly.

# Time for action – getting colorful

To add an option for `ClockWidget` to have a different color, an instance must be obtained, instead of the hardcoded `BLUE` reference. Since `Color` objects are `Resources`, they must be disposed correctly when the widget is disposed.

To avoid passing in a `Color` directly, the constructor will be changed to take an `RGB` value (which is three `int` values), and use that to instantiate a `Color` object to store for later. The lifetime of the `Color` instance can be tied to the lifetime of `ClockWidget`.

*1.* Add a `private final Color` instance called `color` to `ClockWidget`:

```
private final Color color;
```

*2.* Modify the constructor of `ClockWidget` to take an `RGB` instance, and use it to instantiate a `Color` object. Note that the color is leaked at this point, and will be fixed later:

```
public ClockWidget(Composite parent, int style, RGB rgb) {
  super(parent, style);
  // FIXME color is leaked!
  this.color = new Color(parent.getDisplay(),rgb);
  ...
```

*3.* Modify the `paintControl()` method to use this custom color:

```
protected void paintControl(PaintEvent e) {
  ...
  e.gc.setBackground(color);
  e.gc.fillArc(e.x, e.y, e.width-1, e.height-1, arc-1, 2);
```

*4.* Finally, change `ClockView` to instantiate the three clocks with different colors:

```
public void createPartControl(Composite parent) {
  ...
  final ClockWidget clock =
    new ClockWidget(parent, SWT.NONE, new RGB(255,0,0));
  final ClockWidget clock2 =
    new ClockWidget(parent, SWT.NONE, new RGB(0,255,0));
  final ClockWidget clock3 =
    new ClockWidget(parent, SWT.NONE, new RGB(0,0,255));
```

**5.** Now run the application and see the new colors in use:

## What just happened?

The `Color` object was created based on the red/green/blue value passed in to the
`ClockWidget` constructor. Since `RGB` is just a value object, it doesn't need to be
disposed afterwards.

Once the `Color` is created, it is assigned to the instance field. When the clocks are drawn,
the second hands are the appropriate colors.

 The one problem with this approach is that the `Color` instance is leaked.
When the view is disposed, the associated `Color` object is garbage
collected, but the resources associated with the native handle are not.

## Time for action – finding the leak

It is necessary to know how many resources are allocated in order to know if the leak has
been plugged or not. Fortunately, SWT provides a mechanism to do this via the `Display`
and the `DeviceData` classes. Normally, this is done by a separate plug-in, but in this
example `ClockView` will be modified to show this behavior.

**1.** At the start of the `ClockView` class' `createPartControl()` method, add a call to
obtain the number of allocated `Objects`, via `DeviceData` of the `Display` class:

```
public void createPartControl(Composite parent) {
    Object[] oo=parent.getDisplay().getDeviceData().objects;
```

**2.** Iterate through the allocated `objects` counting how many are instances of `Color`:

```
int c = 0;
for (int i = 0; i < oo.length; i++)
  if (oo[i] instanceof Color)
    c++;
```

**3.** Print the count to the standard error stream:

```
System.err.println("There are " + c + " Color instances");
```

**4.** Now run the code in debug mode and show the Clock View. The following will be displayed in the host Eclipse Console View:

```
There are 0 Color instances
There are 0 Color instances
There are 0 Color instances
```

> For efficiency, SWT doesn't log all the allocated resources all the time.
> Instead, it's an option which is enabled at startup through an `options` file,
> which is a text properties file with `name=value` pairs. This can be passed
> to an Eclipse instance at launch via the `-debug` flag.
>
> Fortunately, it is easy to set within Eclipse from the launch configuration's
> tracing tab.

**5.** Close the target Eclipse application, if it is running.

**6.** Go to the launch configuration via the **Debug | Debug Configurations** menu.

**7.** Select the Eclipse Application (if it's not selected already) and go to the **Tracing** tab. Enable the tracing option, and select the `org.eclipse.ui` plugin. Select both the `debug` (at the top) and the `trace/graphics` options:

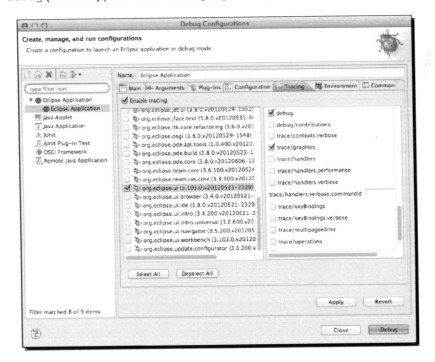

**8.** Now launch the application by hitting **Debug**, and open and close the Clock View a few times:

```
There are 87 Color instances
There are 92 Color instances
There are 95 Color instances
There are 98 Color instances
```

## What just happened?

Clearly, something is leaking three `Color` instances each time the Clock View is opened. Not surprisingly, three instances of the `Color` object are allocated in the three instances of `ClockWidget`. This suggests that there is a resource leak in `ClockView` or `ClockWidget`.

When SWT is running in trace mode, it will keep a list of previously allocated resources in a global list, which is accessible through the `DeviceData` object. When the resource is disposed, it will be removed from the allocated list. This allows the monitoring of the state of resources at play in the Eclipse workbench and discover leaks, typically through repeated actions and noting an increase each time in the resource count.

Other object types are also stored in this list (for example, `Fonts` and `Images`) so it's important to filter by type when looking for a resource set. It's also important to note that Eclipse has its own runtime resources, which are used and so when tracing these are included in the list as well.

By learning how to enable tracing and how to programmatically detect what objects are allocated, it will be possible to discover such leaks, or verify whether they have been fixed afterwards.

## Time for action – plugging the leak

Now that the leak has been discovered, it needs to be fixed. The solution is to `dispose()` the `Color` once it is finished with, which will be when the view itself is removed.

A quick investigation of `ClockWidget` suggests that overriding `dispose()` might work. (Note that this is not the correct solution; see later for why.)

**1.** Create a `dispose()` method in `ClockWidget` with the following code:

```
@Override
public void dispose() {
  if(color != null && !color.isDisposed())
    color.dispose();
  super.dispose();
}
```

**2.** Run the Eclipse application in debug mode (with the tracing enabled, as before) and open and close the view. The output will show something like:

```
There are 87 Color instances
There are 91 Color instances
There are 94 Color instances
There are 98 Color instances
```

**3.** Remove the `dispose()` method (since it doesn't work as intended) and modify the constructor of `ClockWidget` to add an anonymous `DisposeListener` that disposes of the associated `Color` object:

```
public ClockWidget(Composite parent, int style, RGB rgb) {
  super(parent, style);
  this.color = new Color(parent.getDisplay(),rgb);
  addDisposeListener(new DisposeListener() {
    public void widgetDisposed(DisposeEvent e) {
      if(color != null && !color.isDisposed())
        color.dispose();
    }
  });
}
```

**4.** Now run the code and see what happens when the view is opened and closed a few times:

```
There are 87 Color instances
There are 88 Color instances
There are 88 Color instances
There are 88 Color instances
```

The leak has been plugged.

## What just happened?

Once the source of the leak has been identified, the correct course of action is to `dispose()` the `Color` object when no longer needed. However, although it is tempting to think that overriding the `dispose()` method of `ClockWidget` would be all that is needed, in fact it doesn't work. The only time `dispose()` is called is at the top level `Shell` (or `ViewPart`), and if there are no registered listeners then the dispose method is not called on any components beneath. Since this can be quite counter-intuitive, it is of value to have stepped through code to verify that that is the behavior so that it can be avoided in the future.

Detecting, and resolving, resource leaks can be a time-consuming process. There is a plug-in, developed by the SWT team, which can perform a snapshot of resources and verify whether there are any leaks using a similar technique to the preceding one. The plug-in is located at the SWT tools update site (refer to `http://www.eclipse.org/swt/tools.php` and search for Sleak for more information) and can be installed to avoid having to modify code (as was done in this example) for the purposes of monitoring allocated resources.

Don't forget when performing tests that the first one or two runs may give different results by virtue of the fact that other resources may be being initialized at the time. Take a couple of readings first before relying on any data, and bear in mind that other plug-ins (that maybe executing in the background) may be doing resource allocation as well.

Finally, when working with any SWT widget, it is good practice to check whether the resource is already disposed or not. The JavaDoc for `dispose()` says that this is not strictly necessary, and that resources which are already disposed will treat this as a no-op method.

## Pop quiz – understanding resources

Q1. Where do resource leaks come from?

Q2. What are the different types of `Resources`?

Q3. How can you enable SWT resource tracking?

Q4. Once enabled, how do you find out what objects are tracked?

Q5. What's the right way and the wrong way to free resources after use?

## Have a go hero – extending the clock widget

Now that the `ClockWidget` is running, try the following:

- Write a sleak-like view, which periodically counts allocated objects by type.
- Modify any text written by acquiring a `Font` object, with disposal.
- Create a generic dispose listener that takes an instance of `Resource`.
- Provide a `setColor()` method which allows you to change the color.

# Interacting with the user

The whole point of a user interface is to interact with the user. Having a view which displays information may be useful, but it is often necessary to ask the user for data or respond to user actions.

# Time for action – getting in focus

To allow the time zone of the clock widgets to be changed, a drop-down box (known as Combo) as well as a Button will be added to the view. The Combo will be created from an array of String representing TimeZone IDs.

1. Create a timezones field in the ClockView class:

   ```
   private Combo timezones;
   ```

2. At the end of the createPartControl() method, add this snippet to create the drop-down list:

   ```
   public void createPartControl(Composite parent) {
     ...
     String[] ids = TimeZone.getAvailableIDs();
     timezones = new Combo(parent, SWT.SIMPLE);
     timezones.setVisibleItemCount(5);
     for (int i = 0; i < ids.length; i++) {
      timezones.add(ids[i]);
     }
   }
   ```

3. Run the Eclipse and open the Clock View again, and a list of time zones will be shown:

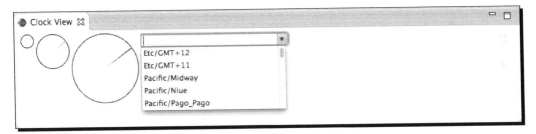

4. It's conventional to set the focus on a particular widget when a view is opened. Implement the appropriate call in the ClockView's setFocus() method:

   ```
   public void setFocus() {
     timezones.setFocus();
   }
   ```

5. Run Eclipse and open the Clock View, and the time zone drop-down widget will be focused automatically.

## What just happened?

Every SWT `Control` has a `setFocus()` method, which is used to switch focus for the application to that particular widget. When the view is focused (which happens both when it's opened, and also when the user switches to it after being in a different view) its `setFocus()` method is called.

 ☞ E4: As will be discussed in *Chapter 7, Understanding the Eclipse 4 Model*, in E4 the `setFocus()` method may be called anything and annotated with the `@Focus` annotation. Conventionally, and to save sanity, it helps to call this method `setFocus()`.

## Time for action – responding to input

To show the effect of changing the `TimeZone`, it is necessary to add an hour hand to the clock. When the time zone is changed in the drop-down box, the hour hand will be updated.

1.  Add an `offset` field to `ClockWidget` along with a setter:

    ```
    private int offset;
    public void setOffset(int offset) {
      this.offset = offset;
    }
    ```

2.  Getters and setters can be generated automatically. Once the field is added, the **Source | Generate Getters and Setters** menu option can be used to generate all missing getters and/or setters; in addition, a single getter/setter can be generated by typing `set` in the class body, followed by *Ctrl* + Space (*Cmd* + Space on OS X).

3.  Add an hour hand in the `paintControl()` method using the following:

    ```
    e.gc.setBackground(e.display.getSystemColor(SWT.COLOR_BLACK));
    int hours = new Date().getHours() + offset;
    arc = (3 - hours) * 30 % 360;
    e.gc.fillArc(e.x, e.y, e.width-1, e.height-1, arc - 5, 10);
    ```

4.  To update the clock when the time zone is changed, register a `SelectionListener` property on the `Combo` in the `createPartControl()` method of the `ClockView` class:

    ```
    timezones.addSelectionListener(new SelectionListener() {
      public void widgetSelected(SelectionEvent e) {
        String z = timezones.getText();
        TimeZone tz = z == null ? null : TimeZone.getTimeZone(z);
        TimeZone dt = TimeZone.getDefault();
    ```

```
        int offset = tz == null ? 0 : (
          tz.getOffset(System.currentTimeMillis()) -
          dt.getOffset(System.currentTimeMillis())) / 3600000;
        clock3.setOffset(offset);
        clock3.redraw();
      }
      public void widgetDefaultSelected(SelectionEvent e) {
        clock3.setOffset(0);
        clock3.redraw();
      }
    });
```

5. Run the Eclipse instance, and modify the time zone. The updates should be drawn on the last clock instance:

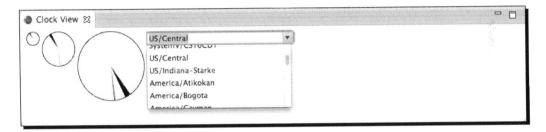

## What just happened?

The Combo box's addSelectionListener() method notifies any changes in the drop-down list. When a notification is received, the text from the Combo box is used to lookup the corresponding time zone offset from the TimeZone class. The difference with the current time zone's offset is subtracted, and since it's in milliseconds, divide by 1000 and then divide by 60 times 60 to convert it to hours. (This also truncates it to an even number of hours.)

If the selection is not found, or the default selection is chosen (in this case, the one with no value) then the offset is reset to zero.

The clock's hour hand doesn't quite behave properly; typically, the hour hand is shorter than the second hand, and the hour hand jumps between hours instead of smoothly moving round as the time progresses. Fixing this is left as an exercise for the reader.

To render the changes immediately, the clock is asked to redraw itself. This could be done inside the ClockView class's setOffset() method; but it would have to check that it was done from the SWT thread, or arrange for it to be posted on the thread asynchronously. Instead, for convenience clock3.redraw() is done immediately after setting the offset, while still inside the SWT thread.

## Pop quiz – understanding widgets

Q1. How do you mark a widget as being the default one for a view?

Q2. How do you update a widget after modifying it?

Q3. What listener can you register with a `Combo`?

Q4. What's the purpose of the `widgetDefaultSelected()` method?

## Have a go hero – updating the clock widget

Now that the `ClockWidget` can handle time zones, do the following:

- Update the hour hand so that the position is calculated based on fractional hours.
- Display the time zone underneath the clock face in the `ClockWidget`.
- Modify the `ClockWidget` so that it can take a `TimeZone` rather than an offset.
- Show if the time displayed is in summer time or not.

# Using other SWT widgets

SWT contains many other widgets other than `Canvas`, and this section covers some of them. JFace will be covered in the next chapter, which provides a Model-View-Controller view to designing GUIs, but it's helpful to know the base SWT classes upon which they are built.

## Time for action – adding items to the tray

Most operating systems have the concept of a **tray** as a set of icons visible from the main window, which can provide quick access components. On OS X, these are represented as icons across the top menu bar; on Windows, as icons on the bottom-right near the clock. Linux systems have various approaches which do similar, and some operating systems have none. Since there is only one `Tray`, it is necessary to add the item only once. The `Activator` class can be used to ensure that `TrayItem` is created at startup and removed at shutdown.

1. Open the `Activator` class and add two private fields:

```
private TrayItem trayItem;
private Image image;
```

2. Add the following to the `start()` method:

```
final Display display = Display.getDefault();
display.asyncExec(new Runnable() {
  public void run() {
```

```
      image = new Image(display, Activator.class
        .getResourceAsStream("/icons/sample.gif"));
      Tray tray = display.getSystemTray();
      if (tray != null && image != null) {
        trayItem = new TrayItem(tray, SWT.NONE);
        trayItem.setToolTipText("Hello World");
        trayItem.setVisible(true);
        trayItem.setText("Hello World");
        trayItem.setImage(new Image(trayItem.getDisplay(),
          Activator.class.getResourceAsStream("/icons/sample.gif")));
      }
    }
  }
});
```

3. Run the test Eclipse instance, and show the Clock View. The small `sample.gif` icon should appear in the task area (top right of OS X, bottom-right of Windows).

4. To test the effect of stopping and restarting the bundle, open the Console View in the test Eclipse instance. Click on the drop-down list on the top-right of the View to create a Host OSGi Console.

```
WARNING: This console is connected to the current running instance
of Eclipse!osgi>
"Framework is launched."
```

5. Type `ss clock` at the `osgi>` prompt and it will show a bundle ID, which can be used to start/stop:

```
osgi> ss clock

id       State        Bundle
4        RESOLVED     com.packtpub.e4.clock.ui_1.0.0.qualifier
```

6. Start and stop the bundle by typing `start` and `stop` into the console with the ID given the preceding output:

```
osgi> stop 4
osgi> start 4
osgi> stop 4
osgi> start 4
```

7. Notice that a new `TrayItem` appears in the `Tray` each time it is started. The clean routine needs to be added in the `Activator` class's `stop()` method:

```
public void stop(BundleContext context) throws Exception {
  if (trayItem != null && !trayItem.isDisposed()) {
    Display.getDefault().asyncExec(new Runnable() {
      public void run() {
        if (trayItem != null && !trayItem.isDisposed())
```

```
            trayItem.dispose();
        }
    });
}
if (image != null && !image.isDisposed()) {
    Display.getDefault().asyncExec(new Runnable() {
        public void run() {
            if (image != null && !image.isDisposed())
                image.dispose();
        }
    });
}
```

8. Re-run the application and start and stop the bundle (probably the same bundle ID as before, but you should check rather than assume); the SWT tray icon should go and come back each time the bundle is stopped and started.

## What just happened?

An SWT `TrayItem` is added to the system's `Tray` when the bundle started, and removed it when the bundle stopped. The icon that came with the sample project was used. To use a different one, don't forget to update the `build.properties` file.

Since the tray is a graphical component, if there's no image then the item isn't shown. The tooltips are optional. Note also that not every system has the concept of a tray, so `null` is a legitimate return value for `display.getSystemTray()`.

A bundle is started automatically when it is loaded, and the loading is triggered by a menu item. If a View is opened, the bundle that class is loaded from is automatically started. They can also be started and stopped programmatically, or through the host OSGi console, which is useful to test whether the `Activator` class's `start()` and `stop()` methods are working correctly.

## Time for action – responding to the user

When the user clicks on the icon, nothing happens. That's because there is not a registered listener on `TrayItem` itself. There are two listeners that can be registered: a `SelectionListener`, called when the icon is clicked, and a `MenuDetectListener` which can respond to a context-sensitive menu. The former will be used to present a clock in its own window, which in SWT terms is called a `Shell`.

1. Open the `Activator` class.

2. Add a field to store a `Shell`:

```
private Shell shell;
```

**3.** Go to the `run()` method inside the `Runnable` in the `Activator` class's `start()` method.

**4.** After the creation of the `TrayItem`, call `addSelectionListener()`, which creates a new `Shell` with a `ClockView`:

```
trayItem.addSelectionListener(new SelectionListener() {
  public void widgetSelected(SelectionEvent e) {
    if (shell == null) {
      shell = new Shell(trayItem.getDisplay());
      shell.setLayout(new FillLayout());
      new ClockWidget(shell, SWT.NONE, new RGB(255, 0, 255));
      shell.pack();
    }
    shell.open();
  }
});
```

**5.** Run the Eclipse instance, open the Clock View and click on the tray icon. A windowed clock will be shown:

**6.** Ensure that the `Shell` is disposed when the bundle is stopped, so add the following to the end of the `Activator` class 's `stop()` method:

```
if (shell != null && !shell.isDisposed()) {
  Display.getDefault().asyncExec(new Runnable() {
    public void run() {
      if (shell != null && !shell.isDisposed())
        shell.dispose();
    }
  });
}
```

**7.** Run the Eclipse instance, click on the `TrayItem`, and use the host OSGi console to stop and start the bundle. The window should disappear when the bundle is stopped.

## What just happened?

When `TrayItem` is installed into the system's `Tray`, event listeners can be registered to respond to user input. The one that gets called when the icon is clicked is the `SelectionListener`, and this gives the opportunity to display the window (or `Shell` in SWT's terminology).

The `Display` associated with the `TrayItem` is used when instantiating the `Shell`. Although either `Display.getDefault()` or `Display.getCurrent()` could be used, neither of these would be the right option. When developers are running in multi-monitor mode, or with a virtual display that spans multiple desktops, it's important to ensure that the `Shell` is shown on the same display as the corresponding `Tray`.

Without a `LayoutManager`, the clock won't show up. `FillLayout` is used here to ensure that the clock is made as large as the window (and resizes accordingly to the window itself). Once the window is created the `pack()` method is called, which sets the size of the window to the preferred size of its children; in this case, `ClockView`.

Finally, the window is shown with the `open()` call.

## Time for action – modal and other effects

There are a number of style bits that are applicable to windows, and some useful methods to affect how the window appears. For example, it might be desirable to make the clock appear semi-transparently, which allows the clock to float above other windows. SWT's `Shell` has a number of these options that can be set.

1.  Modify the instantiation of the `Shell` inside the `widgetSelected()` method in the `Activator` class's inner class to add `SWT.NO_TRIM` (no close/minimize/maximize widgets) and `SWT.ON_TOP` (floating on top of other windows):

    ```
    shell = new Shell(trayItem.getDisplay(),SWT.NO_TRIM|SWT.ON_TOP);
    ```

2.  Set the alpha value as `128`, which is semi-transparent:

    ```
    shell.setAlpha(128);
    ```

3.  Run the Eclipse instance, and click on the tray item to see what kind of window is created.

4.  To create a modal window (and thus, prevent interaction on the main window), change the flag to use `SWT.APPLICATION_MODAL`:

    ```
    shell = new Shell(trayItem.getDisplay(),SWT.APPLICATION_MODAL);
    ```

**5.** To make the application full-screen, call either `setFullScreen()` or `setMaximized()` depending on the platform:

```
shell.setFullScreen(true);
shell.setMaximized(true);
```

**6.** Note that without trims, it may be necessary to add controls such as detecting selection events to close the window.

**7.** Run the Eclipse application and see the effect these flags have on the window.

**8.** Change the `Shell` back to use `SWT.NO_TRIM` and `SWT.ON_TOP`.

**9.** To calculate a circular shape for the floating clock window, add the `circle()` method to the `Activator` class, which has been taken from `Snippet134.java` (taken from the SWT snippets page at `http://www.eclipse.org/swt/snippets/`):

```
private static int[] circle(int r, int offsetX, int offsetY) {
    int[] polygon = new int[8 * r + 4];
    //x^2 + y^2 = r^2
    for (int i = 0; i < 2 * r + 1; i++) {
        int x = i - r;
        int y = (int)Math.sqrt(r*r - x*x);
        polygon[2*i] = offsetX + x;
        polygon[2*i+1] = offsetY + y;
        polygon[8*r - 2*i - 2] = offsetX + x;
        polygon[8*r - 2*i - 1] = offsetY - y;
    }
    return polygon;
}
```

**10.** Finally, change the shape of the window to be circular by setting a `Region` on the `Shell`. This will have the effect of making it look like the clock itself is floating. Add the following code after the `Shell` is created in the `widgetSelected()` method:

```
final Region region = new Region();
region.add(circle(25, 25, 25));
shell.setRegion(region);
```

**11.** When run, the clock will look something like this:

**12.** For completeness, register a dispose listener on the shell to ensure that `Region` is cleaned up:

```
shell.addDisposeListener(new DisposeListener() {
  public void widgetDisposed(DisposeEvent e) {
    if (region != null && !region.isDisposed())
      region.dispose();
  }
});
```

## What just happened?

Varying the flags used to create the shell affects how that window is displayed and interacts with the user. Other calls on the shell can programmatically drive transitions to full-screen and maximized or minimized status, which can be useful in specific circumstances. Some windowing systems differentiate maximized and full-screen; others have distinct characteristics.

The `SWT.NO_TRIM` flag is used to display a window without the normal window furniture. This can be combined with setting a region via `setRegion()`, which allows creation of a non-rectangular shape.

Often, windows without trim are *floating*, that is, they should stay on top of the application window even when it hasn't got the focus. To achieve this, set the `SWT.ON_TOP` flag as well, and adjust the alpha (transparency) value with `setAlpha()`. The alpha value is between 0 (fully transparent) and 255 (fully opaque).

A `Region` can be defined from a set of connected points, or set on a pixel-by-pixel basis. It's important to note that a `Region` is also a `Resource`, and thus must be disposed of after use (which is typically when the `Shell` is closed). The clean-up operation is similar to that of the others discussed earlier, via the `addDisposeListener()` on the `Shell`.

## Time for action – groups and tab folders

A new `TimezoneView` will show a list of clocks in time zones around the world. This time, instead of using the plug-in wizard, the extension will be added manually.

 ☞ E4: The way views are defined for E4 is covered in *Chapter 7*, *Understanding the Eclipse 4 Model*. This chapter discusses how to do it in Eclipse 3.x and the Eclipse 3.x compatibility model of Eclipse 4.x.

**1.** Right-click on the project and navigate to **Plug-in Tools | Open Manifest**, or find the `plugin.xml` file in the navigator and double-click on it.

**2.** Go to the manifest editor's **Extensions** tab. The extensions will list `org.eclipse.` `ui.views`. Expand this, and underneath the **Timekeeping (category)** the **Clock View (view)** will be displayed, added via the plug-in wizard.

**3.** Right-click on `org.eclipse.ui.views` and navigate to **New | view** from the menu. A placeholder entry **name (view)** will be added to the list, and the right-hand side lists properties such as the `id`, `name`, `class`, and `category`. Fill in the following:

  ❑ **ID**: `com.packtpub.e4.clock.ui.views.TimeZoneView`

  ❑ **Name**: `Time Zone View`

  ❑ **Class**: `com.packtpub.e4.clock.ui.views.TimeZoneView`

  ❑ **Category**: `com.packtpub.e4.clock.ui`

  ❑ **Icon**: `icons/sample.gif`

**4.** Save the file. The following will be added into the `plugin.xml` file:

```
<view
  category="com.packtpub.e4.clock.ui"
  class="com.packtpub.e4.clock.ui.views.TimeZoneView"
  icon="icons/sample.gif"
  id="com.packtpub.e4.clock.ui.views.TimeZoneView"
  name="Time Zone View"
  restorable="true">
</view>
```

**5.** Create the `TimeZoneView` class. The easiest way is to go to the `plugin.xml` file's **Extensions** tab, select the **Time Zone View** and click on the hyperlinked **class*** label next to the class name. Alternatively, use the **New Class** wizard by navigating to **File | New | Class** to create `TimeZoneView` as a subclass of `ViewPart`, in the `com.packtpub.e4.clock.ui.views` package.

**6.** Create a class called `TimeZoneComparator`, which implements `Comparator`, in a new package `com.packtpub.e4.clock.ui.internal`. It is conventional to provide utility classes in an internal package to ensure that the implementation is not visible to others. The compare method should delegate to the `TimeZone` class's `compareTo()` method:

```
public class TimeZoneComparator implements Comparator {
  public int compare(Object o1, Object o2) {
    if(o1 instanceof TimeZone && o2 instanceof TimeZone) {
      return ((TimeZone) o1).getID().
       compareTo(((TimeZone) o2).getID());
    } else {
      throw new IllegalArgumentException();
    }
  }
}
```

**7.** Add a `public static` method to the `TimeZoneComparator` class called `getTimeZones()`, which will return a `Map` of `Set`s of `TimeZone`s. The `Map` will be indexed by the first half of the `TimeZone` class's ID. (A `TimeZone` class's ID is something like Europe/Milton_Keynes or America/New_York.) This will group all `TimeZone` in Europe together, and all `TimeZone` in America together:

```
public static Map<String, Set<TimeZone>> getTimeZones(){
  String[] ids = TimeZone.getAvailableIDs();
  Map<String, Set<TimeZone>> timeZones =
   new TreeMap<String, Set<TimeZone>>();
  for (int i = 0; i < ids.length; i++) {
    String[] parts = ids[i].split("/");
    if (parts.length == 2) {
      String region = parts[0];
      Set<TimeZone> zones = timeZones.get(region);
      if (zones == null) {
        zones = new TreeSet<TimeZone>(new TimeZoneComparator());
        timeZones.put(region, zones);
      }
      TimeZone timeZone = TimeZone.getTimeZone(ids[i]);
      zones.add(timeZone);

    }
  }
  return timeZones;
}
```

**8.** In the `createPartControl()` method in `TimeZoneView`, create `CTabFolder` and then iterate through the time zones, creating `CTabItem` for each one:

```
public void createPartControl(Composite parent) {
  Map<String, Set<TimeZone>> timeZones =
  TimeZoneComparator.getTimeZones();
  CTabFolder tabs = new CTabFolder(parent, SWT.BOTTOM);
  Iterator<Entry<String, Set<TimeZone>>> regionIterator =
   timeZones.entrySet().iterator();
  while(regionIterator.hasNext()) {
    Entry<String, Set<TimeZone>> region =
     regionIterator.next();
    CTabItem item = new CTabItem(tabs, SWT.NONE);
    item.setText(region.getKey());
  }
  tabs.setSelection(0);
}
```

**9.** Run this example and show the Time Zone View, and there should be a populated list of tabs along the bottom:

**10.** Inside the `while` loop, add a `Composite` instance to hold multiple `ClockWidget` classes for each `TimeZone` instance:

```
item.setText(region.getKey()); // from before
Composite clocks = new Composite(tabs, SWT.NONE);
clocks.setLayout(new RowLayout());
item.setControl(clocks);
```

**11.** Now iterate through the `TimeZones`, adding a `ClockWidget` for each:

```
RGB rgb = new RGB(128, 128, 128);
TimeZone td = TimeZone.getDefault();
Iterator<TimeZone> timezoneIterator = region.getValue().
iterator();
while (timezoneIterator.hasNext()) {
  TimeZone tz = timezoneIterator.next();
  ClockWidget clock = new ClockWidget(clocks, SWT.NONE, rgb);
  clock.setOffset((
    tz.getOffset(System.currentTimeMillis()) -
    td.getOffset(System.currentTimeMillis())) / 3600000);
}
```

**12.** Run the Eclipse instance and open the Time Zone View to see all of the clocks:

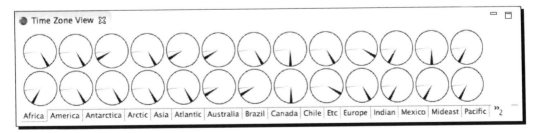

**13.** To make the clocks more identifiable, each will be put into a `Group` with an associated text label, so that the view hierarchy goes from `CTabItem→Composite→ClockWidget` to `CTabItem→Composite→ Group→ClockWidget`. Replace the call to create the the `ClockWidget` with this:

```
ClockWidget clock = new ClockWidget(clocks, SWT.NONE, rgb);
Group group = new Group(clocks,SWT.SHADOW_ETCHED_IN);
group.setText(tz.getID().split("/")[1]);
ClockWidget clock = new ClockWidget(group, SWT.NONE, rgb);
```

**14.** Run it again, and a series of blank elements will be shown:

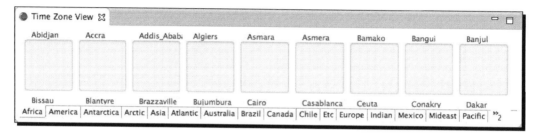

**15.** Since the default layout manager for general `Composite` classes is `null`, `Groups` don't have a layout manager and thus, the clocks are not getting sized appropriately. This can be fixed by setting a layout manager explicitly:

```
group.setLayout(new FillLayout());
```

**16.** Run it again, it looks a little bit more sane:

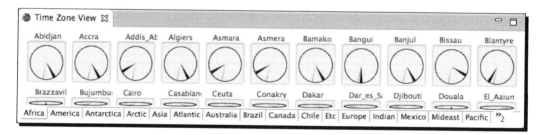

**17.** The clocks at the bottom are squashed and the view can't be scrolled, even though there are clearly more time zones available. To add scrolling to a widget, the `ScrolledComposite` can be used. This provides automatic scroll bars and interaction with the user to permit a much larger virtual area to be scrolled. The View hierarchy will change from `CtabItem→Composite→Group→ClockWidget` to `CTabItem→ScrolledComposite→Composite→Group→ClockWidget` instead:

```
Composite clocks = new Composite(tabs, SWT.NONE);
item.setControl(clocks);
ScrolledComposite scrolled = new
```

```
ScrolledComposite(tabs,SWT.H_SCROLL | SWT.V_SCROLL);
Composite clocks = new Composite(scrolled, SWT.NONE);
item.setControl(scrolled);
scrolled.setContent(clocks);
```

**18.** Run it again, but unfortunately this will be seen:

**19.** The problem is that `ScrolledComposite` has no minimum size. This can be calculated from the `clocks` container. Add this to the bottom of the `while` loop, after the contents of `ScrolledComposite` have been created:

```
Point size = clocks.computeSize(SWT.DEFAULT,SWT.DEFAULT);
scrolled.setMinSize(size);
scrolled.setExpandHorizontal(true);
scrolled.setExpandVertical(true);
```

**20.** Run it again, and the clocks now show up as expected:

**21.** The `ScrolledComposite` has a different background. To change it, add this line after constructing the clock's `Composite`:

```
clocks.setBackground(Display.getDefault()
  .getSystemColor(SWT.COLOR_LIST_BACKGROUND));
```

**22.** Now the Time Zone View is complete:

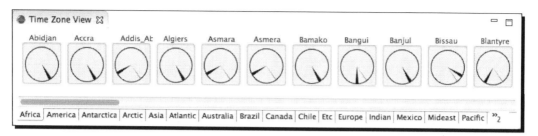

## What just happened?

A combination of `Composite` types created a tabbed environment using `CTabFolder` and `CTabItem` instances. Inside each `CTabItem`, a `ScrolledComposite` contained a `Composite` of multiple `Group` instances, each of which had a single `ClockWidget`. Adding the `ScrolledComposite` provided the scrolling for free, and `Group` allowed us to place text above the `ClockWidget` to display its time zone.

> Some of the components used here lie in the `org.eclipse.swt.custom` package, instead of the `org.eclipse.swt.widgets` package. Several of these begin with `C` as a custom designator to distinguish similarly named widgets. The `CTabFolder/Item` is an SWT-implemented class that provides the tab functionality; the corresponding OS widget `TabFolder/Item` uses a native rendered tab switcher.

## Pop quiz – using SWT

Q1. How do you add an icon to the system menu?

Q2. What does the `SWT.NO_TRIM` style do for `Shell` objects?

Q3. How do you make a `Shell` transparent?

Q4. What do you need to set to create a nonrectangular `Shell`?

Q5. What `Composite` allows you to attach a label to a set of related items?

Q6. What is the default layout manager for a `Group` instance?

Q7. How do you add scrolling to an existing widget?

## Have a go hero – enhancing the time zones

A set of times are displayed in different time zones, but there is scope for enhancements:

- Switch to the tab with the user's default time zone when the view is created
- Sort the clocks by time zone offset, rather than by name of the region
- Create a favorites tab and allow it to be populated by drag-and-drop
- Improve the speed of updates by sharing a single `Thread` to update all clocks
- Improve the sizing of the `ScrollableComposite` so that more than one row is displayed

# Summary

In this chapter, we covered how to create views with SWT widgets. We looked at both standard widget types as well as creating our own, and how those widgets can be assembled into groups with `Composite` and `Layout` classes. We also looked at how resources are managed within SWT, including stepping through the debug procedure for detecting and eliminating leaks.

In the next chapter, we will look at how to use a higher level of abstraction, JFace.

# 3

# Creating JFace Viewers

*In the last chapter, we looked at the basic building blocks of SWT, which provide
a glue layer between the native operating system's widgets and Java. We'll now
look at JFace, which builds upon SWT to provide an MVC architecture as well as
many of the common widgets used by Eclipse.*

In this chapter we will cover:

- Creating a view for showing hierarchical data
- Using image, font, and color resources
- Generating styled text
- Sorting and filtering entries in viewers
- Adding double-click actions
- Selections and property support
- Creating a view for showing tabular data

## Why JFace?

While SWT provides generic implementations for basic widgets (such as trees, buttons,
labels, and so on), these often work at a level that deals with strings and responding to
selection by integer index. To make it easier to display structured content, JFace provides
several viewers, which provide combinations of SWT widgets and event managers to provide
a UI for structured content.

There are many types of viewers (all subclasses of `Viewer`), but the most common ones are `ContentViewers` such as the `TreeViewer` and `TableViewer`. There are also text-based viewers (`TextViewer` has subclasses for `SourceViewer`) as well as operational views (`ConsoleViewer` for the `Console` view, `DetailedProgressViewer` for the `Progress` view). In this chapter, we'll create views based on `TreeViewer` and `TableViewer`. Since JFace is based on SWT, knowing how SWT works is essential to understand how JFace is used.

# Creating TreeViewers

Many widgets in Eclipse are based upon a tree-like view, from a file navigator to class contents. The JFace framework provides a `TreeViewer`, which provides all of this functionality. This will be used to provide a `TimeZoneTreeView`.

## Time for action – creating a TreeViewer

As done in the previous chapter, a new `TimeZoneTreeView` will be created using the `plugin.xml` editor. This view will show the time zones, organized hierarchically by region.

*1.* Right-click on the `com.packtpub.e4.clock.ui` project and select **Plug-in Tools | Open Manifest**, if it's not open already.

*2.* Open the **Extensions** tab and go to the `org.eclipse.ui.views`. Right-click on this and choose **New | View**, and fill in the following fields:

   ◻ **ID**: `com.packtpub.e4.clock.ui.views.TimeZoneTreeView`

   ◻ **Name**: `Time Zone Tree View`

   ◻ **Class**: `com.packtpub.e4.clock.ui.views.TimeZoneTreeView`

   ◻ **Category**: `com.packtpub.e4.clock.ui`

   ◻ **Icon**: `icons/sample.gif`

*3.* An entry is created in the `plugin.xml` file that looks like the following code snippet:

```
<view
   category="com.packtpub.e4.clock.ui"
   class="com.packtpub.e4.clock.ui.views.TimeZoneTreeView"
   icon="icons/sample.gif"
   id="com.packtpub.e4.clock.ui.views.TimeZoneTreeView"
   name="Time Zone Tree View"
   restorable="true">
</view>
```

*4.* As before, create the class `TimeZoneTreeView`, which extends `ViewPart`.

**5.** In the view's `createPartControl()` method, create an instance of a `TreeViewer`, with the `V_SCROLL`, `H_SCROLL`, and `MULTI` flags set and store it in a field. Implement the `setFocus()` method of the view to that of the tree viewer's control:

```
public class TimeZoneTreeView extends ViewPart {
  private TreeViewer treeViewer;
  public void createPartControl(Composite parent) {
    treeViewer = new TreeViewer(parent,
      SWT.MULTI | SWT.H_SCROLL | SWT.V_SCROLL );
  }
  public void setFocus() {
    treeViewer.getControl().setFocus();
  }
}
```

 ☞ E4: Although E4 will be discussed in detail in *Chapter 7, Understanding the Eclipse 4 Model*, in E4 the `@Inject` annotation is needed above the `createPartControl()` method (to supply the parent `Composite`) and `@Focus` above the `setFocus()` method. This allows the view to be a POJO with no Eclipse UI specific references, other than SWT.

**6.** Run the Eclipse application, and show the view by navigating to **Window | Show View | Timekeeping | Time Zone Tree View**:

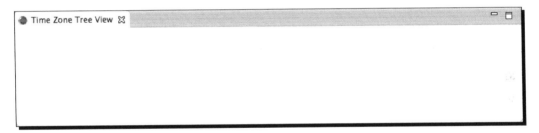

**7.** Unlike Swing, which expects data to be presented in a specific interface, the JFace viewers don't expect any specific data class. Instead, they expect an object value to display (the input), an interface which can read that data (the content provider), and an interface for displaying that data (a label provider).

8.  Create a new class, called `TimeZoneLabelProvider`, which extends `LabelProvider` (from the `org.eclipse.jface.viewers` package). This has a method called `getText()`, which is passed an object and translates that into a textual representation. Instead of a `toString()` call here, return an appropriate value for a `Map.Entry` or a `TimeZone`:

```
public class TimeZoneLabelProvider extends LabelProvider {
  public String getText(Object element) {
    if (element instanceof Map) {
      return "Time Zones";
    } else if (element instanceof Map.Entry) {
      return ((Map.Entry) element).getKey().toString();
    } else if (element instanceof TimeZone) {
      return ((TimeZone) element).getID().split("/")[1];
    } else {
      return "Unknown type: " + element.getClass();
    }
  }
}
```

Since a `TreeViewer` can have multiple roots, the `instanceof Map` test is used to represent the top of the tree, called `Time Zones`.

9.  It's usually a good idea to have a default value—even if it's only an empty string—so that when an unexpected value type is seen in the list, it can be recognized and debugged.

10. Create a new class, `TimeZoneContentProvider`, which implements the `ITreeContentProvider` interface. This requires the implementation of three methods:

    □  `hasChildren()`: returns `true` if the node has children

    □  `getChildren()`: provides the children of a given node

    □  `getElements()`: provides the top-level roots

11. The `hasChildren()` will return `true`, if a `Map` or `Collection` is passed to it, and it's not empty; otherwise, if a `Map.Entry` is passed, recurse. For trees based on nested `Map` or `Collection`, the `hasChildren()` method will look identical:

```
public boolean hasChildren(Object element) {
  if (element instanceof Map) {
    return !((Map) element).isEmpty();
  } else if (element instanceof Map.Entry) {
    return hasChildren(((Map.Entry)element).getValue());
  } else if (element instanceof Collection) {
    return !((Collection) element).isEmpty();
  } else {
```

```
            return false;
        }
    }
```

**12.** The `getChildren()` implementation recurses into a `Map`, `Collection`, or `Map.Entry` following the same pattern. Since the return of this function is an `Object[]`, the built-in functionality of `Map` is used to convert the contents via an `entrySet()` to an array:

```
public Object[] getChildren(Object parentElement) {
    if (parentElement instanceof Map) {
        return ((Map) parentElement).entrySet().toArray();
    } else if (parentElement instanceof Map.Entry) {
        return getChildren(((Map.Entry)parentElement).getValue());
    } else if (parentElement instanceof Collection) {
        return ((Collection) parentElement).toArray();
    } else {
        return new Object[0];
    }
}
```

**13.** The key to implementing a `ITreeContentProvider` is to remember to keep the implementation of the `getChildren()` and `hasChildren()` methods in sync. One way of doing this is to implement the `hasChildren()` method in terms of `getChildren()` returning an empty array, but this may be less performant if the `getChildren()` is an expensive operation.

**14.** Since a `TreeViewer` can have multiple roots, there is a method to get the array of roots from the input element object. A bug in the JFace framework prevents the `getElements()` argument containing its own value. It is therefore, conventional to pass in an array (containing a single element) and return it. This method will be identical for every `TreeContentProvider` that you're ever likely to write:

```
public Object[] getElements(Object inputElement) {
    if (inputElement instanceof Object[]) {
        return (Object[]) inputElement;
    } else {
        return new Object[0];
    }
}
```

Since a `TreeViewer` can have multiple roots, there is a method to get the array of roots from the input element object.

**15.** Now that the providers are complete, in the `createPartControl()` method of `TimeZoneTreeViewer`, connect the providers to the viewer, and finally set the input data object:

```
treeViewer.setLabelProvider(new TimeZoneLabelProvider());
treeViewer.setContentProvider(new TimeZoneContentProvider());
treeViewer.setInput(new Object[]
  {TimeZoneComparator.getTimeZones()});
```

**16.** Run the Eclipse instance, open the view with **Window | Show View | Timekeeping | Time Zone Tree View** and see the results:

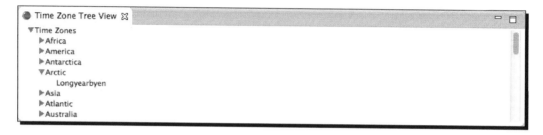

## What just happened?

The data of `TreeViewer` was provided by the `setInput()` method, which is almost always an array of objects, even if it contains only a single element.

To unpack the data structure, the `ITreeContentProvider` interface provides two key methods: `hasChildren()` and `getChildren()`. These allow the data structure to be walked on demand as the user opens and closes nodes in the tree. The rationale for having two separate methods is that the calculation for `getChildren()` may be expensive; the `hasChildren()` is used to show the expandable icon in the node, but the `getChildren()` is deferred until the user opens that node in the tree.

> For data structures that support it, implement the `getParent()` method as well; this makes accessing (or revealing) the object possible. With this method implemented, `viewer.reveal(Object)` will expand the nodes in the hierarchy to reveal that particular object.

To render the labels in the tree, a `LabelProvider` is used. This provides a label (and an optional image) for each element. It is possible to present a different icon for each type of object; this is used by the `Package` view in the Java perspective to present a class icon for the classes, a package icon for the packages, and so on.

The `LabelProvider` can render the messages in different ways; for example, if could append the timezone offset (or only show the difference between that and GMT).

# Time for action – using Images in JFace

The `TimeZoneLabelProvider` can return an `Image`, which is a standard SWT widget. Although the `Image` can be loaded (as in the previous chapter), in JFace there are resource registries, which can be used to manage a set of resources for the application. These include the `ImageRegistry`, `FontRegistry`, and `ColorRegistry` classes. The purpose of a resource registry is to maintain a list of `Resource` instances and ensure that they are correctly disposed, but only when they are no longer needed.

JFace has a set of these global registries; but there are specific ones, such as the ones used by the IDE to maintain a folder and file type icons, for example. These use descriptors to hold a meaning for the resource, and a means to acquire an instance of the resource based on that descriptor. The returned resource is owned by the registry, and as such, should not be disposed by clients that acquire them.

1. In the `TimeZoneLabelProvider`, add a method `getImage()` that uses the Workbench's `ImageRegistry` to provide the folder icon. Implement it as follows:

   ```
   public Image getImage(Object element) {
     if(element instanceof Map.Entry) {
       return PlatformUI.getWorkbench().getSharedImages()
         .getImage(ISharedImages.IMG_OBJ_FOLDER);
     } else {
       return super.getImage(element);
     }
   }
   ```

2. Run the Eclipse instance, and open the Time Zone Tree View. A folder icon will be shown; regions show a folder shown for each of the time zones in your view. The `Image` instance doesn't need to be disposed, because it's owned by the `PlatformUI` plug-in (the images are disposed when the `PlatformUI` shuts down):

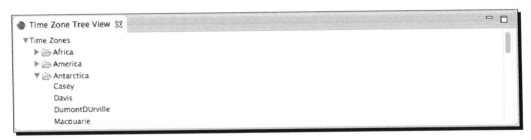

☞ E4: If using E4, the `ISharedImages` instance can be obtained via injection:

```
@Inject
private ISharedImages images;
images.getImage(ISharedImages.IMG_OBJ_FOLDER);
```

3.  To use a different image, either the global `ImageRegistry` of `JFaceRegistry` could be used, or one can be instantiated separately. Using the global one will work, but it means that effectively the `Image` instance never gets disposed, since the `JFaceRegistry` will last for the lifetime of your Eclipse instance.

    Instead, create a `LocalResourceManager` and `ImageRegistry`, which are tied to the lifetime of the control. When the parent control is disposed, the images will be disposed automatically. These should be added to the `createPartControl()` method of `TimeZoneTreeView`.

    ```
    public void createPartControl(Composite parent) {
      ResourceManager rm = JFaceResources.getResources();
      LocalResourceManager lrm = new LocalResourceManager(rm,parent);
    ```

4.  Using the `LocalResourceManger`, create an `ImageRegistry`, and add an `ImageDescriptor` from a URL using `createFromURL()`.

    ```
    ImageRegistry ir = new ImageRegistry(lrm);
    URL sample = getClass().getResource("/icons/sample.gif");
    ir.put("sample", ImageDescriptor.createFromURL(sample));
    ```

5.  Now the `ImageRegistry` is populated, it must be hooked up to the `LabelProvider`, so that it can show the right `Image` on demand. Pass the image registry into the constructor of the `TimeZoneLabelProvider`.

    ```
    treeViewer.setLabelProvider(new TimeZoneLabelProvider());
    treeViewer.setLabelProvider(new TimeZoneLabelProvider(ir));
    ```

6.  Implement the constructor in the `TimeZoneLabelProvider` to store the `ImageRegistry`, and use it to acquire the image in the `getImage()` call:

    ```
    private final ImageRegistry ir;
    public TimeZoneLabelProvider(ImageRegistry ir) {
      this.ir = ir;
    }
    public Image getImage(Object element) {
      if(element instanceof Map.Entry) {
        return ir.get("sample");
      } else if(element instanceof TimeZone) {
        return ir.get("sample");
      } else {
        return super.getImage(element);
      }
    }
    ```

**7.** Now, when opening the view, the sample `gif` is used as a tree icon:

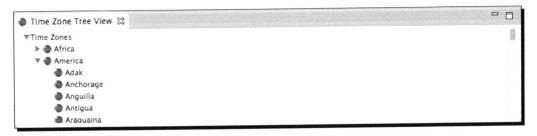

## What just happened?

To start with, standard images from the `PlatformUI` were used, using predefined descriptors from `ISharedImages`. The names of the descriptors begin with `IMG`, and then follow a predefined pattern:

♦ `etool` and `dtool`: Enabled and disabled toolbar icons

♦ `elcl` and `dlcl`: enabled and disabled local toolbar icons

♦ `dec`: decorator

♦ `obj` and `objs`: object(s) (files, folders, and so on)

Other plug-ins have a similar set of images; such as JDT UI, which adds icons for packages, classes, methods, and fields.

To use custom images, an `ImageRegistry` was created backed by a `LocalResourceManager`. When a `Control` is passed into the constructor, it registers itself as a `DisposeListener`—so when the control is disposed, so are the associated images. This also makes the code cleaner, because the `ImageRegistry` can be passed into the `TimeZoneContentProvider`.

Finally, the `ImageRegistry` is initialized with a set of `ImageDescriptors`—in this case, the `icons/sample.gif` that came from the new plug-in project wizard. The same key is used when both initializing and accessing the image. Some Eclipse projects follow a convention of having an `ISharedImages` interface with a set of constants.

# Time for action – styling label providers

The `IStyledLabelProvider` is used to style the representation of the tree viewer, as used by the Java outline viewer for displaying the return type of the method, and by the team's decorator when showing when changes have occurred.

*1.* Add the `IStyledLabelProvider` interface to the `TimeZoneLabelProvider`, and create the `getStyledText()` method. If the selected element is a `Map.Entry` that contains a `TimeZone`, add the offset afterwards in brackets.

```
public class TimeZoneLabelProvider extends LabelProvider
  implements IStyledLabelProvider {
    public StyledString getStyledText(Object element) {
      String text = getText(element);
      StyledString ss = new StyledString(text);
      if (element instanceof TimeZone) {
        int offset = -((TimeZone) element).getOffset(0);
        ss.append(" (" + offset / 3600000 + "h)",
          StyledString.DECORATIONS_STYLER);
      }
      return ss;
    }
}
```

*2.* In order to use the styled label provider, it has to be wrapped within a `DelegatingStyledCellLabelProvider`. Modify the constructor, called from the `createPartControl()` method of `TimeZoneTreeView`.

```
treeViewer.setLabelProvider(
  new DelegatingStyledCellLabelProvider(
    new TimeZoneLabelProvider(ir)));
```

*3.* Run the Eclipse instance, open the view, and the offset is displayed in a different color:

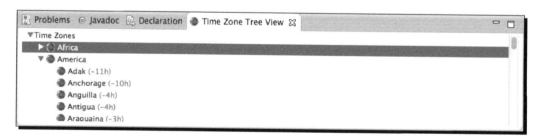

**4.** To change the `Font` used by the view, the `TimeZoneLabelProvider` needs to implement the `IFontProvider` interface. JFace's `FontRegistry` can be used to return an italicized version of the default font. Add a `FontRegistry` parameter to the `TimeZoneLabelProvider` constructor, and implement the `getFont()` method as follows:

```
public class TimeZoneLabelProvider extends LabelProvider
  implements IStyledLabelProvider, IFontProvider {
  private final FontRegistry fr;
  public TimeZoneLabelProvider(ImageRegistry ir, FontRegistry fr){
    this.ir = ir;
    this.fr = fr;
  }
  public Font getFont(Object element) {
    Font italic = fr.getItalic(JFaceResources.DEFAULT_FONT);
    return italic;
  }
}
```

**5.** Modify the `TimeZoneTreeView` to instantiate and pass in the global `FontRegistry` from the `JFaceResources` class.

```
FontRegistry fr = JFaceResources.getFontRegistry();
treeViewer.setLabelProvider(
  new DelegatingStyledCellLabelProvider(
    new TimeZoneLabelProvider(ir)));
treeViewer.setLabelProvider(
  new DelegatingStyledCellLabelProvider(
    new TimeZoneLabelProvider(ir, fr)));
```

**6.** Run the Eclipse instance again, and now the time zones should be shown in an italic font.

## What just happened?

By implementing the `IStyledLabelProvider` and wrapping it with a `DelegatingStyledCellLabelProvider`, the style of the individual elements in the tree can be controlled, including any additions or style/colors of the item. The `StyledText` can render the string in different styles.

Although the `DecorationsStyler` was used here, additional stylers can be defined with `StyledString.createColorRegistryStyler("foreground", "background")`, where the two strings are keys in the global JFace `ColorRegistry`.

Although `Colours` can be changed on a character-by-character basis, the `Font` is global for the string. That's because when the label is calculated, its size is calculated based on the assumption that the string is displayed in a single `Font`.

It's generally good programming practice to have the content or label providers use resource managers that are passed in at construction time. That way, the code can be tested using automated tests or other mock resources. Whether using the Eclipse 3.x or the Eclipse 4.x programming model, decoupling where the resources come from is key to testing.

## Pop quiz – understanding JFace

Q1. What methods are present on `LabelProvider`?

Q2. What is the difference between `hasChildren()` and `getChildren()` on the `ContentProvider`?

Q3. What is an `ImageRegistry` used for?

Q4. How do you style entries in a `TreeView`?

## Have a go hero – adding images for regions

Now that the basics have been covered, try extending the example as follows:

◆ Correct the `TimeZoneLabelProvider` so that it shows hours/minutes offset from GMT

◆ Update the plug-in with a number of flag icons, and then create entries for the image registry (the name of the time zone can be used for the key, which will make accessing it easier)

◆ Display the name of the region in italics, but the time zones themselves in bold font

# Sorting and filtering

One of the features of JFace is that the ordering of the data can be processed by the view, rather than having to require that the data structure do the processing. This makes it easy to present filtered views, where the user either searches for a particular term, or performs a sort in a different manner. These filters are used heavily in the Eclipse IDE, where options such as **Hide libraries from external** and **Hide closed projects** can be found in many of the drop-down actions for the view.

# Time for action – sorting items in a viewer

The `TreeViewer` is already showing data in a sorted format, but this is not a view-imposed sort. Because the data is stored in a `TreeMap`, the sort ordering is created by the `TreeMap` itself, which in turn is sorting on the value of `toString()`. To use a different ordering (say, based on offset) the choices are either to modify the `TreeMap` to add a `Comparator` and sort the data at creation time, or add a sorter to the `TreeViewer`. The first choice is applicable if the data is only used by a single view, or if the data is coming from a large external data store, which can perform the sorting more efficiently (such as a relational database). For smaller data sets, the sorting can be done in the viewer itself.

1. JFace structured viewers allow view-specific sorting with the `ViewerComparator`. Create a new subclass, `TimeZoneViewerComparator`, in the package `com.packtpub.e4.clock.ui.internal`, and implement the `compare()` method as follows:

```
public class TimeZoneViewerComparator extends ViewerComparator {
  public int compare(Viewer viewer, Object o1, Object o2) {
  int compare;
  if (o1 instanceof TimeZone && o2 instanceof TimeZone) {
    compare=((TimeZone)o2).getOffset(System.currentTimeMillis())
    - ((TimeZone)o1).getOffset(System.currentTimeMillis());
  } else {
    compare = o1.toString().compareTo(o2.toString());
  }
  return compare;
  }
}
```

2. Hook it up to the viewer as follows:

```
treeViewer.setComparator(new TimeZoneViewerComparator());
```

3. Run the Eclipse instance, open the Time Zone Tree View, and the `TimeZones` should be sorted first by offset, then alphabetically:

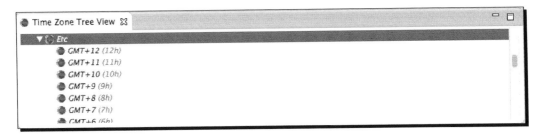

**4.** To add a viewer-specific sort, modify the `compare()` method of
`TimeZoneViewerComparator` to get a `REVERSE` key from the
viewer's data. Use that to invert the results of the sort:

```
return compare;
boolean reverse = Boolean.parseBoolean(
  String.valueOf(viewer.getData("REVERSE")));
return reverse ? -compare : compare;
```

**5.** To see the effect of this sort, set the `REVERSE` key just before the
`setComparator()` call at the end of the `createPartControl()`
method of `TimeZoneTreeView`.

```
treeViewer.setData("REVERSE",Boolean.TRUE);
treeViewer.setComparator(new TimeZoneViewerComparator());
```

**6.** Re-launch the Eclipse instance, and the view should be in the reverse order.

## What just happened?

By adding a `ViewerComparator` to the `Viewer`, the data can be sorted in an appropriate
manner for the viewer in question. Typically, this will be done in conjunction with selecting
an option in the view—for example, an option may be present to reverse the ordering, or to
sort by name or offset.

When implementing a specific `Comparator`, check that the method can handle multiple
object types (including ones that may not be expected). The data in the viewer may change,
or be different at runtime than expected. Use `instanceof` to check that the items are of
the expected type.

To store properties that are specific to a viewer, use the `setData()` and `getData()` calls
on the viewer itself. This allows a generic comparator to be used across views while still
respecting per view filtration/sorting operations.

The preceding example hardcodes the sort data, which requires an Eclipse relaunch to see
the effect. Typically, after modifying properties that may affect the view's sorting or filtering,
the viewer has a `refresh()` invoked to bring the display in line with the new settings.

# Time for action – filtering items in a viewer

Another common feature of viewers is filtering. This is used when performing a manual search as well as for filtering-specific aspects from a view. Quite often, the filtering is connected to the view's menu, which is the drop-down triangle on the top right of the view, using a common name such as **Filters**. The `ViewerFilter` class provides a filtering method, confusingly called `select()`. (There are some `filter()` methods, but these are used to filter the entire array; the `select()` method is used to determine if a specific element is shown or not.)

1. Create a class, `TimeZoneViewerFilter`, in the `com.packtpub.e4.clock.ui.internal` package, which extends `ViewerFilter`. It should take a `String` pattern in the constructor, and return `true` if the element is a `TimeZone` with that pattern in its display name.

```
public class TimeZoneViewerFilter extends ViewerFilter {
  private String pattern;
  public TimeZoneViewerFilter(String pattern) {
    this.pattern = pattern;
  }
  public boolean select(Viewer v, Object parent, Object element) {
    if(element instanceof TimeZone) {
      TimeZone zone = (TimeZone)element;
      return zone.getDisplayName().contains(pattern);
    } else {
      return true;
    }
  }
}
```

2. The filter is set on the viewer; since views can have multiple filters, it set this as an array on the corresponding viewer. The pattern to filter is passed into the constructor in this case, but would normally be taken from the user. Modify the `TimeZoneTreeViewer` class at the bottom of the `createPartControl()` method:

```
treeViewer.setFilters(new ViewerFilter[] {
  new TimeZoneViewerFilter("GMT") });
```

**3.** Now run the Eclipse instance and open the Time Zone Tree View; only time zones in the `etc` region are listed:

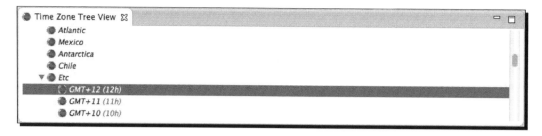

**4.** To remove the expandable nodes next to the tree items, the `TreeViewer` can be configured to expand nodes automatically:

```
treeViewer.setExpandPreCheckFilters(true);
```

**5.** Now run the Eclipse instance and open the Time Zone Tree View. The empty groups are still listed, but the expandable markers only appear on those which have children after filtration.

## What just happened?

The `TimeZoneViewerFilter` class was created as a subclass of `ViewerFilter` and set on the `TreeViewer`. When displaying and filtering the data, the filter is called for every element in the tree (including the root node).

By default, if the `hasChildren()` method returns `true`, the expandable icon is shown. When clicked, it will iterate through the children, applying the filter to them. If all the elements are filtered, the expandable marker will be removed.

By calling `setExpandPreCheckFilters(true)` on the viewer, it will verify that at least one child is left after filtration. This has no negative effect when there aren't any filters set. If there are filters set and there are large data sets, it may take some time to perform the calculation of whether they should be filtered or not.

To show all the tree's elements by default, or collapse it down to a single tree, use `expandAll()` and `collapseAll()` on the viewer. This is typically bound to a local view command with a **[+]** and **[-]** icon (for example, the Synchronize view or the Package Explorer).

If the data is a tree structure, which only needs to show some levels by default, there is an `expandToLevel()` and `collapseToLevel()`, which take an integer and an object (use the `getRoot()` of the tree if not specified) and mark everything as expanded or collapsed to that level. The `expandAll()` method is a short-hand for `expandToLevel(getRoot(), ALL_LEVELS)`.

When responding to a selection event, which contains a hidden object, it is conventional to perform a `reveal()` operation on the object to make it visible in the tree. Note that `reveal()` only works when the `getParent()` is correctly implemented, which isn't the case with this example.

## Pop quiz – understanding sorting and filters

Q1. How can elements of a tree be sorted in an order which isn't its default?

Q2. What method is used to filter elements?

Q3. How can multiple filters be combined?

## Have a go hero – expanding and filtering

Now that views can be sorted and filtered, try the following:

- Add a second filter which removes all time zones, with a negative offset
- When the view is opened, perform an `expandAll()` operation of the elements
- Provide a sort that sorts the regions in reverse order, but the time zones in ascending order
- Provide a dialog that can be used to update the filter and use the empty string, which can be used to reset the filter

# Interaction and properties

Being able to display data is one thing, but invariably views need to be interactive. Whether that's hooking up the sort or filter functionality from the previous chapter, or seeing information about the selected item, views must be interactive not only for exploring data, but also for working with data.

## Time for action – adding a double-click listener

Typically, a tree view is used to show content in a hierarchical manner. However, a tree on its own is not enough to be able to show all the details associated with an object. When the user double-clicks on an element, more details can be shown.

1. At the end of the `createPartControl()` method of `TimeZoneTreeView`, register an anonymous inner class that implements the `IDoubleClickListener` interface with the `addDoubleClickListener()` method on the `treeViewer`. As with the example in *Chapter 1, Creating Your First Plug-in*, this will open a message dialog to verify that it works as expected.

```
treeViewer.addDoubleClickListener(new IDoubleClickListener() {
  public void doubleClick(DoubleClickEvent event) {
    Viewer viewer = event.getViewer();
    Shell shell = viewer.getControl().getShell();
    MessageDialog.openInformation(shell, "Double click",
      "Double click detected");
  }
});
```

2. Run the Eclipse instance, and open the view. Double-click on the tree, and a shell will be displayed with the message **Double click detected**. The dialog is modal and prevents other components in the user interface from being selected until it is dismissed.

3. To find the selected object(s), Eclipse provides an `ISelection` interface (which only provides an `isEmpty()` method) and an `IStructuredSelection` (which provides an iterator and other accessor methods). There's also a couple of specialized subtypes, such as `ITreeSelection`, which can be interrogated for the path that led to the selection in the tree. In the `createPartControl()` method of `TimeZoneTreeView`, where the `doubleClick()` method of the `DoubleClickListener` inner class is present, replace the `MessageDialog` as follows:

```
MessageDialog.openInformation(shell, "Double click",
  "Double click detected");
ISelection sel = viewer.getSelection();
Object selectedValue;
if (!(sel instanceof IStructuredSelection) || sel.isEmpty()) {
  selectedValue = null;
} else {
  selectedValue = ((IStructuredSelection)sel).getFirstElement();
if (selectedValue instanceof TimeZone) {
  TimeZone timeZone = (TimeZone)selectedValue;
  MessageDialog.openInformation(shell, timeZone.getID(),
    timeZone.toString());
}
```

4. Run the Eclipse instance, and open the view. Double-click on the tree, and a shell will be displayed with the string representation of the `TimeZone`.

5. To display more information about the `TimeZone` in the displayed window, create a subclass of `MessageDialog` called `TimeZoneDialog` in the `com.packtpub.e4.clock.ui.internal` package. Implement it as follows:

```
public class TimeZoneDialog extends MessageDialog {
  private TimeZone timeZone;
  public TimeZoneDialog(Shell parentShell, TimeZone timeZone) {
    super(parentShell, timeZone.getID(), null, "Time Zone "
    + timeZone.getID(), INFORMATION,
    new String[] { IDialogConstants.OK_LABEL }, 0);
    this.timeZone = timeZone;
  }
}
```

6. The contents of the `Dialog` are provided by the `customArea()` method, which can be used to build up the view. Add the following `createCustomArea()` method to the `TimeZoneDialog`:

```
protected Control createCustomArea(Composite parent) {
  ClockWidget clock = new ClockWidget(parent,SWT.NONE,
    new RGB(128,255,0));
  clock.setOffset(
    (TimeZone.getDefault().getOffset(System.currentTimeMillis())
    - timeZone.getOffset(System.currentTimeMillis()))
    /3600000);
  return parent;
}
```

7. Finally, modify the call to `MessageDialog.open()` by `TimeZoneTreeView` to use the new implementation:

```
if (selectedValue instanceof TimeZone) {
  TimeZone timeZone = (TimeZone) selectedValue;
  MessageDialog.openInformation(shell, timeZone.getID(),
  timeZone.toString());
  new TimeZoneDialog(shell, timeZone).open();
}
```

**8.** Run the Eclipse instance, double-click on the time zone, and the dialog should appear:

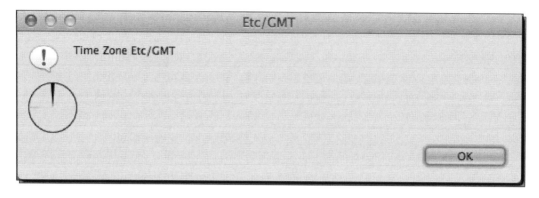

## What just happened?

A double-click listener was added to the viewer by registering it with
addDoubleClickListener(). Initially, a standard information dialog was displayed, but
then a custom subclass of MessageDialog was used which included a ClockWidget. In
order to get the appropriate TimeZone, it was accessed via the currently selected object
from the TreeViewer.

Selection is managed via an ISelection interface. The viewer's getSelection()
method should always return a non-null value, although the value may return true for
the isEmpty() call. There are two relevant subinterfaces; IStructuredSelection and
ITreeSelection.

The ITreeSelection is a subtype of IStructuredSelection, and adds methods specific
to trees. This includes the ability to find out what the selected object(s) are and what their
parents are in the tree.

The IStructuredSelection is the most commanly used interface in dealing with
selection types. If the selection is not empty, it is almost always an instance of an
IStructuredSelection. As a result, the following snippet of code appears regularly:

```
ISelection sel = viewer.getSelection();
Object selectedValue;
if (!(sel instanceof IStructuredSelection) || sel.isEmpty()) {
  selectedValue = null;
} else {
  selectedValue = ((IStructuredSelection)sel).getFirstElement();
}
```

This snippet gets the selection from the viewer, and if it's not an IStructuredSelection, or it's empty, it assigns the variable selectedValue to null. If it's non-empty, it casts it to the IStructuredSelection interface and calls getFirstElement() to get the single selected value.

The selection may have more than one selected value, in which case the getFirstElement() method only returns the first element selected. The IStructuredSelection class provides an iterator to step through all selected objects.

> ☞ E4: In E4, the selected object can be injected via an annotated method:
>
> ```
> @Inject @Optional
> void setTZ(@Named(IServiceConstants.ACTIVE_SELECTION)
> TimeZone timeZone) {
> }
> ```

# Time for action – showing properties

Instead of every object having to have its own custom information dialog, the Eclipse IDE provides a generic Properties view (in the org.eclipse.ui.views plug-in), which can be used to show information about the currently selected object. The properties are discovered generically from an object and accessed through the IPropertySource interface. This allows an object to provide an abstracted way of computing the fields shown in the property view.

The easiest way to create a property source is to let the object in question implement its own IPropertySource interface. This works when the source code can be modified, but in many cases (such as the TimeZone, or a Map.Entry containing a String key and a TimeZone) the source code cannot be modified.

1. Open the MANIFEST/META-INF.MF of the plug-in, and add org.eclipse. ui.views as a dependency via the **Dependencies** tab, or by adding it to the bundles in the Require-Bundle entry. Without this, the IPropertySource interface won't be found.

2. Create a class TimeZonePropertySource in the com.packtpub.e4.clock. ui.internal package that implements the IPropertySource interface. Take a single TimeZone instance in the constructor.

```
public class TimeZonePropertySource implements IPropertySource {
  private TimeZone timeZone;
  public TimeZonePropertySource(TimeZone timeZone) {
   this.timeZone = timeZone;
  }
}
```

**3.** The only methods that need to be implemented are `getPropertyValue()` and `getPropertyDescriptors()`. (The other methods, such as `getEditableValue()` and `isPropertySet()`, can be ignored, because they only get invoked when performing edit operations. These should be left empty or return `null`/`false`.) The accessors are called with an identifier; while the latter returns an array of `PropertyDescriptors` combining pairs of identifiers and a displayable name. Add the following to the `TimeZonePropertySource` class:

```
private static final Object ID = new Object();
private static final Object DAYLIGHT = new Object();
private static final Object NAME = new Object();
public IPropertyDescriptor[] getPropertyDescriptors() {
  return new IPropertyDescriptor[] {
    new PropertyDescriptor(ID, "Time Zone"),
    new PropertyDescriptor(DAYLIGHT, "Daylight Savings"),
    new PropertyDescriptor(NAME, "Name")
  };
}
public Object getPropertyValue(Object id) {
  if (ID.equals(id)) {
    return timeZone.getID();
  } else if(DAYLIGHT.equals(id)) {
    return timeZone.inDaylightTime(new Date());
  } else if (NAME.equals(id)) {
    return timeZone.getDisplayName();
  } else {
    return null;
  }
}
```

**4.** To hook this property source into the Properties view, an adapter is used. It can be specified via a generic `IAdaptable` interface, which allows a class to virtually implement an interface. Since the `TimeZone` cannot implement the `IAdaptable` interface directly, an `IAdapterFactory` is needed.

**5.** Create `TimeZoneAdapterFactory` in the `com.packtpub.e4.clock.ui.internal` package that implements the `IAdapterFactory` interface.

```
public class TimeZoneAdapterFactory implements IAdapterFactory {
  public Class[] getAdapterList() {
    return new Class[] { IPropertySource.class };
  }
  public Object getAdapter(Object o, Class type) {
```

```
      if(type == IPropertySource.class && o instanceof TimeZone) {
        return new TimeZonePropertySource((TimeZone)o);
      } else {
       return null;
      }
    }
  }
```

6.  To register the adaptor factory with Eclipse, add it to the `plugin.xml`
    file declaratively.

    ```
    <extension point="org.eclipse.core.runtime.adapters">
      <factory adaptableType="java.util.TimeZone"
        class=
          "com.packtpub.e4.clock.ui.internal.TimeZoneAdapterFactory">
        <adapter type=
    "org.eclipse.ui.views.properties.IPropertySource"/>
      </factory>
    </extension>
    ```

7.  Run the Eclipse instance, select a time zone in the tree view, and then open the
    properties by navigating to **Window | Show View | Other | General | Properties**.
    Nothing will be shown. To confirm that the adapter has been wired correctly, add
    this at the end of the `createPartControl()` method in the `TimeZoneTreeView`
    view creation:

    ```
    System.out.println("Adapter is " + Platform.getAdapterManager().
      getAdapter(TimeZone.getDefault(),IPropertySource.class));
    ```

8.  Run the Eclipse instance, open the Time Zone Tree View, and check the Console view
    of the host Eclipse instance. The console should contain an output message similar
    to the following:

    ```
    Adapter is com.packtpub.e4.clock.ui.internal.
    TimeZonePropertySource@7f8a6fb0
    ```

9.  So what's the missing link? It turns out in this case that the Properties view
    is not being notified of the change in selection. Adding the following to the
    `createPartControl()` method of the `TimeZoneTreeView` class will solve
    the problem.

    ```
    System.out.println("Adapter is " + Platform.getAdapterManager().
      getAdapter(TimeZone.getDefault(),IPropertySource.class));
    getSite().setSelectionProvider(treeViewer);
    ```

**10.** Now, changes in selection are propagated up to the workbench, so that other views can update themselves. When a `TimeZone` is selected, the Properties, view will be updated automatically. Run the Eclipse instance and open the Time Zone Tree View, select a time zone, and open the **Properties** view:

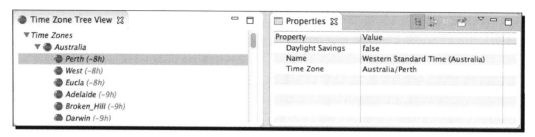

☞ E4: To hook a viewer up to the selection provider, the code looks similar to this:

```
@Inject
ESelectionService selectionService;
ISelectionChangedListener selectionListener;
@PostConstruct
public void postConstruct() {
  selectionListener = new ISelectionChangedListener() {
    public void selectionChanged(SelectionChangedEvent e)
  {
      if (selectionService != null)
        selectionService.setSelection(e.getSelection());
    }
  };
  treeViewer.addSelectionChangedListener(
    selectionListener);
}
@PreDestroy
public void preDestroy() {
  if(selectionListener != null)
    treeViewer.removeSelectionChangedListener
    (selectionListener);
  selectionListener = null;
}
```

# *What just happened?*

To update the state of the Workbench's selection, the view's selection provider was connected with that of the page (via the getSite() method). When the selection in the viewer changes, it sends a message to registered listeners of the page's selection service so that they can update their views, if necessary.

 ☞ E4: The selection listener needs to be (un)registered manually to provide a hook between the viewer and the selection service. Instead of being ISelectionService, it's ESelectionService. The interface is slightly different, because the ISelectionService is tied to the IWorkbenchPart class, but the ESelectionService is not.

To provide information to the Properties view, an IPropertySource was created for the TimeZone and associated with the Platform IAdapterManager through the declaration in the plugin.xml file.

It's generally better to provide hooks declaratively in the plugin.xml file rather than hooking it up with the start() and stop() activator methods. That's because the start on the Activator may not be called until the first class is loaded from the bundle; in the case of the adaptor, the declarative registration can provide the information before it is first required.

The adaptor factory provides the getAdapter() method, which wraps or converts the object being passed into one of the desired type. If the object is already an instance of the given type, it can just be returned as it is—but otherwise return a POJO, proxy, or wrapper object that implements the desired interface. It's quite common to have a class (such as TimeZonePropertySupport) whose sole job is to implement the desired interface, and which wraps an instance of the object (TimeZone) to provide the functionality.

The IPropertySupport interface provides a basic means to acquire properties from the object, and to do so it uses an identifier for each property. These can be any object type; in the preceding example, new Object instances were used. Although it is possible to use String (plenty of other examples do), this is not recommended, since the value of the String has no importance and it takes up space in the JVM's PermGen memory space. In addition, using a plain Object means that the instance can be compared with == without any concerns, whereas doing so with String is likely to fail the code reviews or automated style checkers. (The preceding example uses the .equals() method to encourage its use when not using an Object, but a decent JIT will in-line it—particularly since the code is sending the message to a static final instance.)

## Pop quiz – understanding properties

Q1. How can `TableViewer` instances respond to a click?

Q2. Why are `Dialog` subclasses created?

Q3. What are property descriptors?

Q4. How are properties displayed on the Properties view?

# Tabular data

The tree viewer is used in many situations in Eclipse, but sometimes being able to display more information for a single element is required. JFace provides a `TableViewer` that is similar to the `TreeViewer`, except that instead of a single label there are multiple columns available. There is also a combined `TableTreeViewer`, which combines functionality from the two classes.

## Time for action – viewing time zones in tables

To display the time zones in table form, a new view will be created called Time Zone Table View.

**1.** Right-click on the `com.packtpub.e4.clock.ui` project and select **Plug-in Tools | Open Manifest**. Open the **Extensions** tab and right-click on the **org.eclipse.ui.views**, followed by selecting **New | View** and filling in the following fields:

- ❑ **ID**: `com.packtpub.e4.clock.ui.views.TimeZoneTableView`
- ❑ **Name**: `Time Zone Table View`
- ❑ **Class**: `com.packtpub.e4.clock.ui.views.TimeZoneTableView`
- ❑ **Category**: `com.packtpub.e4.clock.ui`
- ❑ **Icon**: `icons/sample.gif`

**2.** The `plugin.xml` file should now contain the following code snippet:

```
<view
    category="com.packtpub.e4.clock.ui"
    class="com.packtpub.e4.clock.ui.views.TimeZoneTableView"
    icon="icons/sample.gif"
    id="com.packtpub.e4.clock.ui.views.TimeZoneTableView"
    name="Time Zone Table View"
    restorable="true">
</view>
```

**3.** Create the class using the editor's shortcuts to create a new class, `TimeZoneTableView`, which extends `ViewPart`, or with the new class wizard. Once the view is created, add an empty `TableViewer`, and use an `ArrayContentProvider` with the set of available `TimeZone` IDs:

```
public class TimeZoneTableView extends ViewPart {
  private TableViewer tableViewer;
  public void createPartControl(Composite parent) {
    tableViewer=new TableViewer(parent,SWT.H_SCROLL|SWT.V_SCROLL);
    tableViewer.getTable().setHeaderVisible(true);
    tableViewer.setContentProvider(
     ArrayContentProvider.getInstance());
    tableViewer.setInput(TimeZone.getAvailableIDs());
  }
  public void setFocus() {
    tableViewer.getControl().setFocus();
  }
}
```

  E4: If creating a part for an E4 application, remember to use the `@Inject` annotation for the constructor and `@Focus` for the `setFocus()` method.

**4.** Run the Eclipse instance, and a one-dimensional list of time zones will be shown in the Time Zone Table View:

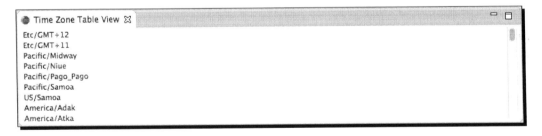

**5.** Convert the array of `Strings` to an array of `TimeZones` and set that as the input:

```
tableViewer.setInput(TimeZone.getAvailableIDs());
String[] ids = TimeZone.getAvailableIDs();
TimeZone[] timeZones = new TimeZone[ids.length];
for(int i=0;i<ids.length;i++) {
  timeZones[i] = TimeZone.getTimeZone(ids[i]);
}
tableViewer.setInput(timeZones);
getSite().setSelectionProvider(tableViewer);
```

**6.** The selection provider is wired up like in the `TimeZoneTreeView` example. Make a selection in the table, and see the change in the Properties view:

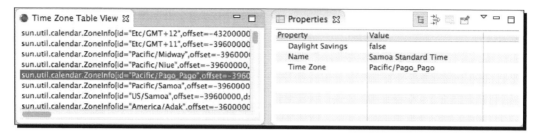

**7.** The table shows a list of the `ZoneInfo` objects. That's because there is no `LabelProvider`, so they're just being rendered with their `toString()` representation. Because a table has multiple columns, `TableViewers` have a number of `TableViewerColumn` instances. Each one represents a column in the `Table`, and each has its own size, title, and label provider. Creating a new column often involves setting up standard features (such as the width) as well as hooking in the required fields to display.

To make it easy to re-use, create an abstract subclass of `ColumnLabelProvider` called `TimeZoneColumn` (in the `com.packtpub.e4.clock.ui.internal` package) with abstract `getText()` and `getTitle()` methods, and a concrete `getWidth()` method.

```
public abstract class TimeZoneColumn extends ColumnLabelProvider {
  public abstract String getText(Object element);
  public abstract String getTitle();
  public int getWidth() {
    return 250;
  }
}
```

**8.** Add a helper method to the `TimeZoneColumn` class, which makes it easier to add it to a viewer:

```
public TableViewerColumn addColumnTo(TableViewer viewer) {
  TableViewerColumn tableViewerColumn =
    new TableViewerColumn(viewer,SWT.NONE);
  TableColumn column = tableViewerColumn.getColumn();
  column.setMoveable(true);
  column.setResizable(true);
  column.setText(getTitle());
  column.setWidth(getWidth());
  tableViewerColumn.setLabelProvider(this);
  return tableViewerColumn;
}
```

**9.** Now create a custom subclass `TimeZoneIDColumn` in the same package that returns the ID column for a `TimeZone`:

```
public class TimeZoneIDColumn extends TimeZoneColumn {
  public String getText(Object element) {
    if (element instanceof TimeZone) {
      return ((TimeZone) element).getID();
    } else {
      return "";
    }
  }
  public String getTitle() {
   return "ID";
  }
}
```

**10.** Modify the `TimeZoneTableView` class, and at the end of the `createPartControl()` method, instantiate the column and call the `addColumnTo()` method, above the call to `setInput()`:

```
new TimeZoneIDColumn().addColumnTo(tableViewer);
tableViewer.setInput(timeZones);
```

 Note that the columns need to be created prior to the `setInput()` call, otherwise they won't display properly.

**11.** Run the Eclipse instance, and show the Time Zone Table View. The ID column should be displayed on its own.

**12.** To add additional columns, copy the `TimeZoneIDColumn` class, modifying the title returned and the returned property of the associated `TimeZone`. For example, create a copy of the `TimeZoneIDColumn` called `TimeZoneDisplayNameColumn`, and modify the `get` method and title.

```
return ((TimeZone) element).getID();
return ((TimeZone) element).getDisplayName();
return "ID";
return "Display Name";
```

**13.** Optionally, do the same with the other properties of `TimeZone`, such as the offset (with `getOffset()`), and whether it's in summer time or not (with `useDaylightTime()`). The columns can then be added to the table.

```
new TimeZoneOffsetColumn().addColumnTo(tableViewer);
new TimeZoneDisplayNameColumn().addColumnTo(tableViewer);
new TimeZoneSummerTimeColumn().addColumnTo(tableViewer);
```

**14.** Run the Eclipse instance, go to the Time Zone Table View, and the additional
column(s) should be seen:

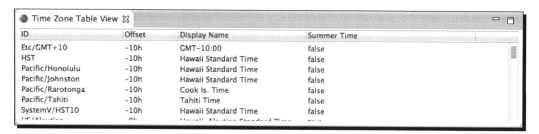

## *What just happened?*

A `TableViewer` was created and multiple `ColumnLabelProviders` were added to it
for displaying individual fields of an object. Subclassing `ColumnLabelProvider` avoids
the need to use anonymous inner classes and it gives a helper function. This can be used
to create and wire in the column (with specified title and width), while delegating those
properties to the concrete subclasses of `TimeZoneIDColumn` and so on. This avoids the
need for tracking columns by ID.

For specific customizations of the columns, the underlying SWT `Column` is used to set
functionality required by the application, including allowing the column to be movable with
`setMovable(true)`, and to be resizable with `setResizable(true)`. Similarly, table-wide
operations (such as showing the header) are performed by manipulating the underlying SWT
`Table` and invoking `setHeaderVisible(true)`.

It's important to note that the columns of the tree viewer are calculated when the
`setInput()` method is called, so columns that are added after this line may not show
properly. Generally, the `setInput()` should be left until the end of the table's construction.

All of the other functionality from the other view is portable, for example, by wiring up the
selection appropriately, the Properties view can show properties of the selected object.

## Time for action – syncing selection

The `TimeZoneTableView` and the `TimeZoneTreeView` can propagate their selection to
the Properties view. Responding to selection changes gives a unified feel despite the fact that
the views are independent entities.

They can be further linked so that when a `TimeZone` is selected in either of these views, it automatically reveals in the other. To do this, a selection listener will need to be registered, and if the selected object is a type of `TimeZone`, display it in the view (with the `reveal()` and `setSelection()` methods).

1. Create a class `TimeZoneSelectionListener` (in the `com.packtpub.e4.clock.ui.internal` package), which implements the `ISelectionListener` interface. This will take a viewer, and an associated part, to implement the `selectionChanged()` method.

```
public class TimeZoneSelectionListener implements
  ISelectionListener {
  private Viewer viewer;
  private IWorkbenchPart part;
  public TimeZoneSelectionListener(Viewer v, IWorkbenchPart p) {
    this.viewer = v;
    this.part = p;
  }
  public void selectionChanged(IWorkbenchPart p, ISelection sel) {
  }
}
```

2. The `selectionChanged()` method needs to:

   - Ignore the event if it was fired by the same part
   - Get the selected object from the event and compare it with the current one
   - If different, and the selected object is a `TimeZone`, update the viewer

3. Implement it as follows:

```
public void selectionChanged(IWorkbenchPart p, ISelection sel) {
  if (p != this.part) {
    IStructuredSelection selected = ((IStructuredSelection)sel)
      .getFirstElement();
    Object current = ((IStructuredSelection)viewer.getSelection())
      .getFirstElement();
    if(selected != current && selected instanceof TimeZone) {
      viewer.setSelection(sel);
      if(viewer instanceof StructuredViewer) {
        ((StructuredViewer) viewer).reveal(selected);
      }
    }
  }
}
```

**4.** The selection listeners need to be registered with the views. Open up the `TimeZoneTableView` class, and at the bottom of the `createPartControl()` method, add the following:

```
selectionListener = new TimeZoneSelectionListener(
   tableViewer, getSite().getPart());
getSite().getWorkbenchWindow().getSelectionService()
   .addSelectionListener(selectionListener);
```

**5.** The `selectionListener` needs to be added as a field, because it will be necessary to remove the listener when the view is disposed:

```
private TimeZoneSelectionListener selectionListener;
public void dispose() {
   if (selectionListener != null) {
     getSite().getWorkbenchWindow().getSelectionService()
       .removeSelectionListener(selectionListener);
     selectionListener = null;
   }
   super.dispose();
}
```

**6.** A very similar change (only the viewer's variable name is different) needs to be added to the `TimeZoneTreeView` class:

```
selectionListener = new TimeZoneSelectionListener(
   tableViewer, getSite().getPart());
getSite().getWorkbenchWindow().getSelectionService()
   .addSelectionListener(selectionListener);
```

**7.** The `dispose` method is the same for the `TimeZoneTreeView` class as the `TimeZoneTableView`.

**8.** Now run the Eclipse instance, select a time zone in the Time Zone Table View, and the Time Zone Tree View should show the same one. Change the selection of the Time Zone Tree View and the Time Zone Table View should show the same one.

## What just happened?

Selection events occur a lot in the Eclipse workspace, so it is important that the selection listeners be performant. By filtering events fired from the same part, or filtering uninteresting types, the event delivery will be more efficient. In this case, the selection is checked to ensure that the selection contains (at least) one element, which is a `TimeZone`, before performing any UI updates.

The selection of the viewer can be synchronized with the `setSelection()` call; this saves having to instantiate a new selection object and set the data appropriately. However, setting the selection alone is not enough; the `reveal()` method needs to be called to ensure that it is appropriately highlighted. If multiple objects are selected, this will only reveal the first element.

The `reveal()` method is only available to `StructuredViewers`, so the selection stamps the selection as it is, and explicitly sets the `IStructuredSelection` for those that are `StructuredViewers`.

Finally, the listeners are registered when the view is created, and removed when the view is disposed. To do this, get hold of the `ISelectionService` via the part and then invoke the `addSelectionListener()` method to add it, and invoke the `removeSelectionListener()` method to remove it.

>  ☞ E4: If using E4, instead of using the `ISelectionService`, the `ESelectionService` is used. This provides a similar, but not identical, interface in that the `WorkbenchPart` is no longer present. Typically, the `ESelectionService` is injected into the view and the listener is wired in the `@PostConstruct` and removed in the `@PreDestroy` call.

## Pop quiz – understanding tables

Q1. How are a columns' headers enabled in a `TableViewer`?

Q2. What is a `TableViewerColumn` for?

Q3. How is selection synchronized between two views?

# Summary

This chapter covered how to use JFace to build viewers for structured data; both tree-based views (with a `TreeViewer`) and table-based views (with a `TableViewer`). It also covered some JFace built-in features for managing fonts and images.

To synchronise data between views in Eclipse, services such as the `ISelectionService` are used (or for E4 the `ESelectionService` is used). Having views generate and consume selection events provides a visual consistency, even though the views may be exposed by different plug-ins.

# 4
# Interacting with the User

*In the previous chapter, we looked at some of the basic JFace viewers, which provide a representation of data. However, we need to interact with the user and we can do this in multiple ways, from responding to mouse clicks to processing data-intensive operations in the background.*

In this chapter we will cover:

- ◆ Creating a menu in response to a user pop up
- ◆ Adding a command and a handler in a menu
- ◆ Using progress managers to report work
- ◆ Adding actions to the progress manager
- ◆ Showing errors and dealing with failure

## Creating actions, commands, and handlers

The first few releases of the Eclipse framework provided `Action` as a means of contributing to menu items. These were defined declaratively via `actionSets` in the `plugin.xml` file, and many tutorials still reference those today. At the programming level, when creating views, `Actions` are still used to provide context menus programmatically.

They were replaced with commands in Eclipse 3, as a more abstract way of decoupling the operation of a command with its representation of the menu. To connect these two together, a handler is used.

☞ E4: Eclipse 4.x uses the command's model, and decouples it further using the `@Execute` annotation on the `handler` class. Commands and views are hooked up with entries on the application's model. The basic ideas covered in this chapter will translate into examples in the E4 in Chapter 7.

# Time for action – adding context menus

A context menu can be added to the `TimeZoneTableView` class and respond to it dynamically in the view's creation. The typical pattern for Eclipse 3 applications is to create a `hookContextMenu()` method, which is used to wire up the context menu operation with displaying the menu. A default implementation can be seen by creating an example view, or one can be created from first principles.

Eclipse menus are managed by a `MenuManager`. This is a specialized subclass of a more general `ContributionManager`, which looks after a dynamic set of contributions that can be made from other sources. When the menu manager is connected to a control, it responds in the standard ways for the platform for showing the menu (typically a context-sensitive click or short key). Menus can also be displayed in other locations, such as a view's or the workspace's coolbar (toolbar). The same `MenuManager` approach works in these different locations.

1. Open the `TimeZoneTableView` class and go to the `createPartControl()` method.

2. At the bottom of the method, add a new `MenuManager` with the ID `#PopupMenu` and associate it to the viewer's control.

```
MenuManager manager = new MenuManager("#PopupMenu");
Menu menu = manager.createContextMenu(tableViewer.getControl());
tableViewer.getControl().setMenu(menu);
```

3. If the `Menu` is empty, the `MenuManager` won't show any content, so this currently has no effect. To demonstrate this, an `Action` will be added to the `Menu`. An `Action` has text (for rendering in the pop-up menu, or the menu at the top of the screen), as well as a state (enabled/disabled, selected) and a behavior. These are typically created as subclasses and (although the `Action` doesn't strictly require it) an implementation of the `run()` method. Add this to the bottom of the `createPartControl()` method.

```
Action deprecated = new Action() {
  public void run() {
    MessageDialog.openInformation(null, "Hello", "World");
  }
};
deprecated.setText("Hello");
manager.add(deprecated);
```

**4.** Run the Eclipse instance, open the Time Zone Table View, and right-click on the table. The Hello menu can be seen, and when selected, an informational dialog is shown.

## What just happened?

The `MenuManager` (with the id `#PopupMenu`) was bound to the control, which means when that particular control's context sensitive menu is invoked, the manager will be able to ask to display a menu. The manager is associated with a single `Menu` object (which is also stamped on the underlying control itself) and is responsible for updating the status of the menu.

 Actions are deprecated. They are included here since examples on the Internet may have preferred references to them, but it's important to note that while they still work, the way of building user interfaces are with the commands and handlers, shown in the next section.

When the menu is shown, the actions that the menu contains are rendered in the order in which they are added. `Action` are usually subclasses that implement a `run()` method, which performs a certain operation, and have text which is displayed.

`Action` instances also have other metadata, such as whether they are enabled or disabled. Although it is tempting to override the accessor methods, this behavior doesn't work—the setters cause an event to be sent out to registered listeners, which causes side effects, such as updating any displayed controls.

## Time for action – creating commands and handlers

Since the `Action` class is deprecated, the supported mechanism is to create a command, a handler, and a menu to display the command in the menu bar.

**1.** Open the plug-in manifest for the project, or double-click on the **plugin.xml** file.

**2.** Edit the source on the **plugin.xml** tab, and add a definition of a `Hello` command as follows:

```
<extension point="org.eclipse.ui.commands">
  <command name="Hello"
    description="Says Hello World"
    id="com.packtpub.e4.clock.ui.command.hello"/>
</extension>
```

**3.** This creates a command, which is just an identifier and a name. To specify what it does, it must be connected to a handler, which is done by adding the following extension:

```
<extension point="org.eclipse.ui.handlers">
  <handler class=
  "com.packtpub.e4.clock.ui.handlers.HelloHandler"
   commandId="com.packtpub.e4.clock.ui.command.hello"/>
</extension>
```

**4.** The handler joins the processing of the command to a class that implements `IHandler`, typically `AbstractHandler`. Create a class `HelloHandler` in a new `com.packtpub.e4.clock.ui.handlers` package, which implements `AbstractHandler` (from the `org.eclipse.core.commands` package).

```
public class HelloHandler extends AbstractHandler {
  public Object execute(ExecutionEvent event) {
    MessageDialog.openInformation(null, "Hello", "World");
    return null;
  }
}
```

**5.** The command's ID `com.packtpub.e4.clock.ui.command.hello` is used to refer to it from menus or other locations. To place the contribution in an existing menu structure, it needs to be specified by its `locationURI`, which is a URL that begins with `menu:` such as `menu:window?after=additions` or `menu:file?after=additions`. To place it in the **Help** menu, add this to the `plugin.xml` file.

```
<extension point="org.eclipse.ui.menus">
  <menuContribution allPopups="false"
   locationURI="menu:help?after=additions">
    <command commandId="com.packtpub.e4.clock.ui.command.hello"
     label="Hello"
     style="push">
    </command>
  </menuContribution>
</extension>
```

**6.** Run the Eclipse instance, and there will be a **Hello** menu item under the **Help** menu. When selected, it will pop up the `Hello World` message. If the **Hello** menu is disabled, verify that the handler extension point is defined, which connects the command to the handler class.

# What just happened?

The main issue with the actions framework was that it tightly coupled the state of the command with the user interface. Although an action could be used uniformly between different menu locations, the `Action` superclass still lives in the JFace package, which has dependencies on both SWT and other UI components. As a result, `Action` cannot be used in a headless environment.

Eclipse 3.x introduced the concept of commands and handlers, as a means of separating their interface from their implementation. This allows a generic command (such as `Copy`) to be overridden by specific views. Unlike the traditional command design pattern, which provides implementation as subclasses, the command in Eclipse 3.x uses a final class and then a retargetable `IHandler` to perform the actual execution.

 ☞ E4: In Eclipse 4.x, the concepts of commands and handlers are used extensively to provide the components of the user interface. The key difference is in their definition; for Eclipse 3.x, this typically occurs in the `plugin.xml` file, whereas in E4 it is part of the application model.

In the example, a specific handler was defined for the command, which is valid in all contexts. The handler's class is the implementation; the command ID is the reference.

The `org.eclipse.ui.menus` extension point allows `menuContributions` to be added anywhere in the user interface. To address where the menu can be contributed to, the `locationURI` object defines where the menu item can be created. The syntax for the URI is as follows:

- `menu:` Menus begin with the `menu:` protocol (can also be `toolbar:` or `popup:`)
- `identifier:` This can be a known short name (such as `file`, `window`, and `help`), the global menu (`org.eclipse.ui.main.menu`), the global toolbar (`org.eclipse.ui.main.toolbar`), a view identifier (`org.eclipse.ui.views.ContentOutline`), or an ID explicitly defined in a pop-up menu's `registerContextMenu()` call.
- `?after(or before)=key:` This is the placement instruction to put this after or before other items; typically additions is used as an extensible location for others to contribute to.

The `locationURI` allows plug-ins to contribute to other menus, regardless of where they are ultimately located.

Note, that if the handler implements the `IHandler` interface directly instead of subclassing `AbstractHandler`, the `isEnabled()` method will need to be overridden as otherwise the command won't be enabled, and the menu won't have any effect.

# Time for action – binding commands to keys

To hook up the command to a keystroke a binding is used. This allows a key (or series of keys) to be used to invoke the command, instead of only via the menu. Bindings are set up via an extension point `org.eclipse.ui.bindings`, and connect a sequence of keystrokes to a command ID.

**1.** Open the `plugin.xml` in the `clock.ui` project.

**2.** In the `plugin.xml` tab, add the following:

```
<extension point="org.eclipse.ui.bindings">
  <key commandId="com.packtpub.e4.clock.ui.command.hello"
    sequence="M1+9"
    contextId="org.eclipse.ui.contexts.window"
    schemeId=
    "org.eclipse.ui.defaultAcceleratorConfiguration"/>
</extension>
```

**3.** Run the Eclipse instance, and press *Cmd + 9* (for OS X) or *Ctrl + 9* (for Windows/Linux). The same `Hello` dialog should be displayed, as if it was shown from the menu. The same keystroke should be displayed in the `Help` menu.

## What just happened?

The `M1` key is the primary meta key, which is *Cmd* on OS X and *Ctrl* on Windows/Linux. This is typically used for the main operations; for example `M1 + C` is copy and `M1 + V` is paste on all systems. The sequence notation `M1 + 9` is used to indicate pressing both keys at the same time.

The command that gets invoked is referenced by its `commandId`. This may be defined in the same plug-in, but does not have to be; it is possible for one application to provide a set of commands and another plug-in to provide keystrokes that bind them.

It is also possible to set up a sequence of key presses; for example, `M1 + 9  8  7` would require pressing *Cmd + 9* or *Ctrl + 9* followed by *8* and then *7* before the command is executed. This allows a set of keystrokes to be used to invoke a command; for example, it's possible to emulate an Emacs quit operation with the keybinding `Ctrl + X Ctrl + C` to the quit command.

Other modifier keys include `M2` (*Shift*), `M3` (*Alt/Option*), and `M4` (*Ctrl* on OS X). It is possible to use `CTRL`, `SHIFT`, or `ALT` as long names, but the meta names are preferred, since `M1` tends to be bound to different keys on different operating systems.

The non-modifier keys themselves can either be single characters (A to Z), numbers (0 to 9), or one of a set of longer name key-codes, such as F12, ARROW_UP, TAB, and PAGE_UP. Certain common variations are allowed; for example, ESC/ESCAPE, ENTER/RETURN, and so on.

Finally, bindings are associated with a scheme, which in the default case should be `org.eclipse.ui.defaultAcceleratorConfiguration`. Schemes exist to allow the user to switch in and out of keybindings and replace them with others, which is how tools like "vrapper" (a vi emulator) and the Emacs bindings that come with Eclipse by default can be used. (This can be changed via **Window | Preferences | Keys** menu in Eclipse.)

## Time for action – changing contexts

The context is the location in which this binding is valid. For commands that are visible everywhere—typically the kind of options in the default menu—they can be associated with the `org.eclipse.ui.contexts.window` context. If the command should also be invoked from dialogs as well, then the `org.eclipse.ui.context.dialogAndWindow` context would be used instead.

1. Open the `plugin.xml` file of the `clock.ui` project.

2. To enable the command only for Java editors, go to the **plugin.xml** tab, and modify the `contextId` as follows:

```
<extension point="org.eclipse.ui.bindings">
  <key commandId="com.packtpub.e4.clock.ui.command.hello"
       sequence="M1+9"
       contextId="org.eclipse.ui.contexts.window"
       contextId="org.eclipse.jdt.ui.javaEditorScope"
       schemeId="org.eclipse.ui.defaultAcceleratorConfiguration"/>
</extension>
```

3. Run the Eclipse instance, and create a Java project, a test Java class, and an empty text file.

4. Open both of these in editors. When the focus is on the Java editor, the *Cmd + 9* or *Ctrl + 9* operation will run the command, but when the focus is on the text editor, the keybinding will have no effect.

Unfortunately, it also highlights the fact that just because the keybinding is disabled when in the Java scope, it doesn't disable the underlying command.

If there is no change in behavior, try cleaning the workspace of the test instance at launch, by going to the **Run | Run ...** menu, and choosing **Clear** on the workspace. This is sometimes necessary when making changes to the `plugin. xml` file, as some extensions are cached and may lead to strange behavior.

## What just happened?

Context scopes allow bindings to be valid for certain situations, such as when a Java editor is open. This allows the same keybinding to be used for different situations, such as a **Format** operation—which may have a different effect in a Java editor than an XML editor, for instance.

Since scopes are hierarchical, they can be specifically targeted for the contexts in which they may be used. The Java editor context is a subcontext of the general text editor, which in turn is a subcontext of the window context, which in turn is a subcontext of the `windowAndDialog` context.

The available contexts can be seen by editing the `plugin.xml` file in the plug-in editor; in the extensions tab the binding shows an editor window with a form:

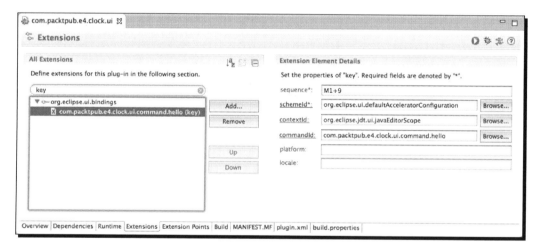

Clicking on the **Browse…** button next to the **contextId** brings up a dialog, which presents the available contexts:

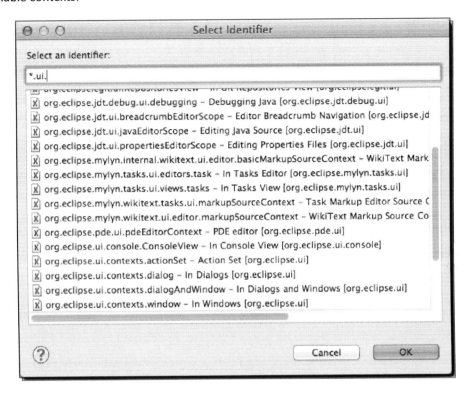

It's also possible to find out all the contexts programmatically or via the running OSGi instance, by navigating to **Window | Show View | Console**, and then using **New Host OSGi Console** in the drop-down menu, and then running the following code snippet:

```
osgi> pt -v org.eclipse.ui.contexts

Extension point: org.eclipse.ui.contexts [from org.eclipse.ui]

Extension(s):
-------------------
null [from org.eclipse.ant.ui]
    <context>
        name = Editing Ant Buildfiles
        description = Editing Ant Buildfiles Context
        parentId = org.eclipse.ui.textEditorScope
        id = org.eclipse.ant.ui.AntEditorScope
```

```
        </context>

    null [from org.eclipse.compare]
        <context>
          name = Comparing in an Editor
          description = Comparing in an Editor
          parentId = org.eclipse.ui.contexts.window
          id = org.eclipse.compare.compareEditorScope
        </context>
```

## Time for action – enabling and disabling the menu's items

The previous section showed how to hide or show a specific keybinding depending on the open editor type. However, it doesn't stop the command being called via the menu, or from it showing up in the menu itself. Instead of just hiding the keybinding, the menu can be hidden as well by adding a visibleWhen block to the command.

The expressions framework provides a number of variables, including activeContexts, which contains a list of the active contexts at the time. Since many contexts can be active simultaneously, the active contexts is a list (for example, [dialogAndWindows, windows, textEditor, javaEditor]). So, to find an entry (in effect, a contains operation) an iterate operator with the equals expression is used.

*1.* Open up the plugin.xml file, and update the the Hello command by adding a visibleWhen expression.

```xml
<extension point="org.eclipse.ui.menus">
  <menuContribution allPopups="false"
  locationURI="menu:help?after=additions">
   <command commandId="com.packtpub.e4.clock.ui.command.hello"
    label="Hello" style="push">
     <visibleWhen>
       <with variable="activeContexts">
         <iterate operator="or">
           <equals value="org.eclipse.jdt.ui.javaEditorScope"/>
         </iterate>
       </with>
     </visibleWhen>
   </command>
  </menuContribution>
</extension>
```

2.  Run the Eclipse instance, and verify that the menu is hidden until a Java editor is opened. If this behavior is not seen, run the Eclipse application with the `clean` argument to clear the workspace. After clearing, it will be necessary to create a new Java project with a Java class, as well as an empty text file, to verify that the menu's visibility is correct.

## What just happened?

Menus have a `visibleWhen` guard that is evaluated when the menu is shown. If it is `false`, the menu is hidden.

The `expressions` syntax is based on nested XML elements with certain conditions. For example, an `<and>` block is `true` if all of its children are `true`, whereas an `<or>` block is `true` if one of its children is `true`. Variables can also be used with a property test using a combination of a `<with>` block (which binds the specified variable to the stack) and an `<equals>` block or other comparison.

In the case of variables that have lists, an `<iterate>` can be used to step through elements using either `operator="or"` or `operator="and"` to dynamically calculate enablement.

To find out if a list contains an element, a combination of `<iterate>` and `<equals>` operators is the standard pattern.

There are a number of variables that can be used in tests; these are listed in the Eclipse help documentation under the *Workbench Core Expressions* chapter, and include the following variables:

*   `activeContexts`: List of context IDs that are active at the time
*   `activeShell`: The active shell (dialog or window)
*   `activeWorkbenchWindow`: The active window
*   `activeEditor`: The current or last active editor
*   `activePart`: The active part (editor or view)
*   `selection`: The current selection
*   `org.eclipse.core.runtime.Platform`: The `Platform` object

The `Platform` object is useful for performing dynamic tests using test, such as the following:

```
<test value="ACTIVE"
  property="org.eclipse.core.runtime.bundleState"
  args="org.eclipse.core.expressions"/>
<test
  property="org.eclipse.core.runtime.isBundleInstalled"
  args="org.eclipse.core.expressions"/>
```

Knowing if a bundle is installed is often useful; it's better to only enable functionality if a bundle is started (or in OSGi terminology, `ACTIVE`). As a result, use of `isBundleInstalled` has been replaced by the `bundleState=ACTIVE` tests.

# Time for action – reusing expressions

Although it's possible to copy and paste expressions between places where they are used, it is preferable to re-use an identical expression.

***1.*** Declare an expression using the expression's extension point, by opening the `plugin.xml` file of the `clock.ui` project.

```
<extension point="org.eclipse.core.expressions.definitions">
  <definition id="when.hello.is.active">
    <with variable="activeContexts">
      <iterate operator="or">
        <equals value="org.eclipse.jdt.ui.javaEditorScope"/>
      </iterate>
    </with>
  </definition>
</extension>
```

If defined via the extension wizard, it will prompt to add dependency on the `org.eclipse.core.expressions` bundle. This isn't strictly necessary for this example to work.

***2.*** To use the definition, the enablement expressions needs to use the reference.

```
<extension point="org.eclipse.ui.menus">
  <menuContribution allPopups="false"
   locationURI="menu:help?after=additions">
    <command commandId="com.packtpub.e4.clock.ui.command.hello"
     label="Hello" style="push">
      <visibleWhen>
        <with variable="activeContexts">
          <iterate operator="or">
            <equals value="org.eclipse.jdt.ui.javaEditorScope"/>
          </iterate>
        </with>
        <reference definitionId="when.hello.is.active"/>
      </visibleWhen>
    </command>
  </menuContribution>
</extension>
```

**3.** Now that the reference has been defined, it can be used to modify the handler as well, so that the handler and menu become active and visible together. Add the following to the `Hello` handler in the `plugin.xml` file:

```
<extension point="org.eclipse.ui.handlers">
  <handler class="com.packtpub.e4.clock.ui.handlers.Hello"
   commandId="com.packtpub.e4.clock.ui.command.hello">
    <enabledWhen>
      <reference definitionId="when.hello.is.active"/>
    </enabledWhen>
  </handler>
</extension>
```

**4.** Run the Eclipse application and exactly the same behavior will occur; but should the enablement change, it can be done in one place.

## What just happened?

The `org.eclipse.core.expressions` extension point defined a virtual condition that could be evaluated when the user's context changes, so both the menu and the handler can be made visible and enabled at the same time. The reference was bound in the `enabledWhen` condition for the handler, and the `visibleWhen` condition for the menu.

Since references can be used anywhere, expressions can also be defined in terms of other expressions. As long as the expressions aren't recursive, they can be built up in any manner.

## Time for action – contributing commands to pop-up menus

It's useful to be able to add contributions to pop-up menus so that they can be used by different places. Fortunately, this can be done fairly easily with the `menuContribution` element and a combination of enablement tests. This allows the removal of the `Action` introduced in the first part of this chapter with a more generic command and handler pairing.

There is a deprecated extension point—which still works in Eclipse 4.2 today—called `objectContribution`, which is a single specialized hook for contributing a pop-up menu to an object. This has been deprecated for some time, but often older tutorials or examples may refer to it.

**1.** Open the `TimeZoneTableView` class and add the `hookContextMenu()` method as follows:

```
private void hookContextMenu(Viewer viewer) {
  MenuManager manager = new MenuManager("#PopupMenu");
  Menu menu = manager.createContextMenu(viewer.getControl());
  viewer.getControl().setMenu(menu);
  getSite().registerContextMenu(manager, viewer);
}
```

**2.** Add the same `hookContextMenu()` method to the `TimeZoneTreeView` class.

**3.** In the `TimeZoneTreeView` class, at the end of the `createPartControl()` method, call `hookContextMenu(tableViewer)`.

**4.** In the `TimeZoneTableView` class, at the end of the `createPartControl()` method, replace the call to the action with a call to `hookContextMenu()` instead:

```
hookContextMenu(tableViewer);
MenuManager manager = new MenuManager("#PopupMenu");
Menu menu = manager.createContextMenu(tableViewer.getControl());
tableViewer.getControl().setMenu(menu);
Action deprecated = new Action() {
  public void run() {
    MessageDialog.openInformation(null, "Hello", "World");
  }
};
deprecated.setText("Hello");
manager.add(deprecated);
```

**5.** Running the Eclipse instance now and showing the menu results in nothing being displayed, because no menu items have been added to it yet.

**6.** Create a command and a handler `Show the Time`.

```
<extension point="org.eclipse.ui.commands">
  <command name="Show the Time" description="Shows the Time"
    id="com.packtpub.e4.clock.ui.command.showTheTime"/>
</extension>
<extension point="org.eclipse.ui.handlers">
  <handler class=
    "com.packtpub.e4.clock.ui.handlers.ShowTheTime"
    commandId="com.packtpub.e4.clock.ui.command.showTheTime"/>
</extension>
```

**7.** Create a class `ShowTheTime`, in the `com.packtpub.e4.clock.ui.handlers` package, which extends `org.eclipse.core.commands.AbstractHandler`, to show the time in a specific time zone.

```
public class ShowTheTime extends AbstractHandler {
  public Object execute(ExecutionEvent event) {
    ISelection sel = HandlerUtil.getActiveWorkbenchWindow(event)
      .getSelectionService().getSelection();
    if (sel instanceof IStructuredSelection && !sel.isEmpty()) {
      Object value =
        ((IStructuredSelection)sel).getFirstElement();
      if (value instanceof TimeZone) {
        SimpleDateFormat sdf = new SimpleDateFormat();
```

```
          sdf.setTimeZone((TimeZone) value);
          MessageDialog.openInformation(null, "The time is",
            sdf.format(new Date()));
        }
      }
      return null;
    }
}
```

**8.** Finally, to hook it up, a menu needs to be added to the special `locationURI` `popup:org.eclipse.ui.popup.any`.

```
<extension point="org.eclipse.ui.menus">
  <menuContribution allPopups="false"
    locationURI="popup:org.eclipse.ui.popup.any">
    <command label="Show the Time" style="push"
      commandId="com.packtpub.e4.clock.ui.command.showTheTime">
      <visibleWhen checkEnabled="false">
        <with variable="selection">
          <iterate ifEmpty="false">
            <adapt type="java.util.TimeZone"/>
          </iterate>
        </with>
      </visibleWhen>
    </command>
  </menuContribution>
</extension>
```

**9.** Run the Eclipse instance, and open the **Time Zone Table view** or **Time Zone Table view**. Right-click on a `TimeZone`, and the command **Show the Time** will be displayed (that is, one of the leaves of the tree or one of the rows of the table). Select the command and a dialog should show the time.

## What just happened?

The views from the previous chapter and the knowledge of how to wire up commands in this chapter provided a unified means of adding commands, based on the selected object type. This approach of registering commands is powerful, because any time a time zone is exposed as a selection in the future it will now have a **Show the Time** menu added to it automatically.

The commands define a generic operation, and handlers bind those commands to implementations. The context-sensitive menu is provided by the pop-up menu extension point using the `locationURI popup:org.eclipse.ui.popup.any`. This allows the menu to be added to any pop-up menu that uses a `MenuManager` and when the selection contains a `TimeZone`. The `MenuManager` is responsible for listening to the mouse gestures to show a menu, and filling it with details when it is shown.

In the example, the command was enabled when the object was an instance of a `TimeZone`, and also if it could be adapted to a `TimeZone`. This would allow another object type (say, a contact card) to have an adapter to convert it to a `TimeZone`, and thus show the time in that contact's location.

## Have a go hero – using view menus and toolbars

The way to add a view menu is similar to adding a pop-up menu; the `locationURI` used is the view's ID rather than the menu item itself. Add a **Show the Time** menu to the `TimeZone` view as a view menu.

Another way of adding the menu is to add it as a toolbar, which is an icon in the main Eclipse window. Add the **Show the Time** icon by adding it to the global toolbar instead.

To facilitate testing of views, add a menu item that allows you to show the `TimeZone` views with `PlatformUI.getActiveWorkbenchWindow().getActivePage().showView(id)`.

## Pop quiz – understanding menus

Q1. What's the difference between an `Action` and a `Command`, and which one should be used?

Q2. How can a `Command` be connected to a menu?

Q3. What is the `M1` key?

Q4. How are keystrokes bound to commands?

Q5. What is a menu `locationURI`?

Q6. How is a pop-up menu created?

# Jobs and progress

Since the user interface is single threaded, if a command takes a long amount of time it will block the user interface from being redrawn or processed. As a result, it is necessary to run long-running operations in a background thread to prevent the UI from hanging.

Although the core Java library contains `java.util.Timer`, the Eclipse Jobs API provides a mechanism to both run jobs and report progress. It also allows jobs to be grouped together and paused or joined as a whole.

# Time for action – running operations in the background

If the command takes a long time to execute, the user interface can be blocked. This happens because there is only one user interface thread, and because the command is launched from the UI, it will run in the UI thread. Instead, long running operations should run in a background thread, and then once finished, be able to display the results instead. Clearly creating a new `Thread` (like the clock updates initially) or other techniques like a `Timer` would work. However, the Eclipse system has a mechanism to provide a `Job` to do the work instead, or a `UIJob` to run in the context of the UI thread.

*1.* Open the `HelloHandler` and go to the `execute()` method. Replace its contents with the following code snippet:

```
public Object execute(ExecutionEvent event) {
  Job job = new Job("About to say hello") {
    protected IStatus run(IProgressMonitor monitor) {
      try {
        Thread.sleep(5000);
      } catch (InterruptedException e) {
      }
      MessageDialog.openInformation(null, "Hello", "World");
      return Status.OK_STATUS;
    }
  };
  job.schedule();
  return null;
}
```

*2.* Run the Eclipse instance, and click on the **Help | Hello** menu item. (It may be necessary to open a Java file to enable the menu). Open the Progress view, and a `Job` will be listed with `About to say hello` running. Unfortunately, an error dialog is then shown:

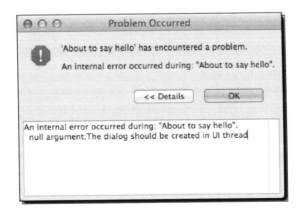

**3.** This occurs because the `Job` runs on a non-UI background thread, so when the `MessageDialog` is shown an exception occurs. To fix this, instead of showing the `MessageDialog` directly, a second `Job` or `Runnable` can be created to run specifically on the UI thread. Replace the call to the `MessageDialog` with the following code snippet:

```
MessageDialog.openInformation(null, "Hello", "World");
Display.getDefault().asyncExec(new Runnable() {
  public void run() {
    MessageDialog.openInformation(null, "Hello", "World");
  }
});
```

This example uses the `asyncExec()` to run a runnable on the UI thread (similar to the `SwingUtilities.invokeLater()` method in Swing).

**4.** Run the Eclipse instance, select the **Hello** menu, and after a five second pause, the dialog should be shown.

## What just happened?

Every action in the Eclipse UI must run on the UI thread, so if the action takes a significant time to run, it will give the impression that the user interface is blocked or hung. The way to avoid this is to drop out of the UI thread before doing any long term work. Any updates that need to be done involving the UI should be scheduled back on the UI thread.

The example used both `Job` (a mechanism for scheduling named processes that can be monitored via the Progress view), as well as the display's `asyncExec()` method to launch the resulting message dialog.

Both of these situations require the use of inner classes, which can increase the verbosity of the code. With future versions of Java and use of lambda expressions this will be significantly reduced.

 ☞ E4: Since E4 can use different renderers, the `Display` is not a good target for submitting background `UIJob`. Instead, use a `UISynchronize` instance to acquire the `asyncExec()` or `syncExec()` method.

### Have a go hero – using a UI job

Instead of scheduling the UI notification piece as a `Display.asyncExec()` method, create it as a `UIJob` instead. This works in exactly the same way as a `Job` does, but you need to override the `runInUIThread()` method instead of the `run()` method. This may be useful when there is more UI interaction required, such as asking the user for more information.

# Time for action – reporting progress

Normally when a `Job` is running, it is necessary to periodically update the user to let them know the state of progress. By default, if a `Job` provides no information, a generic `busy` indicator is shown. When a `Job` is executed, it is passed an `IProgressMonitor` object, which can be used to notify the user of progress (and provide a way to cancel the operation). A progress monitor has a number of tasks, each of which has a total unit of work that it can do. For jobs that don't have a known amount of work, `UNKNOWN` can be specified and it will be displayed in a generic `busy` indicator.

1. Open the `HelloHandler` and go to the `execute()` method. In the `run()` method of the inner `Job`, add a `beginTask()` at the beginning, and a `worked()` method in the loop after each second's sleep, for five iterations. The code will look like the following:

```
protected IStatus run(IProgressMonitor monitor) {
  try {
    monitor.beginTask("Preparing", 5000);
    for(int i=0;i<5;i++) {
      Thread.sleep(1000);
      monitor.worked(1000);
    }
  } catch (InterruptedException e) {
  } finally {
    monitor.done();
  }
  MessageDialog.openInformation(null, "Hello", "World");
  return Status.OK_STATUS;
}
```

2. Run the Eclipse instance, and open the Progress view by navigating to **Windows | Show View | Other | General | Progress**. Now, go to **Help | Hello**; the Progress view should show the progress as the sleep occurs.

3. To make the reporting more accurate, report the status more frequently.

```
for(int i=0;i<50;i++) {
  Thread.sleep(100);
  monitor.worked(100);
}
```

4. Run the Eclipse instance again. When the job is run via the **Help | Hello** menu, the status will be updated in the Progress view more frequently.

# What just happened?

When running a `Job`, the progress monitor can be used to indicate how much work has been done. It must start with a `beginTask()` method—this gives both the total number of work units as well as a textual name that can be used to identify what's happening.

If the amount of work is unknown, use `IProgressMonitor.UNKNOWN`.

The unit scale doesn't really matter; it could have been 50 or 50,000. As long as the total number of work units add up, and they're appropriately used, it will give the user a good idea of the operation.

Don't just report based on the number of lines (or tasks). If there are four work items but the fifth one takes as long as the previous four, then the amount of work reported needs to be balanced; for example, provide a total of 8 units, with 1 unit for each of the first four and then the remaining four for the fifth item.

Finally, `done()` was called on the progress monitor. This signifies that the `Job` has been completed, and can be removed from any views that are reporting the status. This is wrapped inside a `finally` block to ensure that the monitor is completed even if the `Job` finishes abnormally (for example, if an exception occurs).

# Time for action – dealing with cancellation

Sometimes the user will change their mind; they may have selected the wrong option, or something more important may have come up. The progress monitor allows for two-way communication; the user can signify when they want to cancel as well. There is a method, `isCancelled()`, which returns `true` if the user has signified in some way that he/she wishes the `Job` to finish early. Periodically checking this during the operation of the `Job` allows the user to cancel a long-running `Job` before it reaches the end.

1. Modify the `for` loop in the `HelloHandler` to check on each iteration whether the monitor is cancelled or not.

```
for(int i=0;i<50 && !monitor.isCanceled(); i++) {
  ...
}
if(!monitor.isCancelled()) {
  Display.getDefault().asyncExec(new Runnable() {...});
}
```

**2.** Run the Eclipse instance and click on the **Hello** command. This time, go into the Progress view and click on the red stop square next to the job. The job should cancel and the dialog showing the message shouldn't be shown:

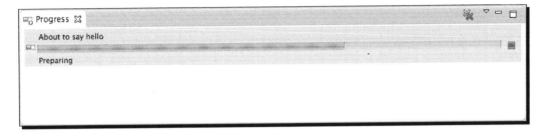

## What just happened?

Being responsive to the user is a key point in implementing plug-ins. If there are long running operations, make sure to check to see if the user has cancelled the operation—there's no point in tying up the CPU if the user doesn't want it to continue.

The monitor.isCancelled() method is generally implemented with a single field access, so calling it frequently often has no negative performance implications. Calling the isCancelled() method too many times is never noticed by users, however, not calling it enough certainly is noticed.

## Time for action – using subtasks and subprogress monitors

When performing a set of operations, subtasks can give the user additional details about the state of the operation. A subtask is merely a named message, which is displayed along with the task name in the Progress view.

**1.** Add monitor.subTask() during the operation to give feedback.

```
for (int i=0; i<50 && !monitor.isCanceled(); i++) {
  if(i==10) {
    monitor.subTask("Doing something");
  } else if (i==25) {
    monitor.subTask("Doing something else");
  } else if (i==40) {
    monitor.subTask("Nearly there");
  }
  Thread.sleep(100);
  monitor.worked(100);
}
```

**2.** Run the Eclipse instance, and look at the Progress view. The subtask should be shown underneath the status bar:

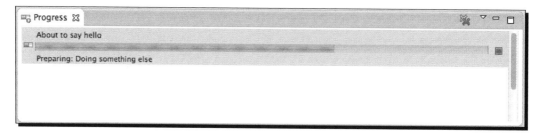

**3.** When calling another method with a progress monitor, if the monitor is passed as it is, it can have undesirable effects. Add a new method, checkDozen(), to the Job of HelloHandler and add a condition in the for loop that breaks out if the number of execution reaches 12.

```
protected IStatus run(IProgressMonitor monitor) {
  ...
  } else if (i == 12) {
    checkDozen(monitor);
  }
  ...
}
private void checkDozen(IProgressMonitor monitor) {
  try {
    monitor.beginTask("Checking a dozen", 12);
    for (int i = 0; i < 12; i++) {
      Thread.sleep(10);
      monitor.worked(1);
    }
  } catch (InterruptedException e) {
  } finally {
    monitor.done();
  }
}
```

**4.** Run the Eclipse instance, select the **Hello** menu and open the Progress view and the progress status completely disappears after it reaches that point:

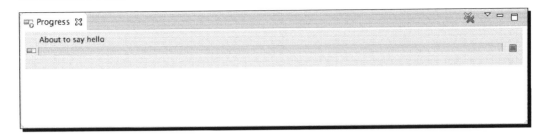

5. To solve this problem, create another IProgressMonitor instance and pass that into the method call using a SubProgressMonitor instance.

```
} else if (i == 12) {
    checkDozen(new SubProgressMonitor(monitor, 100));
    continue;
}
```

6. Now, run the action, and the progress will update as expected. Note, that the continue statement is used here to avoid calling monitor.worked(100).

## What just happened?

The checkDozen() method took an IProgressMonitor instance, and simulated a set of different tasks (with different units of work). Passing the same monitor instance causes problems as the work gets missed between the two.

To fix this behavior, a SubProgressMonitor instance was passed in. Because the SubProgressMonitor got 100 units of work from its parent, when the done() method was called on the SubProgressMonitor, the parent saw the completion of the 100 units of work.

Importantly, this also allows the child to use a completely different scale of work units and be completely decoupled from the parent's use of work units.

## Time for action – using null progress monitors and submonitors

When a method uses progress monitors extensively, it is inelegant to keep checking whether the monitor is null or not. Instead, the progress monitor can be replaced with a NullProgressMonitor, which acts as a no-op for all monitor calls.

1. Update the checkDozen() method to use a NullProgressMonitor, if null is passed.

```
private void checkDozen(IProgressMonitor monitor) {
    if(monitor == null)
        monitor = new NullProgressMonitor();
```

This allows the remainder of the method to run without modification, and saves any `NullPointerExceptions` that may result.

2. A similar result is obtained for both the `NullProgressMonitor` and `SubProgressMonitor` with a wrapper/factory class called `SubMonitor`. This provides factory methods to wrap the monitor and creates child progress monitors.

```
protected IStatus run(IProgressMonitor monitor) {
  try {
    SubMonitor subMonitor =
      SubMonitor.convert(monitor,"Preparing", 5000);
    for (int i = 0; i < 50 && !subMonitor.isCanceled(); i++) {
      if (i == 10) {
        subMonitor.subTask("Doing something");
      } else if (i == 25) {
        subMonitor.subTask("Doing something else");
      } else if (i == 40) {
        subMonitor.subTask("Nearly there");
      } else if (i == 12) {
        checkDozen(subMonitor.newChild(100));
        continue;
      }
      Thread.sleep(100);
      subMonitor.worked(100);
    }
  } catch (InterruptedException e) {
  } finally {
    if(monitor != null)
      monitor.done();
  }
}
```

3. Running the code has the same effect as the previous one, but it's more efficient. Note that the `subMonitor` object is used everywhere in the method until the end, where `monitor` is used to invoke `done()`. Since `monitor` may be `null`, it is guarded with a test.

## What just happened?

The `NullProgressMonitor` was replaced with a `SubProgressMonitor` with a `SubMonitor`. To convert an arbitrary `IProgessMonitor` into a `SubMonitor`, use the `convert()` factory method. This has the advantage of testing for `null` (and using an embedded `NullProgressMonitor` if necessary) as well as facilitating the construction of `SubProgressMonitor` instances with the `newChild()` call.

Note that the contract of `SubMonitor` requires the caller to invoke `done()` on the underlying progress monitor at the end of the method, so it gives an error when it's done an assignment such as `monitor = SubMonitor.convert(monitor)` in code.

Since the `isCancelled()` check will ultimately call the parent monitor, it doesn't strictly matter whether it is called on the submonitor or the parent monitor. However, if the parent monitor is `null`, invoking it on the parent will result in a `NullPointerException`, whereas the `SubProgressMonitor` will never be `null`.

In situations where there will be lots of recursive tasks, the `SubProgessMonitor` will handle nesting better than instantiating a `SubProgressMonitor` each time. That's because the implementation of the `newChild()` method doesn't necessarily need to create a new `SubMonitor` instance each time; it can keep track of how many times it has been called recursively.

The `SubMonitor` also has a `setWorkRemaining()` call, which can be used to reset the amount of work for the outstanding progress monitor. This can be useful if the job doesn't know at the start how much work there is to be done, but it does become known later in the process.

# Time for action – setting job properties

It is possible to associate arbitrary properties with a `Job`, which can be used to present its progress in different ways. For example, by specifying a command it's possible to click on a running `Job` and then execute something in the user interface, such as a detailed job description. `Job` properties are set with `setProperty()`, and can include any key/value combination. The keys use a `QualifiedName`, which is like a pair of strings for namespace/value. In the case of the Progress view, there is an `IProgressConstants2` interface, which defines values that can be set, including `COMMAND_PROPERTY`, which can be used to invoke a command.

1. Open the `HelloHandler` and go to the end of the `execute()` method. Just before the `Job` is scheduled, acquire the `Command` from the `ICommandService` and then stamp it on the `Job` as a property.

```
ICommandService service = (ICommandService)
  PlatformUI.getWorkbench().getService(ICommandService.class);
Command command = service == null ? null :
  service.getCommand("com.packtpub.e4.clock.ui.command.hello");
if(command != null) {
  job.setProperty(IProgressConstants2.COMMAND_PROPERTY,command);
}
job.schedule()
return null;
```

☞ **E4:** In E4, the `ICommandService` can be obtained via injection, using `@Inject ICommandService service`. Injection will be covered in more detail in *Chapter 7, Understanding the Eclipse 4 Model*.

2. Run the Eclipse instance, open the **Hello** command and go to the Progress view. Nothing will be shown, because the Job expects a `ParameterizedCommand` instead. Modify the property value, and using the `generateCommand()` factory of `ParameterizedCommand`.

```
if(command != null) {
job.setProperty(IProgressConstants2.COMMAND_PROPERTY,command);
  job.setProperty(IProgressConstants2.COMMAND_PROPERTY,
    ParameterizedCommand.generateCommand(command, null));
}
```

3. Now run the Eclipse instance, go to the Progress view, and click on the **Hello** command. Underneath the Progress view, a hyperlink will be provided to allow firing off another **Hello** command:

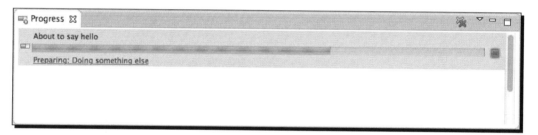

4. If the command has no handler (or the handler is disabled), a pop-up error message will be shown:

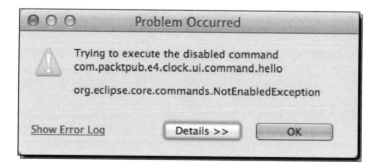

**5.** If the command is handled, clicking on the link will run the command, which in this case runs the `HelloHandler` and launches another job instance. Each click will spawn off a new `Job`:

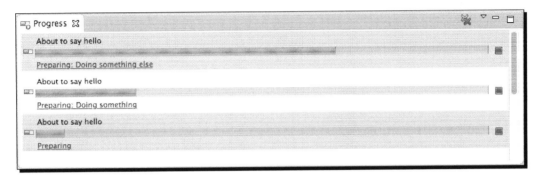

**6.** It's possible to change the icon shown in the view by specifying an `ImageDescriptor` as a `Job` property with the key `ICON_PROPERTY`. The image descriptor can be loaded from the `createFromURL()` method of `ImageDescriptor` and set as a property.

```
job.setProperty(IProgressConstants2.ICON_PROPERTY,
  ImageDescriptor.createFromURL(
    HelloHandler.class.getResource("/icons/sample.gif")));
```

**7.** Run the Eclipse instance, go to the Progress view, and then click on the **Hello** menu. The icon should be shown against the job:

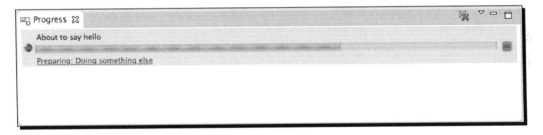

## What just happened?

Setting properties on the running `Job` allows viewers to extract information and present it in different ways. Properties are specified with a `QualifiedName` key and the value is passed in as an object, which is property specific.

The purpose of the `QualifiedName` key is to act as a string identifier, but partitioned into different namespaces. For example, the properties used by the `IProgressConstants` use `org.eclipse.ui.workbench.progress` as the namespace qualifier, and shorter strings such as `command` and `icon` for individual properties. The benefit of this (instead of `org.eclipse.ui.workbench.properties.command`) is that the long prefix string is stored once in memory and so doesn't take up repeated space in either the class file or the PermGen space, which can be limited on JDK 7. (JDK 8 will remove the PermGen, so it should be less of an issue in the future.)

Valid values for the `Job` in the Progress view can be found in the `IProgressConstants` and `IProgressContstants2` interfaces. Note that this is not a fixed set; additional `Job` properties can be added for use both elsewhere in the Eclipse platform and by independent extensions.

To associate a `Command` with a `Job`, set a property which contains a `ParameterizedCommand`. The factory method `generateCommand()` on the `ParameterizedCommand` class can be used to convert a command into a `ParameterizedCommand`.

The `Command` can be acquired from the `ICommandService`, which is acquired via the `PlatformUI` workbench or through injection in E4.

## Have a go hero – displaying in the taskbar

The `IProgressConstants2` interface also defines a property name `SHOW_IN_TASKBAR_ICON_PROPERTY`, which shows whether the progress of the `Job` is exposed to those operating systems that support it. On OS X, a bar will be shown over the Eclipse application icon. Set the property to the value `Boolean.TRUE` and see the effect it has on the `Job`.

The `Job` can also indicate if it is running in the foreground or the background, and can query its state via the `Job` property `PROPERTY_IN_DIALOG`. This is not intended to be set by clients, but can be read and displayed (or different actions be taken).

## Pop quiz: understanding jobs

Q1. What is the difference between `Display.syncExec()` and `Display.asyncExec()`?

Q2. What is the difference between `Display` and `UISynchronize`?

Q3. What is the difference between `Job` and `UIJob`?

Q4. What is the singleton `Status` object that indicates everything is ok?

Q5. How is the `CommandService` obtained in Eclipse?

Q6. How is an icon associated with a `Job` in the Progress view?

Q7. When should a `SubMonitor` instead of a `SubProgressMonitor` be used?

Q8. How frequently should the `Job` cancellation status be checked?

# Reporting errors

As long as everything works as expected, the IDE won't need to tell the user that something has gone wrong. Unfortunately, even the most optimistic programmer won't believe that the code will work in every situation. Bad data, threading issues, simple bugs and environmental issues can result in operations failing, and when it fails, the user needs to be notified.

Eclipse has built-in mechanisms to report problems, and these should be used in response to a user interaction that has failed.

## Time for action – showing errors

So far, the code has been using an information dialog as the demonstration of the handler. There's an equivalent method that can be used to create an error message instead. Instead of calling `MessageDialog.openInformation()`, there's an `openError()` method, which presents the same kind of dialog, but with an error message instead:

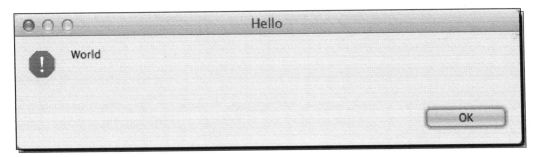

Using dialogs to report errors may be useful for certain environments, but unless the user has just invoked something (and the UI is blocked while doing it), reporting errors via a dialog is not a very useful thing to do. Instead, Eclipse offers a standard way to encapsulate both success and failure, in the `Status` object and the interface `IStatus` that it implements. When a `Job` completes, it returns an `IStatus` object to denote success or failure of the `Job` execution.

1. Introduce an error into the `run()` method of `HelloHandler`, whch will generate a `NullPointerException`. Add a `catch` to the existing `try` block and use that to return an error status. Since the `OK_STATUS` is a singleton instance of `Status` that can be used for all successful operations, it is necessary to instantiate a new `Status` object with the error information enclosed.

```
protected IStatus run(IProgressMonitor monitor) {
  try {
    SubMonitor subMonitor =
     SubMonitor.convert(monitor,"Preparing", 5000);
    subMonitor = null; // the bug
    ...
  } catch (NullPointerException e) {
    return new Status(IStatus.ERROR,
     Activator.PLUGIN_ID, "Programming bug?", e);
  } finally {
```

2. Run the Eclipse instance, and invoke the **Hello** command. An exception will be generated, and the status object containing the information needed will be passed to Eclipse. If the `Job` is running in the foreground, the job scheduler will present the status message if it is an error:

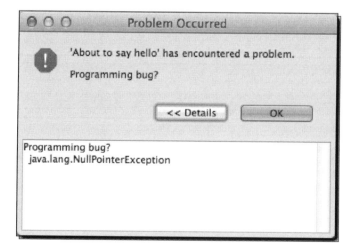

3. Go to **Window | Other | Error Log** in the target Eclipse instance to see the error, which has also been written into the `workspace/.metadata/.log` file:

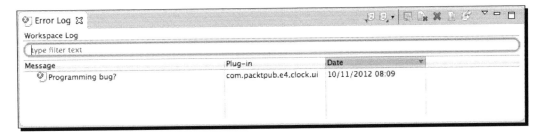

4. Double-click on the entry in the error log to bring up specific details:

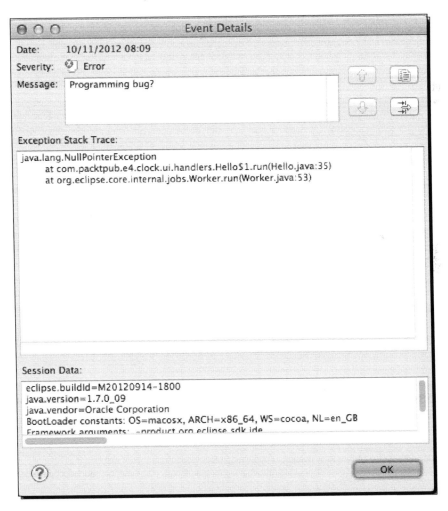

**5.** Instead of returning an error status, it's also possible to log the error message programmatically, using `StatusManager`. The `StatusManager` is a service that can be acquired from a static factory or injected from a service. To just log the information but keep going, execute the following code snippet:

```
} catch (NullPointerException e) {
    return new Status(IStatus.ERROR,
        Activator.PLUGIN_ID, "Programming bug?", e);
    StatusManager statusManager = StatusManager.getManager();
    Status status = new Status(IStatus.ERROR,
     Activator.PLUGIN_ID, "Programming bug?", e);
    statusManager.handle(status,
     StatusManager.LOG);
} ...
```

 ☞ E4: `StatusManager` has been replaced with `StatusReporter`, which has a `report()` method that is equivalent to the `handle()` method.

**6.** Run the Eclipse instance, invoke the **Hello** action and see the error being logged without displaying a dialog.

**7.** Modify the status flags to add `SHOW` as well:

```
statusManager.handle(status,
    StatusManager.LOG | StatusManager.SHOW );
```

**8.** Re-run the Eclipse instance, invoke the **Hello** action and the error will be shown as well as logged.

**9.** Finally, remove the bug from the `HelloHandler` so that it doesn't cause errors.

```
subMonitor = null; // the bug
```

## What just happened?

First, `openError()` was used to show an error, which is useful for specific cases—such as when the user is interacting with the UI and has just done an operation that is problematic.

The next step looked at status reporting and handling in Eclipse, including how exceptions are captured and associated with a specific plug-in. A `Status` object was used to indicate a single issue—though there's a `MultiStatus`, which can be used to add additional `Status` instances, if required. Generally, the status should be logged but not shown as dialogs popping up in the user's screen (especially from a background job) are a UX anti-pattern.

These flags can be combined, so LOG indicates that the status message should be logged but not otherwise displayed to the user, while SHOW indicates that the message should be shown in the standard dialog. Both of these happen asynchronously; the code will continue executing after invoking these calls, regardless of how the messages are shown to the user. There is a BLOCK flag as well, which prevents continued execution of the thread, but this should not be used as it may lead to inadvertent deadlocks.

## Pop quiz – understanding errors

Q1. How is an info/warning/error dialog shown?

Q2. What is the difference between StatusManager and StatusReporter?

Q3. Are status reports asynchronous or synchronous by default?

Q4. How can more than one problem be reported at the same time?

# Summary

This chapter covered how the user interfaces respond to user input by defining menus associated with abstract commands that are associated with handlers to execute code. It also covered how to run code in the background with jobs, and report the errors via the standard error reporting mechanism.

The next chapter will look at how to store preferences so that configuration items can be kept between restarts of the Eclipse platform.

# 5

# Storing Preferences and Settings

*An IDE is powerful as it provides a number of different utility windows to help the developer as they do their job. It becomes more powerful when they can customize it to their own taste, whether it is something as simple as colors, or something more targeted such as filters. The preference store in Eclipse allows users to customize it in the way they want.*

In this chapter we shall:

- Read and write preferences from a `PreferenceStore`
- Create a `PreferencePage` using `FieldEditors`
- Implement additional `FieldEditors`
- Explain the difference between `IEclipsePreferences` and `IPreferenceStore`
- Cover settings and mementos for storing transient state

## Storing preferences

A user preference is a stored configuration option that persists between different Eclipse runtimes. Preferences are simple values (`int`, `String`, `boolean`, and so on) and are identified with a `String` key, typically prefixed with the plug-in's identifier. Preferences can also be edited via a standard preference panel injected with an extension point. They can also be imported and exported from an Eclipse workbench using **File | Import/Export | Preferences** and saved as an **epf** (**Eclipse Preference File**).

# Time for action – persisting a value

To save and load preferences, an instance of `IPreferenceStore` is typically obtained from the `AbstractUIPlugin` subclass, in this case, the `Activator` of the clock plug-in. The `getPreferenceStore()` method returns a store which can be used to persist key/value pairs. Perform the following steps:

1. Open the `Activator` of the `clock.ui` plug-in.

2. Add the following to the `start()` method to count the number of times the plug-in has been launched:

```
int launchCount = getPreferenceStore().getInt("launchCount");
System.out.println("I have been launched "
+ launchCount + "times");
getPreferenceStore().setValue("launchCount",launchCount+1);
```

3. Run the Eclipse instance and open the Time Zone View.

4. In the host Eclipse, open the Console view. It should say "**I have been launched 0 times**".

5. Close the Eclipse instance down and run it again (but do not clear the workspace). Open the Time Zone View again.

6. In the host Eclipse open the Console view. It should now say "**I have been launched 1 times**".

## What just happened?

The `IPreferenceStore` is usually loaded via the `AbstractUIPlugin`, which provides a `getPreferenceStore()`. This API provides get/set methods for primitive types (`getInt()`, `getBoolean()`, `getString()`, and so on) as well as `setValue()` methods for the same types.

If the class does not have `AbstractUIPlugin` subclass, it can also be acquired by using the following code:

```
IPreferenceStore preferenceStore = new
    ScopedPreferenceStore(InstanceScope.INSTANCE,ID);
```

In the previous code, `ID` is the name of the identifier prefix used, typically the bundle's ID. (In `AbstractUIPlugin` it is calculated as `bundle.getSymbolicName()`).

 ☞ E4: If using E4, `IPreferenceStore` can be obtained via injection. Alternatively, a single preference value can be bound with `@Preference(name)` or `@Preference` to get the `IEclipsePreferences` object. It is also possible to track individual preferences being changed with a method parameter injection.

The number of times the plug-in is launched will be stored as a value in the preferences store. If run from Eclipse, the message, "**I have been launched 0 times**" is shown the first time the application is run; the second time, "**I have been launched 1 times**"; and each restart will update the counter.

Note that the preferences API generally shouldn't be used to store plug-in specific state. There's a method `getStateLocation()` which returns an `IPath` that can be used for storing such transient state.

If "**I have been launched 0 times**" is displayed repeatedly, **Clear workspace before launching** may be selected in the launch configurations menu. To disable this, go to **Run | Run Configurations...** and in the **Main** tab ensure that the **Clear** checkbox is deselected.

## Time for action – creating a preference page

Although preferences can be stored, providing a user interface is necessary for end users. A preference page implements the `IPreferencePage` interface. The easiest way is to use `FieldEditorPreferencePage` as a super class, which provides most of the standard plug-in behavior needed. Perform the following steps:

1. Open the `plugin.xml` of the `clock.ui` plug-in. In order to declare a new preference page, use the `org.eclipse.ui.preferencePages` extension point. Add the following code:

```
<extension point="org.eclipse.ui.preferencePages">
  <page name="Clock"
        class="com.packtpub.e4.clock.ui.ClockPreferencePage"
        id="com.packtpub.e4.clock.ui.preference.page"/>
</extension>
```

2. The same effect can be achieved by editing the `plugin.xml` in the editor and clicking on **Add** in the **Extensions** tab and selecting the **preferencePages** extension point.

3. Create a class `ClockPreferencePage` that extends `FieldEditorPreferencePage` in the `com.packtpub.e4.clock.ui` package as follows:

```
public class ClockPreferencePage extends
  FieldEditorPreferencePage
  implements IWorkbenchPreferencePage {
  protected void createFieldEditors() {
  }
  public void init(IWorkbench workbench) {
  }
}
```

**4.** Run the Eclipse application. Go to the preferences window by clicking on **Eclipse | Preferences** for OS X, or **Window | Preferences** for Windows/Linux. In the preferences list a **Clock** page should be displayed, although at present there will be no content.

**5.** Add a new `IntegerFieldEditor` for storing the launch count by adding it to the `createFieldEditors()` method as follows:

```
protected void createFieldEditors() {
    addField(new IntegerFieldEditor("launchCount",
      "Number of times it has been launched"
      ,getFieldEditorParent()));
}
```

**6.** Run the Eclipse application, go to Preferences and look at the **Clock** page. To get it to display the correct value, the `FieldEditorPreferencePage` needs to be connected to the plug-in's `PreferenceStore` as follows:

```
public void init(IWorkbench workbench){
    setPreferenceStore(
      Activator.getDefault().getPreferenceStore());
}
```

**7.** Now run the Eclipse application, go to the Preferences and look at the **Clock** page. The number will update based on the number of times the Eclipse application has launched.

## What just happened?

The preferences page was created and connected to the preferences window and the correct preference store (obtained from the plug-in's `Activator`). Instances of `FieldEditor` were added to display properties on a per-property basis.

The implementation of `getFieldEditorParent()` is something that needs to be called each time a field editor is created. It might be tempting to refactor this into a common variable, but the JavaDoc says that the value cannot be cached. If the `FLAT` style is used, then it will create a new instance of the parent each time it is called.

# Time for action – creating warning and error messages

In free-form text fields it's sometimes possible to input a value that doesn't make sense. For example, when asking someone for their e-mail address it might be necessary to validate it against some kind of regular expression like .+@.+ to provide a simplistic test. Perform the following steps:

1. To test the default validation, run the Eclipse instance and go to the Clock preference page. Type some text in the numeric field. A warning message will be displayed as shown in the following screenshot:

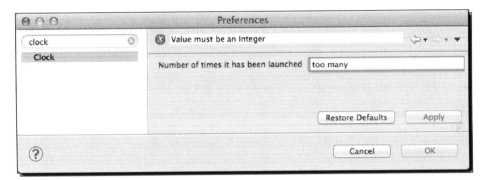

2. To add validation, create a new field called `offset` which allows valid values between `-14` and `+12`. (By default, `IntegerFieldEditor` validates against the range `0` to `MAX_INT`.) Add the following to the `createFieldEditors()` method:

```
IntegerFieldEditor offset = new IntegerFieldEditor("offset",
    "Current offset from GMT", getFieldEditorParent());
offset.setValidRange(-14, +12);
addField(offset);
```

3. Run the Eclipse instance, go to the Clock preference page and type in an invalid value as follows:

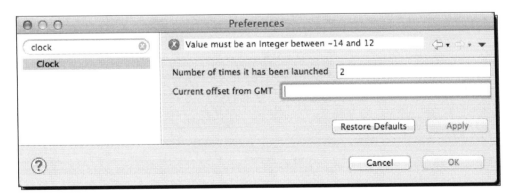

## What just happened?

Each field editor can determine what is (or is not) valid, and the validity of the page as a whole is a conjunction of all of the individual field editors' validity. It's also possible to create custom validation rules by creating a subclass of the appropriate `FieldEditor` by overriding the `isValid()` method appropriately.

The error message will display the warning, **"Value must be an Integer between -14 and 12"** at the top of the preference page."

## Time for action – choosing from a list

Although free text may be appropriate for some types of preferences, for others, choosing from a set of values may be more appropriate. `ComboFieldEditor` can be used to present the user with a selection, which can be used to represent the user's favourite `TimeZone`. The combo dropdown is built from an array of pairs of strings. The first string is the displayed label in the dropdown, while the second value is the string identifier that will be persisted to (and loaded from) the preferences store. Perform the following steps:

1.  In the `createFieldEditors()` method of the `ClockPreferencePage` class, add the following code to populate a `ComboFieldEditor` with the list of `TimeZone` IDs:

    ```
    protected void createFieldEditors() {
      String[][] data;
      String[] ids = TimeZone.getAvailableIDs();
      Arrays.sort(ids);
      data = new String[ids.length][];
      for (int i = 0; i < ids.length; i++) {
        data[i] = new String[] { ids[i], ids[i] };
      }
      addField(new ComboFieldEditor("favourite",
        "Favourite time zone", data, getFieldEditorParent()));
    }
    ```

2.  Run the Eclipse instance and go to the Clock preference page. A new dropdown will allow the user to select their favourite `TimeZone`. Choose a value, then close and re-open the Eclipse instance; the previous value should be stored as seen in the following screenshot:

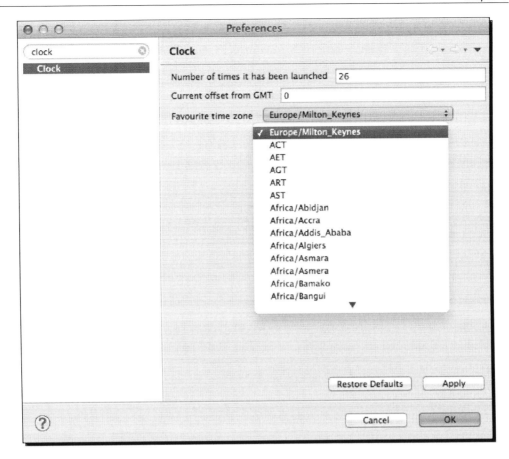

## What just happened?

Adding new types of field editor allows different types of data to be edited. Since all of the preferences are saved as a string, the `ComboFieldEditor` takes a set of pairs of strings; one for the display label, and one for the persisted value.

The `ComboFieldEditor` was initialized with a list of the `TimeZone` IDs, using the ID for both the display label and the persisted value. The display could present more information such as the display name, the offset from GMT, or other metadata. However, the string value which is persisted to the preferences should be unique and not subject to parsing or loading errors. In this case, using the ID means that a later iteration of the preferences plug-in could render the display text in a different form while still persisting the same ID in the preference store.

# Time for action – using a grid

The preference values weren't lined up as expected. This is because the default preference field editor uses a FLAT style of rendering, which simply lays out the fields similar to a vertical RowLayout. Perform the following steps:

1. Change it to a more natural look by specifying a GRID style of rendering:

```
public ClockPreferencePage() {
  super(GRID);
}
```

2. Now when the preference page is displayed, it will look more natural as seen in the following screenshot:

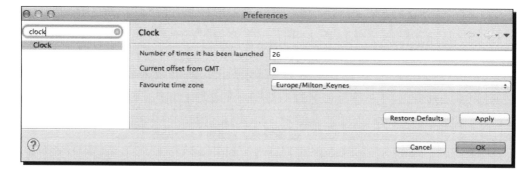

## What just happened?

The default or FLAT style does not render well. It was added in 2007 (see Eclipse bug 163281) before the popularity of the grid layout increased, and typically needs to be overridden to provide a decent user interface experience. Switching to GRID does this by working out the label length, field lengths, and setting up the split accordingly. Furthermore, the view is resizable with the fields taking up the additional stretch space.

If the layout needs further customization, or the widget set needs to be extended, then it is possible to create a plain subclass of PreferencePage and create the contents in the createContents() method. Then apply any changes in the performOk() method or performApply() methods.

# Time for action – placing the preferences page

When the preference page is created, if it does not specify a location (known as a category in the `plugin.xml` file and manifest editor), it is inserted into the top level. This is appropriate for some kinds of projects (for example, Mylyn, Java, Plug-in Development); but many plug-ins should contribute to an existing location in the preference page tree. Complete the following steps:

1. Preference pages can be nested by specifying the parent preference page's ID. To move the Clock preference page underneath the General preference page, specify `org.eclipse.ui.preferencePages.Workbench` as the category as shown in the following code:

```
<extension point="org.eclipse.ui.preferencePages">
  <page name="Clock"
  id="com.packtpub.clock.ui.preference.page"
  category="org.eclipse.ui.preferencePages.Workbench"
  class="com.packtpub.e4.clock.ui.ClockPreferencePage"/>
</extension>
```

2. Run the Eclipse instance and look in **Preferences**. The Clock preference page should now be under the General tree node instead, as seen in the following screenshot:

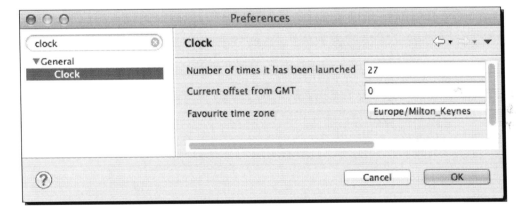

# What just happened?

The preference page can be placed anywhere in the hierarchy by specifying the parent page's ID in the category attribute. The parent pages can be listed using **Window | Show View | Other | Console**, then opening a **Host OSGi console** followed by running the following command:

```
osgi> pt -v org.eclipse.ui.preferencePages
Extension point: org.eclipse.ui.preferencePages [from org.eclipse.ui]

Extension(s):
-------------------
null [from org.eclipse.ant.ui]
  <page>
    name = Ant
    class = org.eclipse.ant.internal.ui.preferences.AntPreferencePage
    id = org.eclipse.ant.ui.AntPreferencePage
  </page>
```

Another way of listing the IDs is to use the **Browse** button via the `plugin.xml` editor. From the extension point defining the Clock preference page, the **Browse** button next to the category field will bring up a dialog containing all of the valid IDs, including a search filter to reduce the number of matches, as shown in the following screenshot:

# Time for action – using other field editors

The `FieldEditorPreferencePage` supports other types of field editor. These different types of editor include `BooleanFieldEditor`, `ColorFieldEditor`, `ScaleFieldEditor`, `FileFieldEditor`, `DirectoryFieldEditor`, `PathEditor`, and `RadioGroupFieldEditor`. Add a sample of each of these types to the `ClockPreferencePage` page to find out what they can store. Perform the following steps:

1. Open the `createFieldEditors()` method of the `ClockPreferencePage` and add the following code at the bottom of the method:

```
addField(new BooleanFieldEditor("tick","Boolean value",
  getFieldEditorParent()));
addField(new ColorFieldEditor("colour", "Favourite colour",
  getFieldEditorParent()));
addField(new ScaleFieldEditor("scale", "Scale",
  getFieldEditorParent(), 0, 360, 10, 90));
 addField(new FileFieldEditor("file", "Pick a file",
  getFieldEditorParent()));
addField(new DirectoryFieldEditor("dir", "Pick a directory",
  getFieldEditorParent()));
addField(new PathEditor("path","Path",
  "Directory",getFieldEditorParent()));
addField(new RadioGroupFieldEditor("group", "Radio choices", 3,
  data,getFieldEditorParent(),true));
```

2. Run the Eclipse instance and go to the Clock preference page. It should look similar to the following screenshot:

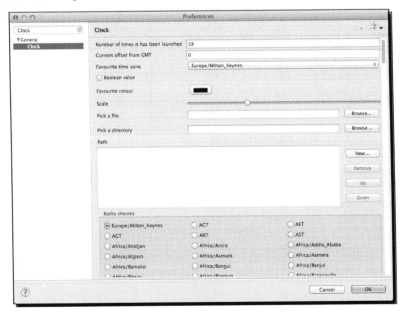

## What just happened?

This change added different types of standard field editors provided by the JFace package, to give a flavor of the types of data entry element that can be shown.

Some of the editors are specific to the kinds of entry points that are used in Eclipse itself, such as file, directory, or path editors. Others are more general such as colour, scale, boolean, or radio choices.

The values are persisted in the preferences format in a text values, appropriate to the data type. To see where the values are written to, go to the `runtime-EclipseApplication/.metadata/.plugins/org.eclipse.core.runtime/.settings/com.packtpub.e4.clock.ui.prefs` file. The contents look similar to the following code:

```
colour=49,241,180
eclipse.preferences.version=1
favourite=Europe/Milton_Keynes
group=Europe/Milton_Keynes
launchCount=28
scale=78
tick=true
```

The persisted colour value is stored as a red/green/blue triple, while the boolean value is stored as a `true` or `false` value.

## Time for action – adding keywords

Eclipse had a search field in the preferences list since version 3.1. This is defined not from UI but from a separate keyword extension instead. The keyword has an ID and a label, but the label isn't shown; rather, it's a space separated list of words which can be used in the filtering dialog. Perform the following steps:

**1.** To add the keywords `offset` and `timezone` to the `ClockPreferencePage`, create a new extension point in `plugin.xml` for `org.eclipse.ui.keywords`:

```
<extension point="org.eclipse.ui.keywords">
  <keyword id="com.packtpub.e4.clock.ui.keywords"
    label="offset timezone"/>
</extension>
```

**2.** Now associate these keywords with the preference page itself as follows:

```
<extension point="org.eclipse.ui.preferencePages">
  <page name="Clock" ... >
    <keywordReference id="com.packtpub.e4.clock.ui.keywords"/>
  </page>
</extension>
```

**3.** Run the Eclipse instance, go to the Preferences page and type `timezone` and `offset` in the search box. The Clock preference page should be shown in both cases:

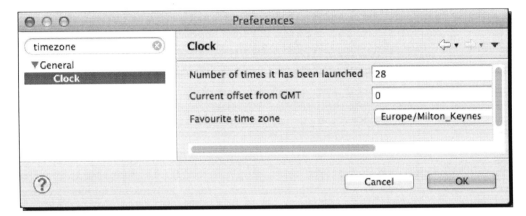

## What just happened?

By providing a list of keywords and associating them with the preferences page the user can search for the item in the preferences tree. The same keyword support is used to search for items in other places such as the New dialog wizards and the properties page.

Furthermore, these keywords are internationalizable. By specifying a key with a % name, Eclipse can load the keywords from an externalized file called `plugin.properties`. If `%clock.keywords` was used as the label and `plugin.properties` had an entry `clock.keywords=timezone offset`, then a French translation of the keywords could be provided in a `plugin_fr.properties` file.

# Time for action: using IEclipsePreferences

Although JFace defines `IPreferenceStore`, there's a lower-level interface called `IEclipsePreferences`. The key difference between `IPreferenceStore` and `IEclipsePreferences` is that the latter has support for arbitrary nodes similar to nested `HashMaps`. `IEclipsePreferences` is also based upon the OSGi `Preferences` service and can be used without any UI or JFace involvement. When the `IPreferenceStore` is obtained from `AbstractUIPlugin`, it lazily creates a `ScopedPreferenceStore` using `InstanceScope` and the bundle's symbolic name as the node name. Perform the following steps:

1. Modify `clock.ui`'s `Activator`:

   ```
   int launchCount = getPreferenceStore().getInt("launchCount");
   IEclipsePreferences eclipsePreferences =
     InstanceScope.INSTANCE. getNode(PLUGIN_ID);
   int launchCount2 = eclipsePreferences.getInt("launchCount",-1);
   System.out.println("I have been launched " + launchCount +
     " times and " + launchCount2);
   ```

2. Run the Eclipse instance and open the Time Zone View.

3. In the host Eclipse instance, go to the Console view, and the output should show the same value being displayed **I have been launched 6 times** and **6**.

## What just happened?

The same preference value was accessed through both as JFace's `IPreferenceStore`, which is used by UI plug-ins and extension points such as the `PreferencePage` and through the `IEclipsePreferences` API that can be used by headless plug-ins.

 ☞ E4: The `IEclipsePreferences` is used by E4 as the default preferences store.

To pass in an existing `IEclipsePreferences` to an API (like the preference page), an inverse adaptor can be created using the following code:

```java
public class EclipsePreferencesScope implements IScopeContext {
  private IEclipsePreferences preferences;
  public EclipsePreferencesScope(IEclipsePreferences preferences) {
    this.preferences = preferences;
  }
  public String getName() {
    return "";
  }
```

```
    public IPath getLocation() {
      return new Path(preferences.absolutePath());
    }
    public IEclipsePreferences getNode(String qualifier) {
      return preferences;
    }
  }
```

Finally the IEclipsePreferences interface is a subtype of Preferences, which is a
standard OSGi service. To compile against just the OSGi runtime, use Preferences as the
declared type for variables instead of IEclipsePreferences. That way, the code can be
compatible with both Eclipse and standard OSGi libraries.

## Have a go hero – translating into different languages

Eclipse's internationalization support is provided by a plugin.properties file. In the
plugin.xml, instead of using strings for the values, use %keys. The % instructs the engine
to look up a corresponding entry in plugin.properties to display the value.

To support different languages use plugin_fr.properties, plugin_de.properties
for French and German respectively (don't forget to add these to build.properties
otherwise they won't be found). The keys are still the same, but the values can be localized
appropriately. The search keywords are an example of something that can be searched as
well, so use an online translation service or make-up a translation to test out the effect of
running Eclipse in a different language. (Eclipse can be launched in different languages with
eclipse -nl de on the command line.)

# Using IMemento and DialogSettings

Preferences are designed to be values persisted in the workspace (or project) that can be
consumed by both UI and non-UI components. The preference support also handles changes
and default values.

However, it's not always the case that values need to be persisted in the preference store.
Certain values are specific to views such as the order of columns in a table view, or whether
the sort order is increasing or decreasing. Furthermore, it's possible to have multiple views in
different windows that have different sort orders.

IMementos are a means to store view-specific rendering data in a way that can be saved
by the workbench when the window closes, and re-opened when the perspective is
brought back.

DialogSettings are a more general way of storing values. Despite the name, these are
not limited to dialogs.

# Time for action – adding a memento for the Time Zone View

The `TimeZoneView`, created in *Chapter 2, Creating views with SWT*, presents a list of regions as tabs and allows the user to select a region of interest. When the view is closed and then re-opened, the previously selected tab is not remembered. This is the kind of nugget that could be persisted in a memento for later re-use. Perform the following steps:

**1.** To record what the last selected tab was when it is changed; add the variable `lastTabSelected`, which contains the last selected tab name, to the `TimeZoneView` as follows:

```
private transient String lastTabSelected;
```

**2.** At the end of `createPartControl()`, add a selection listener to the tab, such that any time the tab's selection is changed, the name of the tab is remembered:

```
tabs.addSelectionListener(new SelectionAdapter() {
  public void widgetSelected(SelectionEvent e) {
    if(e.item instanceof CTabItem) {
      lastTabSelected = ((CTabItem)e.item).getText();
    }
  }
});
```

**3.** When the workbench is closed, save the state by adding a `saveState()` method:

```
public void saveState(IMemento memento) {
  super.saveState(memento);
  memento.putString("lastTabSelected", lastTabSelected);
}
```

**4.** Restore the data when the view is opened:

```
public void init(IViewSite site, IMemento memento) throws
PartInitException {
  super.init(site, memento);
  if(memento != null) {
    lastTabSelected = memento.getString("lastTabSelected");
  }
}
```

**5.** Finally, update `createPartControl()` to set the selected tab when it's opened:

```
if(lastTabSelected == null) {
  tabs.setSelection(0);
} else {
  CTabItem[] items = tabs.getItems();
  for (CTabItem item : items) {
    if(lastTabSelected.equals(item.getText())) {
```

```
            tabs.setSelection(item);
            break;
        }
    }
}
```

6. Run the workbench, show the Time Zone View, select a tab, close the workbench and re-open, and the last selected tab should be restored.

## What just happened?

The `IMemento` is a way of storing content between launches of the workbench. When the workbench shuts down, it sends `save()` to each of the open views and persists the state such that the workbench state is restored when it is re-opened.

If this behavior is not seen while testing, check that the Eclipse workspace isn't being automatically cleaned at startup in the launch configuration.

Unfortunately, although the view is saved if it is open when the workbench is closed, if the view is closed first then nothing is saved. This makes the memento pattern one of the most useless patterns in Eclipse. The `IMemento` pattern should not generally be used; instead, use the preferences store, or the `DialogSettings` as explained next.

 ☞ E4: In E4, the `@PostConstruct` annotation can be used to set up values that were saved prior to a view being shut down, and a `@PreDestroy` to save any state that is required for next time. It is not as fragile as the `IMemento` pattern.

## Time for action – using DialogSettings

A more useful alternative to the Memento pattern is `DialogSettings`, which provides a properties-like interface for storing strings and other basic primitive values. This stores its information in an XML file, and can be acquired as a standard extension to the UI plug-in or created from a file location. The settings store is used to store values persistently, and is saved automatically when the plug-in shuts down. At startup, it is loaded automatically. Perform the following steps:

1. To migrate the settings for the last tab selected to use `DialogSettings`, remove the `init()` and `save()` methods from the `TimeZoneView` and replace them with the following in the `createPartControl()`:

```
final IDialogSettings settings =
 Activator.getDefault().getDialogSettings();
lastTabSelected = settings.get("lastTabSelected");
```

**2.** The call to `getDialogSettings()` comes from the `UIPlugin` class. Once the `DialogSettings` have been acquired, it can be used to store and retrieve values. Update the selection listener to store this in the settings instead:

```
tabs.addSelectionListener(new SelectionAdapter() {
  public void widgetSelected(SelectionEvent e) {
    if (e.item instanceof CTabItem) {
      lastTabSelected = ((CTabItem) e.item).getText();
      settings.put("lastTabSelected", lastTabSelected);
    }
  }
});
```

**3.** Now run the Eclipse instance, go to the Time Zone View and note how the settings are saved when either the view is closed or the application shuts down.

## What just happened?

The calls to `IMemento` were replaced with `DialogSettings`, a much more useful mechanism for storing values. In addition, we created a separate group of settings to create a nested namespace with `settings.addNewSection("name")` and with `settings.getSection("name")`.

The name `DialogSettings` comes from the fact that was initially used by dialogs with warnings such as "Do not show this message again". In fact, this is so common that a Dialog with a "Do not show this message again" can be created with a `MessageDialogWithToggle` as follows:

```
if (settings.getBoolean("spamalot")) {
  MessageDialogWithToggle dialog = MessageDialogWithToggle.
   openInformation(Display.getCurrent().getActiveShell(),
    "Spam", "Keep being spammed?", "Do not show this spam again",
    false, null, null);
  boolean spamalot = !dialog.getToggleState();
  settings.put("spamalot",spamalot);
}
```

The `MessageDialogWithToggle` also has an option to write this to a preference store using the store and the key value in the last two values (`null` in the example).

The `DialogSettings` can also be used to store items such as the last-value-used or to restore selection.

The key difference between using an `IPreferenceStore` and using `DialogSettings` is that the former can be used for importing/exporting preferences between Eclipse instances, using the **File | Import/Export | Preferences** menu. The `DialogSettings`, on the other hand, are supposed to be transient and recreatable if they are lost.

 ☞ E4: As E4 takes off and provides default support for reading and writing preferences, expect to see more uses of the preferences for storing both transient and non-transient preference data.

## Pop quiz – understanding preferences

Q1. What is the default style used for the `FieldEditorPreferencePage`, and how can it be changed to something more aesthetically pleasing?

Q2. What kinds of primitive values can be edited with a `FieldEditorPreferencePage`?

Q3. How can a preference value be searched for in the preference page?

Q4. Which is the preferred API for storing view-specific information; `IMemento` or `IEclipsePreferences`?

Q5. Which class provides the "Do not show this message again" support?

# Summary

We have covered the mechanisms that Eclipse uses to store metadata values. A preference store is the key/value pair mechanism used by preference pages, as well as being interacted programmatically from headless plug-ins. It is also possible to use `IMementos` or `DialogSettings` to store transient information about a view or plug-in. While some code examples demonstrate `IMemento`, they are essentially useless and can be substituted with `DialogSettings` without any loss of generality. Some plug-ins just use `PreferenceStore` and ignore `DialogSettings`, even though information may not be strictly necessary to persist or share between instances. For that reason, the `MessageDialogWithToggle` also includes the ability to persist into an associated `PreferenceStore`.

In the next chapter, we will look at how to work with `Resources` inside Eclipse.

# 6

# Working with Resources

*As an IDE, Eclipse is used to work with files and folders. Eclipse creates the concept of a workspace (a group of related projects), a number of projects, and then files and folders underneath each. These resources are then used by builders to be able to create derived resources upon change, which is how Eclipse compiles* `.java` *source files into* `.class` *files.*

In this chapter we shall:

- ◆ Create a custom editor
- ◆ Read the contents of a file
- ◆ Create a resource file
- ◆ Use a builder to automatically process changes
- ◆ Integrate the builder with a nature
- ◆ Highlight problems in the editor with markers

## Using the workspace and resources

Everything in the Eclipse IDE is based on the concept of a workspace which contains a number of projects, which in turn contain files and folders. Generically, these are all resources which are represented with a path and then with either a set of contents or a set of children.

# Time for action – creating an editor

The example will be based on a (made-up) markup language called minimark, which is essentially a plain text file with blank delimited paragraphs that can be translated into an HTML file. This will involve creating an editor for text-based content, for minimark files. Perform the following steps:

**1.** Create a new plug-in project called `com.packtpub.e4.minimark.ui` by going to **File | New | Project | Plug-in project** and filling in the following details:

   - **Project name**: `com.packtpub.e4.minimark.ui`

**2.** Click on **Next** and fill in the following details:

   - **ID**: `com.packtpub.e4.minimark.ui`
   - **Version**: `1.0.0.qualifier`
   - **Name**: `Minimark`
   - **Vendor**: `PACKTPUB`
   - Select the checkbox for **Create an Activator**
   - Select the checkbox for **This plug-in will make contributions to the UI**
   - Unselect the checkbox for **Create a Rich Client Application**

**3.** Click on **Finish** and a new plug-in will be created.

**4.** The next step is to create an editor for the minimark files. Open the plug-in's manifest by right-clicking on the project and selecting **Plug-in Tools | Open Manifest** or by double-clicking on the `plugin.xml` file.

**5.** Go to the **Extensions** tab and click on **Add**. The extension points dialog will show; search for **editors** and it should show up in the list. (If it doesn't, uncheck the **Show only extension points from the required plug-ins** and it will prompt to add `org.eclipse.ui.editors` to the required dependencies.)

**6.** Once the extension point has been added, right-click on the extension point and select **New | Editor** from the menu. This will add a template extension point; fill it in as follows:

   - **id**: `com.packtpub.e4.minimark.ui.minimarkeditor`
   - **name**: `Minimark`
   - **extensions**: `minimark`
   - **class**: `com.packtpub.e4.minimark.ui.MinimarkEditor`

**7.** The resulting `plugin.xml` will look like the following code:

```
<extension point="org.eclipse.ui.editors">
  <editor name="Minimark" extensions="minimark" default="false"
    class="com.packtpub.e4.minimark.ui.MinimarkEditor"
    id="com.packtpub.e4.minimark.ui.minimarkeditor"/>
</extension>
```

**8.** Now, add the required dependencies in the **Dependencies** tab:

- ❑ `org.eclipse.jface.text`: Provides text-processing libraries
- ❑ `org.eclipse.ui.editors`: The general editor support
- ❑ `org.eclipse.ui.workbench.texteditor`: The general text editor

**9.** Use the **File | New | Class** wizard to create `MinimarkEditor` in the `com.packtpub.e4.minimark.ui` package as a subclass of `AbstractTextEditor`:

```
public class MinimarkEditor extends AbstractTextEditor {
}
```

**10.** Run the Eclipse instance, and create a project with **File | New | Project | General Project** called `EditorTest`. Then use the **File | New | File** to create a file called `test.minimark`. Double-click on this file and an error will be seen, as shown in the following screenshot:

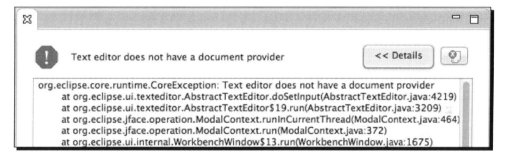

**11.** This happens because an editor needs to be hooked up to a document provider which synchronizes the content of the document with any other open editors. (This allows Eclipse to open multiple editors on the same file and still show the same changes in both.) To solve the error, add a constructor that sets the editor's document provider to a general `TextFileDocumentProvider`:

```
import org.eclipse.ui.editors.text.TextFileDocumentProvider;
public class MinimarkEditor extends AbstractTextEditor {
  public MinimarkEditor() {
    setDocumentProvider(new TextFileDocumentProvider());
  }
}
```

***12.*** Run the Eclipse instance again, double-click on the `test.minimark` file and an empty text editor will be opened.

## What just happened?

A basic text editor was created and associated with files ending in `.minimark`.

To add an editor type, the following bundles are needed:

- `org.eclipse.core.runtime`
- `org.eclipse.jface.text`
- `org.eclipse.ui`
- `org.eclipse.ui.editors`
- `org.eclipse.ui.workbench.texteditor`

The editor needs to be a subtype of an `EditorPart`. In this case, `AbstractTextEditor` provides the basic functionality for editing text-based files. It also needs to be registered with the `org.eclipse.ui.editors` extension point.

Note that building editors and the document providers that underpin them is a book in its own right; the implementation of the editor here is to support the resource-processing examples. More information on writing custom editors is available in the online help.

## Time for action – writing the markup parser

First, the format of the markup language needs to be explained. The first line will be a title, and then subsequent paragraphs are blank-line separated. This can be translated into an HTML file as follows:

| minimark source | Translated HTML |
| --- | --- |
| **This is the title** | `<html><head><title>This is the title</title></head><body><h1>This is the title</h1><p>` |
| **A paragraph with some text** | `A paragraph with some text` |
| | `</p><p>` |
| **Another paragraph** | `Another paragraph` |
| | `</p></body></html>` |

Perform the following steps:

**1.** Create a class called `MinimarkTranslator` in the `com.packtpub.`
`e4.minimark.ui` **package as follows:**

```
public class MinimarkTranslator {
  public static void convert(Reader reader, Writer writer)
  throws IOException {
    BufferedReader lines = new BufferedReader(reader);
    String line;
    String title = String.valueOf(lines.readLine());
    writer.write("<html><head><title>");
    writer.write(title);
    writer.write("</title></head><body><h1>");
    writer.write("</h1><p>");
    while (null != (line = lines.readLine())) {
      if ("".equals(line)) {
        writer.write("</p><p>");
      } else {
        writer.write(line);
        writer.write('\n');
      }
    }
    writer.write("</p></body></html>");
    writer.flush();
  }
}
```

**2.** Copy the example text from the start of this section and save it as a file `input.txt` in the `com.packtpub.e4.minimark.ui` **project.**

**3.** Add a `main()` method to `MinimarkTranslator` to read in the `input.txt` file and write it out as `output.txt`:

```
public static void main(String[] args) throws IOException {
  convert(
    new FileReader("in.txt"),
    new FileWriter("out.txt"));
}
```

**4.** Run this as a Java application and refresh the project. The file `out.txt` should be shown, and opening it should show an HTML file like the one at the start of this section.

**5.** After testing `MinimarkConverter` works as expected, delete the `main()` method. Automated plug-in testing will be covered in more detail in *Chapter 9, Automated Testing of Plug-ins*.

## *What just happened?*

The minimal markup language can take plain ASCII text and be translated into an HTML file. The purpose of this exercise is not to define a fully comprehensive markup processor, but rather to provide a simple translator that can be shown to generate HTML as rendered in a browser from a plain text file.

Note that the translator has at least one bug; if the file is empty then the title may well be `null`, which would result in a title of `null` in the HTML browser.

The reader is invited to replace the translator with a different implementation, such as one of the Markdown parsers available on GitHub or Maven Central.

## Time for action – building the builder

Compilers (and every other kind of translator) in Eclipse are implemented with builders. These are notified when a file or a set of files are changed and can take appropriate action. In the case of the Java builder, it translates the `.java` source files into the `.class` files. Perform the following steps:

**1.** Open the `minimark.ui` project's `.project` file. This is visible in the Navigator view, but not in the Package Explorer or other views. Builders are associated to a project within the `.project` file. The builder ID is referenced via `buildCommand`, for example have a look at the following code:

```
<projectDescription>
  <name>com.packtpub.e4.minimark.ui</name>
  <buildSpec>
    <buildCommand>
      <name>org.eclipse.jdt.core.javabuilder</name>
    </buildCommand>
...
```

**2.** To translate a `.minimark` file into HTML automatically, a builder is needed. A builder is a class that extends `IncrementalProjectBuilder` and implements a `build()` method. This is called by the framework when files are saved and either gives a list of changed files or asks that the full project is built. Since this is defined in the core resources bundle, open `plugin.xml` and add the `org.eclipse.core.resources` bundle to `plugin.xml` in the dependency list.

**3.** Create a class in the `com.packtpub.e4.minimark.ui` package called `MinimarkBuilder`:

```
public class MinimarkBuilder extends IncrementalProjectBuilder {
  protected IProject[] build(int kind, Map<String, String> args,
    IProgressMonitor monitor) throws CoreException {
    return null;
  }
}
```

**4.** Builds are called with different kinds of flag, which indicates whether the entire project is being built, or if a subset of the project is being built. For builds that aren't `FULL_BUILD` there's also a resource delta, which contains the set of resources that have been changed. Calculating a resource delta is a non-free operation so should only be done if needed. The `build()` method is typically implemented as follows:

```
protected IProject[] build(int kind, Map<String, String> args,
  IProgressMonitor monitor) throws CoreException {
  if (kind == FULL_BUILD) {
    fullBuild(getProject(), monitor);
  } else {
    incrementalBuild(getProject(), monitor,
      getDelta(getProject()));
  }
  return null;
}
```

**5.** The `fullBuild()` and `incrementalBuild()` methods need to be defined. It is also necessary to handle the case where `getDelta()` returns a `null` value, and invoke the full builder accordingly:

```
private void incrementalBuild(IProject project, IProgressMonitor
  monitor, IResourceDelta delta) throws CoreException {
  if (delta == null) {
    fullBuild(project, monitor);
  } else {
    System.out.println("Doing an incremental build");
  }
}
private void fullBuild(IProject project, IProgressMonitor monitor)
  throws CoreException {
  System.out.println("Doing a full build");
}
```

**6.** Finally, to hook up a builder, declare its reference in an extension point `org.eclipse.core.resources.builders`. This defines a reference (via an ID) to a class that implements `IncrementalProjectBuilder`. Add the following code to `plugin.xml`:

```
<extension id="MinimarkBuilder"
 point="org.eclipse.core.resources.builders">
  <builder
  callOnEmptyDelta="false"
  hasNature="false"
  isConfigurable="false"
  supportsConfigurations="false">
    <run class="com.packtpub.e4.minimark.ui.MinimarkBuilder"/>
  </builder>
</extension>
```

This extension point requires an ID to be given, since the name defined in the `.project` file will be the plug-in's ID concatenated with the extension ID. It is conventional, but not necessary, for the full ID to be the name of the class.

**7.** Run the Eclipse instance. Create a new General project in the test workspace, and once created open the `.project` file. Add the builder manually by adding in a `buildCommand` with the ID from the extension point:

```
<buildSpec>
  <buildCommand>
    <name>com.packtpub.e4.minimark.ui.MinimarkBuilder</name>
  </buildCommand>
</buildSpec>
```

**8.** The message **Doing a full build** can be seen in the host console when the builder is added, or if the project is cleaned. Edit and save a `.minimark` file, and the message **Doing an incremental build** should be displayed.

## What just happened?

The builder is capable of being invoked when files in a project are changed. To associate the builder with the project, it was added as a build command to the project, which is contained in the `.project` file. The name used for the builder is the extension's unique ID, which is formed as a dot-separated concatenation of the plug-in's ID and the element in the `plugin.xml` file.

The incremental builder has a standard pattern which allows an implementation to determine if it is doing a full or incremental build. There is also a `clean()` method (which wasn't implemented here) that is used to remove all resources that have been created by a builder.

## Time for action – iterating through resources

A project (`IProject`) is a top-level unit in the workspace (`IWorkspaceRoot`). These can contain resources (`IResource`), which are either folder (`IFolder`) or file (`IFile`) objects. They can be iterated with the `members()` function, but this will result in the creation of `IResource` for every element processed, even if they aren't relevant. Instead, defer to the platform's internal tree by passing it a visitor that will step through each element required. Perform the following steps:

**1.** Create a class, `MinimarkVisitor`, in the `com.packtpub.e4.minimark.ui` package, that implements `IResourceProxyVisitor` and `IResourceDeltaVisitor` interfaces.

**2.** Implement the `visit(IResourceProxy)` method to get the name of the resource, and display a message if it finds a file whose name ends with `.minimark`. It should return `true` to allow child resources to be processed:

```
public boolean visit(IResourceProxy proxy) throws CoreException {
  String name = proxy.getName();
  if(name != null && name.endsWith(".minimark")) {
    // found a source file
    System.out.println("Processing " + name);
  }
  return true;
}
```

**3.** Modify `incrementalBuild()` and `fullBuild()` to connect the builder to the `MinimarkVisitor` class as follows:

```
private void incrementalBuild(IProject project, IProgressMonitor
monitor, IResourceDelta delta) throws CoreException {
  if (delta == null) {
    fullBuild(project, monitor);
  } else {
    delta.accept(new MinimarkVisitor());
  }
}
private void fullBuild(IProject project, IProgressMonitor monitor)
throws CoreException {
  project.accept(new MinimarkVisitor(),IResource.NONE);
}
```

**4.** Run the Eclipse, select a project that has the `minimark` builder configured and a `.minimark` file, and do **Project | Clean**. The host Eclipse instance should have a message saying **Processing test.minimark** in the Console view.

**5.** Now create a method in `MinimarkVisitor` called `processResource()`. This will get the contents of the file and pass them to the translator. To start with, the translated file will be written to `System.out`:

```
private void processResource(IResource resource) throws
CoreException {
  if (resource instanceof IFile) {
    try {
      IFile file = (IFile) resource;
      InputStream in = file.getContents();
      MinimarkTranslator.convert(new InputStreamReader(in),
        new OutputStreamWriter(System.out));
    } catch (IOException e) {
      throw new CoreException(new Status(Status.ERROR,
        Activator.PLUGIN_ID, "Failed to generate resource", e));
```

```
            }
        }
    }
```

**6.** Now modify the `visit()` method to invoke `processResource()`:

```
public boolean visit(IResourceProxy proxy) throws CoreException {
    String name = proxy.getName();
    if (name != null && name.endsWith(".minimark") {
        System.out.println("Processing " + name);
        processResource(proxy.requestResource());
    }
    return true;
}
```

> The method is called `requestResource()` instead of `getResource()` to signify that it isn't just a simple accessor, but that objects are created in calling the method.

**7.** Run the Eclipse instance, make a change to a `.minimark` file, and perform a clean build with **Project | Clean**. The host Eclipse instance should print the translated output in the Console view.

## What just happened?

When notified of changes in the build, the files are processed with a visitor. This abstracts away the need to know how the resources are organized. Resources such as team-private files (`.git`, `.svn`, or CVS directories) are automatically excluded from the caller.

Using `IResourceProxyVisitor` to obtain the content is faster than using `IResourceVisitor`, since the former can be used to test for properties on the name. This provides a much faster way of getting resources that follow a naming pattern as it does not require the creation of an `IResource` object for every item, some of which may not be necessary.

The builder communicates errors through `CoreException`, which is the standard exception for many of Eclipse's errors. This takes as its parameter a `Status` object (with an associated exception and plug-in ID).

Finally, when a full build is invoked (by performing **Project | Clean** on the project) the output is seen in the Console view of the development Eclipse.

# Time for action – creating resources

The next step is to create an IFile resource for the .html file (based on the name of the .minimark file). Eclipse uses an IPath object to represent a filename from the root of the workspace. An IPath of /project/folder/file.txt refers to the file.txt file in a folder called folder contained within the project called project. The root path represents the IWorkspaceRoot. Perform the following steps:

**1.** In the processResource() method of MinimarkVisitor, calculate the new filename, and use it to create an IFile from the file's parent IContainer:

```
try {
    IFile file = (IFile) resource;
    String htmlName = file.getName().replace(".minimark", ".html");
    IContainer container = file.getParent();
    IFile htmlFile = container.getFile(new Path(htmlName));
```

**2.** To create the contents of the file, an InputStream has to be passed to the setContents() method. The easiest way to create this is to pass a ByteArrayOutputStream to MinimarkTranslator, and then use a ByteArrayInputStream to get the contents to set on the file.

 PipedInput/OutputStream are inherently broken because they use a fixed width pipeline and will block when full.

Make the following changes:

```
ByteArrayOutputStream baos = new ByteArrayOutputStream();
MinimarkTranslator.convert(new InputStreamReader(in),
  new OutputStreamWriter(System.out));
  new OutputStreamWriter(baos));
ByteArrayInputStream contents =
new ByteArrayInputStream(baos.toByteArray());
```

**3.** Now the contents need to be set on the file. If the file exists, the contents are set with setContents(), but if it doesn't create() needs to be called instead:

```
if (htmlFile.exists()) {
  htmlFile.setContents(contents, true, false, null);
} else {
  htmlFile.create(contents, true, null);
}
```

The `true` parameter is to force the change; that is, the contents will be written even if the resource has been updated elsewhere. The `false` parameter for the `setContents()` method is to indicate that changes should not be recorded, and the final `null` parameter for both methods is to pass an optional `ProgressMonitor`.

**4.** Finally the resource needs to be marked as derived, which tells Eclipse that this is an automatically generated file and not a user-edited one:

```
htmlFile.setDerived(true,null);
```

**5.** Run the Eclipse instance, do **Project | Clean** and the corresponding HTML file should be generated. Modify the `.minimark` file, do a clean again, and the HTML file should be regenerated.

## What just happened?

The build was modified to invoke `MinimarkTranslator` and create a resource in the filesystem. Since it uses a stream to set the contents a `ByteArrayOutputStream` is used to build up the translated contents, and a `ByteArrayInputStream` is used to read it back for the purposes of setting the file's contents.

The `exists()` method check is necessary because setting the contents on a non-existent file throws a `CoreException`.

The files are represented as a generic `IPath` object, which is concretely implemented with the `Path` class. `Path` classes are represented as slash (/) separated filenames, regardless of the operating system, but each path component needs to obey the local filesystem's constraints, such as not allowing colons on Windows.

## Time for action – implementing incremental builds

The final part of the puzzle is to implement the incremental part of the builder. Most of the builds that Eclipse performs are incremental, which means that it only compiles the files that are needed at each point. An incremental build gives a resource delta which says what files have been modified, added, or removed. This is implemented in `IResourceDelta` which is handed to the `IResourceDeltaVisitor visit()` method. A resource delta combines an `IResource` with a flag that says whether it was added or removed. Perform the following steps:

**1.** Open `MinimarkBuilder` and go to the `visit(IResourceDelta)` method. This is used by the incremental build when individual files are changed. Since the delta already has a resource, it can be used to determine if the file is relevant, and if so pass it to the `processResource()` method:

```
public boolean visit(IResourceDelta delta) throws CoreException {
```

```
    IResource resource = delta.getResource();
    if(resource.getName().endsWith(".minimark")) {
      processResource(resource);
    }
    return true;
    }
```

2.  Run the Eclipse instance, and edit and save the `.minimark` file. The builder's incremental builder will be invoked with the given resource and the file will be updated. Eclipse's HTML editor won't automatically refresh the change, but if the `.html` file is opened with a text editor, a side-by-side view shows that the file is being updated with each save.

## What just happened?

An incremental build and a full build are very similar; they both process a set of resources. In the former case, it's the set of files that were changed in a workspace update operation (such as a **Save** or **Save All**). In the latter case, it's all files in an individual project. If building is done on independent resources which are unrelated then breaking it apart to a single `processResource()` method is an efficient way of building new resources.

## Time for action – handling deletion

The incremental builder does not handle deletions in its current implementation. To handle deletion, `IResourceDelta` needs to be inspected to find out what kind of delta took place, and the delete handled accordingly.

Perform the following steps:

1.  Run the Eclipse instance and delete a `.minimark` file. An exception is thrown and reported to the user:

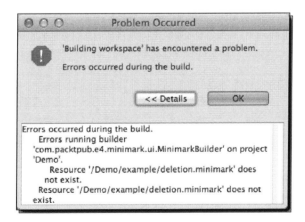

**2.** To fix this issue, modify the check in `MinimarkVisitor` class' `processResource()` method to see if the resource exists or not:

```
private void processResource(IResource resource) throws
CoreException {
    if (resource instanceof IFile && resource.exists()) {
```

**3.** This solves the `NullPointerException`, but the generated HTML file is left behind. To clean up the associated `.html` file if the `.minimark` file is being deleted, the resource delta's flags can be inspected to see if it is deleted, and if so, the corresponding HTML file can be deleted as well. Modify the `visit(IResourceDelta)` method as follows:

```
public boolean visit(IResourceDelta delta) throws CoreException {
    boolean deleted = (IResourceDelta.REMOVED & delta.getKind())!=0;
    IResource resource = delta.getResource();
    String name = resource.getName();
    if (deleted) {
        String htmlName = name.replace(".minimark",".html");
        IFile htmlFile = resource.getParent().
          getFile(new Path(htmlName));
        if (htmlFile.exists()) {
            htmlFile.delete(true, null);
        }
    } else {
        processResource(resource);
    }
    return true;
}
```

**4.** Run the Eclipse instance, and create a new `test.minimark` file. Save it, and a corresponding `test.html` file will be created. Delete the `test.minimark` file, and the `test.html` file should also be deleted.

**5.** Create the `test.minimark` file again, and the `test.html` file will be generated. Delete the `test.html` file, and it won't be regenerated automatically. To fix this, `IResourceDelta` needs to track deletions of `.html` files as well, and process the corresponding `.minimark` resource. Modify the `visit(IResourceDelta)` as follows:

```
public boolean visit(IResourceDelta delta) throws CoreException {
    boolean deleted = (IResourceDelta.REMOVED & delta.getKind())!=0;
    IResource resource = delta.getResource();
    String name = resource.getName();
    if (name.endsWith(".minimark")) {
        if (deleted) {
            String htmlName = name.replace(".minimark",".html");
```

```
        IFile htmlFile = resource.getParent().getFile(
        new Path(htmlName));
        if (htmlFile.exists()) {
          htmlFile.delete(true, null);
        }
      } else {
        processResource(resource);
      }
    } else if (name.endsWith(".html")) {
      String minimarkName = name.replace(".html",".minimark");
      IFile minimarkFile = resource.getParent().getFile(
       new Path(minimarkName));
      if (minimarkFile.exists()) {
        processResource(minimarkFile);
      }
    }
  }
  return true;
}
```

**6.** Run the Eclipse instance and delete the generated `test.html` file. It should be automatically regenerated by the `MinimarkBuilder/MinimarkVisitor`. Now, delete the `test.html` file and the corresponding `test.minimark` file should be deleted as well.

## What just happened?

When a `.minimark` file was deleted, a `NullPointerException` was seen. This was fixed by guarding `visit()` with a check to see if the resource existed or not.

For consistency, the deletion of associated resources was also handled. If the `.html` file is deleted, it is regenerated (but only if a corresponding `.minimark` file is present). When the `.minimark` file is deleted, the corresponding `.html` file is also deleted.

## Have a go hero – builder upgrades

Along with reacting to changes and creating content, builders are also responsible for removing content when the project is cleaned. The `IncrementalProjectBuilder` defines a `clean()` method, which is invoked when the user performs **Project | Clean** on either that specific project or the workspace as a whole.

Implement a `clean()` method on the `MinimarkBuilder` which walks the project, and for each `.minimark` file, deletes any corresponding `.html` file. Note that not all `.html` files should be deleted as some may be legitimate source files in a project.

# Using natures

Although builders can be configured on a project manually, they aren't usually added directly. Instead, a project may have natures which represent a type of dimension that a project has; and natures can be automatically associated with builders. For example, a Java project is identified with a Java nature and others (such as the PDE project) are identified as both a Java project and an additional nature for PDE processing. Other languages have their own natures, such as C.

## Time for action – creating a nature

A nature is created by implementing the `IProjectNature` interface. This will be used to create a `MinimarkNature`, which will allow projects to be associated with the `MinimarkBuilder`. Perform the following steps:

**1.** Create a class called `MinimarkNature` in the `com.packtpub.e4.minimark.ui` package:

```
public class MinimarkNature implements IProjectNature {
  public static final String ID =
    "com.packtpub.e4.minimark.ui.MinimarkNature";
  private IProject project;
  public IProject getProject() {
    return project;
  }
  public void setProject(IProject project) {
    this.project = project;
  }
  public void configure() throws CoreException {
  }
  public void deconfigure() throws CoreException {
  }
}
```

**2.** The purpose of a nature is to assist by adding (or configuring) the builders, which are associated by an ID. To make cross-referencing possible, define a constant in the `MinimarkBuilder` which can be used to refer to it by the nature:

```
public class MinimarkBuilder extends IncrementalProjectBuilder {
  public static final String ID =
    "com.packtpub.e4.minimark.ui.MinimarkBuilder";
```

**3.** The way a builder is added to the project is by accessing the project descriptor and adding a build command. There is no easy way of adding or removing a builder, so acquire the set of commands, search to see if it is present, and then add or remove it. Using the `Arrays` class takes away some of the pain. Implement the `configure()` method as follows:

```
public void configure() throws CoreException {
  IProjectDescription desc = project.getDescription();
  List<ICommand> commands = new ArrayList<ICommand>(
    Arrays.asList(desc.getBuildSpec()));
  Iterator<ICommand> iterator = commands.iterator();
  while (iterator.hasNext()) {
    ICommand command = iterator.next();
    if (MinimarkBuilder.ID.equals(command.getBuilderName())) {
      return;
    }
  }
  ICommand newCommand = desc.newCommand();
  newCommand.setBuilderName(MinimarkBuilder.ID);
  commands.add(newCommand);
  desc.setBuildSpec(commands.toArray(new ICommand[0]));
  project.setDescription(desc,null);
}
```

**4.** To deconfigure a project, the reverse is done. Implement the `deconfigure()` method as follows:

```
public void deconfigure() throws CoreException {
  IProjectDescription desc = project.getDescription();
  List<ICommand> commands = new ArrayList<ICommand>(
  Arrays.asList(desc.getBuildSpec()));
  Iterator<ICommand> iterator = commands.iterator();
  while (iterator.hasNext()) {
    ICommand command = iterator.next();
    if (MinimarkBuilder.ID.equals(command.getBuilderName())) {
      iterator.remove();
    }
  }
  desc.setBuildSpec(commands.toArray(new ICommand[0]));
  project.setDescription(desc,null);
}
```

**5.** Having implemented the nature, it needs to be defined as an extension point within the `plugin.xml` of the `minimark.ui` project:

```
<extension id="MinimarkNature"
  point="org.eclipse.core.resources.natures">
  <runtime>
    <run class="com.packtpub.e4.minimark.ui.MinimarkNature"/>
  </runtime>
</extension>
```

**6.** To associate the nature with a project, a menu needs to be added to the **Configure** menu associated with projects. Create an entry in the `plugin.xml` file for the **Add Minimark Nature** command, and put it in the `projectConfigure` menu:

```
<extension point="org.eclipse.ui.commands">
  <command name="Add Minimark Nature"
  defaultHandler="com.packtpub.e4.minimark.ui.AddMinimarkHandler"
  id="com.packtpub.e4.minimark.ui.AddMinimarkNature"/>
</extension>
<extension point="org.eclipse.ui.menus">
  <menuContribution allPopups="false" locationURI=
  "popup:org.eclipse.ui.projectConfigure?after=additions">
    <command label="Add Minimark Nature" style="push"
      commandId="com.packtpub.e4.minimark.ui.AddMinimarkNature"/>
  </menuContribution>
</extension>
```

**7.** Create a new class in the `com.packtpub.e4.minimark.ui` package called `AddMinimarkNature`, as follows:

```
public class AddMinimarkHandler extends AbstractHandler {
  public Object execute(ExecutionEvent event)
  throws ExecutionException {
    ISelection sel = HandlerUtil.getCurrentSelection(event);
    if (sel instanceof IStructuredSelection) {
      Iterator<?> it = ((IStructuredSelection)sel).iterator();
      while (it.hasNext()) {
        Object object = (Object) it.next();
        if(object instanceof IProject) {
          try {
            addProjectNature((IProject) object,MinimarkNature.ID);
          } catch (CoreException e) {
            throw new ExecutionException("Failed to set nature on"
            + object,e);
          }
        }
      }
    }
```

```
      return null;
    }
    private void addProjectNature(IProject project, String nature)
    throws CoreException {
      IProjectDescription description = project.getDescription();
      List<String> natures = new ArrayList<String>(
        Arrays.asList(description.getNatureIds()));
      if(!natures.contains(nature)) {
        natures.add(nature);
        description.setNatureIds(natures.toArray(new String[0]));
        project.setDescription(description, null);
      }
    }
  }
```

8. Run the Eclipse instance, create a new General project, and open the `.project` file using the Navigator view. Now right-click on the project, and select **Configure | Add Minimark Nature** to add the nature. When the nature is added, it will add the commands automatically and the changes will be visible in the `.project` file.

## What just happened?

The `MinimarkNature` class was created to inject a builder into the project description when added. Changing the `.project` file manually does not add the builder, so an action to programmatically add the nature was created and added to the standard **Configure** menu.

Both the Nature and the Builder are referred to via IDs; these are stored in the `.project` and `.classpath` files. Since these may be checked into a version control system, the names of these IDs should be consistent between releases. (It's best practice to add these to version control.)

The project descriptor contains the content from the `.project` file and stores an array of nature IDs and commands. To add a nature to a project, its identifier is appended to this list. Note that the change only takes effect when the updated project descriptor is set on the project.

Since the nature's modifications only take effect when set programmatically, the `Add Minimark Nature` command was created to add the nature. The command was put into the menu popup `org.eclipse.ui.projectConfigure?after=additions`, which is the standard location for adding and configuring natures. Conventionally, either a separate command to **Add Minimark Nature** and **Remove Minimark Nature** is used, or a **Toggle Minimark Nature** could be used for both actions. The advantage of the separate Add/Remove menu items is that their visibility can be controlled based on whether the project already has the nature or not.

The handler class used `HandlerUtil` to extract the current selection; though this just extracts the object from the parameter map via the variable name `selection`.

To avoid spelling errors, it makes sense to define constants as static final variables. If they are related with class names, it can be better to use `class.getName()` as the identifier so that if they are renamed then the identifiers are automatically updated as well. Alternatively, they can be created from a concatenation with the plug-in's ID (in this case, via `Activator.ID`).

## Have a go hero – enabling for a selected object type

It is conventional to only show the configure option if it is strictly necessary. In the case where projects already have `MinimarkNature`, we should not show the command. Use the `visibleWhen` property to target the selection and only enable it if the `projectNature` of the selected object is that of the `minimark` builder.

# Using markers

The final section in this chapter is devoted to markers. These are the errors and warnings that the compiler shows when it detects problems in files. They can be created automatically, typically from a builder.

## Time for action – error markers if the file is empty

Errors and warning markers are used to indicate if there are problems in the source files. These are used by the Eclipse compiler to indicate Java compile errors, but they are also used for non-Java errors as well. For example, text editors also show warnings when words are misspelled. A warning can be shown if the `.minimark` file is empty and the title is missing.

There isn't a simple way of accessing the file's size in Eclipse, so we'll use a heuristic that if the generated HTML file is less than about 100 bytes then there probably wasn't much to start with anyway. Perform the following steps:

1. Open `MinimarkVisitor` and go to the `processResource()` method.

2. When the HTML file is generated, put in a test to determine if the size is less than 100 bytes:

```
ByteArrayOutputStream baos = new ByteArrayOutputStream();
MinimarkTranslator.convert(new InputStreamReader(in),
  new OutputStreamWriter(baos));
ByteArrayInputStream contents = new ByteArrayInputStream(
  baos.toByteArray());
if(baos.size() < 100) {
  System.out.println("Minimark file is empty");
}
```

**3.** The problem with printing out an error message is that it won't be seen by the user. Instead, it can represented with an `IMarker` object, created on the source resource, and with additional properties to set the type and location of the error:

```
System.out.println("Minimark file is empty");
IMarker marker = resource.createMarker(IMarker.PROBLEM);
marker.setAttribute(IMarker.SEVERITY,IMarker.SEVERITY_ERROR);
marker.setAttribute(IMarker.MESSAGE,"Minimark file is empty");
marker.setAttribute(IMarker.LINE_NUMBER,0);
marker.setAttribute(IMarker.CHAR_START,0);
marker.setAttribute(IMarker.CHAR_END,0);
```

**4.** Run the Eclipse instance and create a new empty `.minimark` file. When it is saved, an error will be reported in the Problems view. If it's not shown, it can be opened with **Window | Show View | Other | General | Problems**:

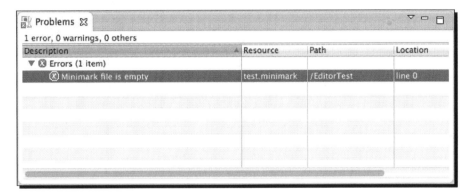

# *What just happened?*

A heuristic that detected when the input file was likely to be empty was used to generate a marker in the build view. While creating an empty file, the builder runs and the problem is generated in the problems view.

The marker also allows additional fields to be set if the location of the problem is known. These are optional fields but can be used to give a user more information as to the source of the problem. In the case of a misspelled word, the `CHAR_START` and `CHAR_END` can be used to pinpoint the exact word on a line; in the case of more general errors the `LINE_NUMBER` can be used to indicate the approximate location in the file.

Each time the file is changed, additional markers are created in the problems view. Even if content is added, the existing errors aren't removed. That will be fixed in the next section.

# Time for action – registering a marker type

The current implementation has a flaw, in that it doesn't appear to fix the problems after they have been resolved. That's because the marker types are kept associated with a resource, even if that resource is changed. The reason this isn't seen in Java files is that the builder wipes out all (Java) errors prior to the start of a build, and then adds new ones as applicable. To avoid wiping out other plug-in's markers, each marker has an associated marker type. JDT uses this to distinguish between its markers and others contributed by different systems. This can be done for `MinimarkMarkers` as well. Perform the following steps:

**1.** Open `plugin.xml` of the `minimark.ui` project. Add the following extension to define a `MinimarkMarker`:

```
<extension id="com.packtpub.e4.minimark.ui.MinimarkMarker"
    name="Minimark Marker"
    point="org.eclipse.core.resources.markers">
    <persistent value="false"/>
    <super type="org.eclipse.core.resources.problemmarker"/>
</extension>
```

**2.** To use this marker when the error is created, instead of using `IMarker.PROBLEM`, use its extension ID from `plugin.xml` in the `processResource()` method of the `MinimarkVisitor`:

```
IMarker marker = resource.createMarker(IMarker.PROBLEM);
IMarker marker = resource.createMarker(
    "com.packtpub.e4.minimark.ui.MinimarkMarker");
```

**3.** At the start of the `processResource()` method, flush all the markers associated with the resource of this type:

```
resource.deleteMarkers(
    "com.packtpub.e4.minimark.ui.MinimarkMarker",
    true, IResource.DEPTH_INFINITE);
```

**4.** Run the Eclipse instance and verify that as soon as some content is put in a `.minimark` file that the errors are cleared. Delete the content, save the file, and the errors should reappear.

**5.** Finally, the editor doesn't show up warnings in the column. To make that happen, change the super class of `MinimarkEditor` from `AbstractEditor` to `AbstractDecoratedTextEditor`. Run the Eclipse instance again. Now errors will be reported in the editor as well:

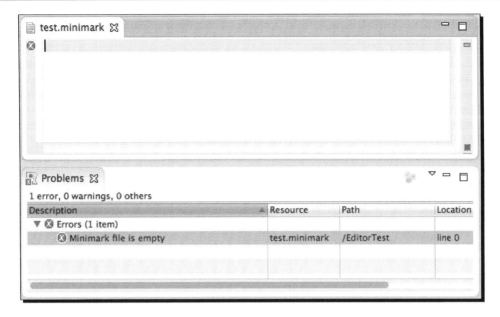

## What just happened?

Now the custom markers for the resource are being deleted at the start of a build and if there's a problem a marker will be automatically added. When the problem is resolved, the resource's markers are automatically deleted anyway.

In the deletion code, the boolean argument says whether to delete markers that are a subtype of that marker type or not. The second argument says what happens in the case that it's a folder or other container, and if deletion should recurse.

Generally, builders delete and create a specific type of problem marker so that they do not affect the other that may be associated with that resource. This allows other contributors (such as the spell checking editor) to raise warnings or informational dialogs that are not cleaned by a particular builder.

### Have a go hero – working out when the file is really empty

Fix the file detection so that it works out when the source file is really empty. Do this by using EFS and the file's locationURI to get a FileInfo, which contains the file's size.

## Pop quiz – understanding resources, builders, and markers

Q1. How is an error with a missing document provider fixed?

Q2. What is an `IResourceProxy` and why is it useful?

Q3. What is an `IPath`?

Q4. What is a nature, and how is one set on a project?

Q5. How are markers created on a project?

# Summary

In this chapter we looked at how resources are accessed, created, and processed. We used an example of a markup language to associate a builder that translated markup items into HTML when the source files were saved. We then hooked up the builder with a nature so that a project can automatically be configured with content when needed.

The next chapter will look at the E4 model, and how it differs from Eclipse 3.x in creating views and contributing to a Rich Client Platform.

# 7

# Understanding the Eclipse 4 Model

*The last major change to Eclipse was with the 3.0 release when it migrated to OSGi. The Eclipse 4 model provides a significant departure from the Eclipse 3.x line, with the user interface being represented as a dynamic EMF model. In addition, both the model and views can be represented as simple POJOs with services provided by dependency injection. There is also a separate rendering mechanism which allows an E4 application to be hosted by different UIs, although we'll look at the SWT renderer specifically. In this chapter, we'll take a look at the differences and how you can evolve Eclipse plug-ins forward.*

In this chapter we shall:

- ◆ Set up an Eclipse 4 instance for development
- ◆ Create an E4 application with parts
- ◆ Style UI with CSS
- ◆ Send and receive events
- ◆ Create commands, handlers, and menus
- ◆ Integrate with preferences
- ◆ Inject custom POJOs

# Working with the Eclipse 4 model

Since Eclipse was first released in November 2001, its user interface has remained mostly static. Each window has a perspective, which contains zero or one editor area, and zero or more view parts. In early releases, every perspective had exactly one editor area, and it was not until the release of Eclipse RCP with Eclipse 3.0 in 2004 that it was possible to disable the editor, and have a custom application suitable for a non-IDE use.

However, the presentation of the perspective always proved difficult to customize, such as changing the background color or arrangement of the windows or toolbars.

The Eclipse 4 model provides a way to model an application both at design time, and also interpret and modify it at runtime. An application has a top-level model, but may also have additional model fragments contributed by different bundles. Additionally, the separate rendering framework allows the UI to be represented with different tools such as JavaFX and HTML. In this book, the default SWT rendering tool will be used, since that closely matches the existing Eclipse 3.x UI.

The other significant change is that it is no longer necessary to create subclasses of specific classes to contribute to the Eclipse infrastructure. Instead, classes are created with dependency injection (similar to how Spring components are configured) and may consume platform-level services separately to the user interface. Instead of referring to global singletons through accessor methods, these are now available through injection. This allows components to be built as simple POJOs (Plain Old Java Objects) which allows them to be tested headlessly and provides a looser binding to the services that they consume.

## Time for action – installing E4 tooling

To work with Eclipse 4 modeled applications, it is necessary to install the E4 tools to allow the application XMI to be edited through an editor. These are not shipped with the standard Eclipse distribution package, and must be installed separately.

*1.* Add the following update site by going to **Window | Preferences | Install/Update | Available Software Sites**, then click on **Add...** and put in:

 In OS X, the **Preferences** menu is located under the **Eclipse** menu.

- ❏ Juno (4.2): `http://download.eclipse.org/e4/updates/0.13`
- ❏ Kepler (4.3): `http://download.eclipse.org/e4/updates/0.14`

Alternatively, the tools can be found by installation through the Eclipse Marketplace.

2. Click on **OK** in the **Add Site** dialog and on **OK** in the **Preferences** page to add it. Once added, go to **Help | Install New Software** and then select the newly added site in the list. Select the the following features:

- CSS file editor
- CSS spy for Eclipse 4
- Eclipse 4 core tools

These add the ability to edit both `css` and `e4xmi` files, and create Eclipse 4 applications by a wizard, which are used to create and render the user interface in Eclipse 4.

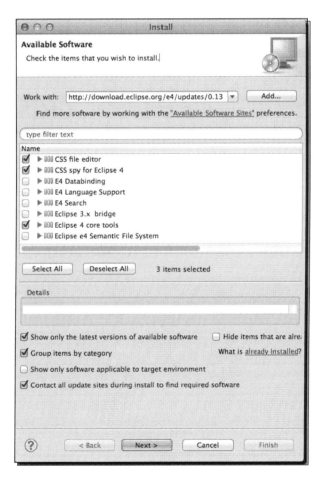

3.  Restart Eclipse after the install has completed.

4.  Go to **File | New | Project** and verify that **Eclipse 4 | Eclipse 4 Application Project** is seen in the new project wizard's choices.

## *What just happened?*

Installing the Eclipse E4 tools and E4 CSS spy provides a custom editor for `e4xmi` files, as well as `css` files. In addition, the CSS spy can be called with *Alt + Shift + F5*, or via the Quick Access search bar.

To run the CSS spy in a launched application, add `org.eclipse.e4.tools.css.spy` to the required bundles in the launch configuration. (Don't add them to the product definition unless the product's end users need to be able to invoke the CSS spy.)

There is also a live EMF editor which can be called with *Alt + Shift + F9*. This is useful for exploring the Eclipse runtime, either in the IDE or in the launched application. To add the live EMF editor, add `org.eclipse.e4.tools.emf.liveeditor` to the launch configuration.

Don't forget to click on **Validate plug-ins** and if necessary **Add required plug-ins** to ensure that the tools' dependencies are present in the launched product.

## Time for action – creating an E4 application

Eclipse applications use an application ID to launch and start execution. For E4 applications, `org.eclipse.e4.ui.workbench.swt.E4Application` is used. Since this is specified within a product, to start with a new E4 application will be created.

1.  Go to the **File | New | Project...** menu and choose **Eclipse 4 | Eclipse 4 Application Project** from the list.

 If the **Eclipse 4 Application Project** is not shown here, check that the E4 tools are installed correctly.

2. Create a project with the name `com.packtpub.e4.application`, and step through the wizard. Choose the default values for each field.

**3.** On the last page, ensure that the **Create sample contents** option is selected. This will ensure that the E4 tools creates standard parts and menus for the default application.

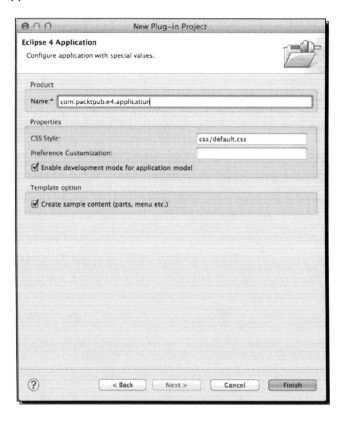

**4.** Click on **Finish** and the project will be created.

**5.** Right-click on the **com.packtpub.e4.application** project and choose **Run As | Eclipse Application**. This launches a new version of the IDE, which isn't what might be expected.

**6.** Double-click on the product file (called **com.packtpub.e4.application.product**) and click on the run icon in the top-right corner:

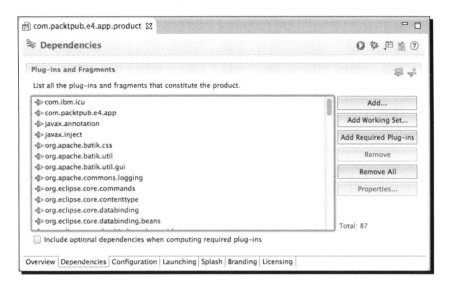

If you get a web browser launched when invoking the product, it may be that RAP is installed. If this happens, the product can be launched by going to the **Run | Run As...** and selecting the **Eclipse Application** type, followed by **Run a product: com.packtpub.e4.application.product**. Alternatively, the **Overview** tab has a **Testing** section, which includes a link to **Launch an Eclipse Application**.

**7.** When the application runs, an error may be seen:

```
!MESSAGE Application error
!STACK 1
java.lang.RuntimeException: No application id has been found.
```

This indicates that the product was missing one or more dependencies in the product list. Some older versions of the E4 tools did not include required plug-ins such as `javax.xml`. As a result, the runtime application fails to install, with the cryptic error that it can't find the application.

**8.** To resolve the problem, click on the **Add Required Plug-ins** for the product (the button on the right of the product editor, as seen in the preceding screenshot). Now, when it is run, the default window should be shown:

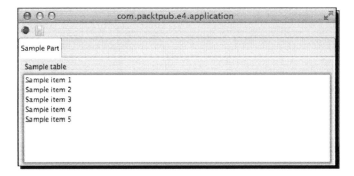

## What just happened?

The new E4 wizard created a simple E4 rich client application, including creating some sample content (menus, commands, and so on). After fixing issues with missing dependencies, product launch operation starts the application successfully.

When running any kind of Eclipse application, it is good practice to stop the launch when there are missing dependencies. The launch configuration, visible via the **Run | Run Configurations...** menu, has an option on the plug-ins tab **Validate plug-ins automatically prior to launching**:

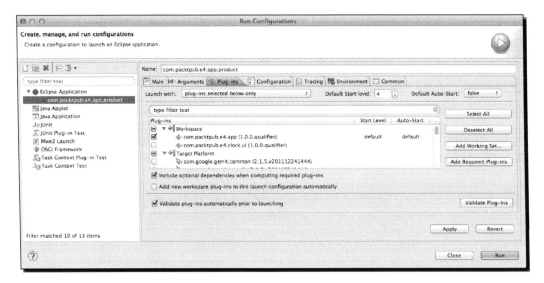

Now, when launching the product without adding the necessary plug-ins, a warning will be shown. Clicking on the **Validate Plug-ins** button can run this validation at any time.

## Time for action – creating a part

Having created a sample application, the next step is to create a view, known as a part in E4. Parts are the generic name for views, editors, and other grouping components in an E4 application. Unlike views in Eclipse 3, the view class doesn't have to have any references to the Eclipse APIs. This makes it particularly easy to build and test in isolation.

**1.** Open the `plugin.xml` file of the `com.packtpub.e4.application` project, and go to the **Dependencies** tab. Add a dependency to the `org.eclipse.ui.di` bundle, if it's not already added.

**2.** Create a new class called `Hello` in the `com.packtpub.e4.application.parts` package.

**3.** Add a field called `label` of type `Label`.

**4.** Add a `create()` method, annotated with `@PostConstruct` that instantiates the `Label` and sets its text to `Hello`.

 If `@PostConstruct` appears not to work, ensure `javax.annotation` is added as a package import to the bundle (see `http://www.vogella.com/articles/EclipseRCP/article.html#tutorial_api2`).

**5.** Add a `focus()` method, annotated with `@Focus`.

 The `focus()` method is required in Eclipse 4.2 but optional in 4.3 onwards.

**6.** The class will look like:

```
package com.packtpub.e4.application.parts;
import javax.annotation.PostConstruct;
import org.eclipse.e4.ui.di.Focus;
import org.eclipse.swt.SWT;
import org.eclipse.swt.widgets.Composite;
import org.eclipse.swt.widgets.Label;
public class Hello {
  private Label label;
  @PostConstruct
  public void create(Composite parent) {
    label = new Label(parent, SWT.NONE);
```

```
      label.setText("Hello");
   }
   @Focus
   public void focus() {
      label.setFocus();
   }
}
```

7.  Double-click on the `Application.e4xmi` file and it should open up in the application editor (if it doesn't, install the E4 tools from the update site earlier in this chapter).

8.  Navigate to **Application** | **Windows** | **Trimmed Window** | **Controls** | **Perspective Stack** | **Perspective** | **Controls** | **PartSashContainer** | **Part Stack**.

9.  Delete the **Sample Part**, if present, by right-clicking on it and choosing **Remove**.

10. Right-click on the **Part Stack**, and select **Add child** followed by **Part**. The part should be created as follows:

    ❏   **ID:** `com.packtpub.e4.application.part.0`

    ❏   **Label:** `Hello`

    ❏   **Class URI:** Click on **Find** and enter `Hello` as the class name, and it will add `bundleclass://com.packtpub.e4.application/com.packtpub.e4.application.parts.Hello`

    ❏   **Closeable:** Ensure **Closeable** is not selected

    ❏   **To Be Rendered:** Ensure To Be **Rendered** is selected

    ❏   **Visible:** Keep **Visible** selected

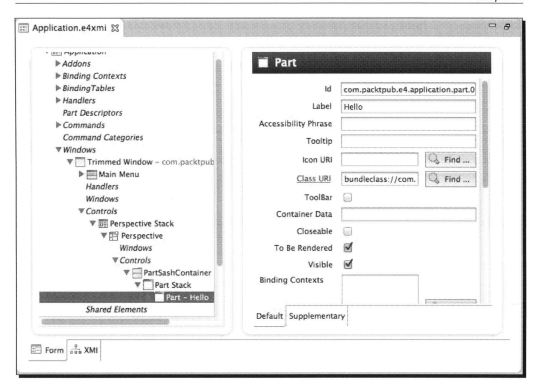

**11.** Finally, save the `e4xmi` file and then launch the product. If all has gone well, **Hello** should be displayed in the generated window:

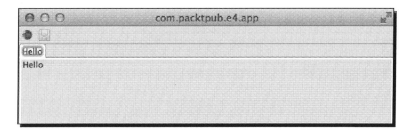

**12.** If nothing is shown, the first debug point is to delete the workspace of the runtime application. The launch configuration can be set to clear the contents of the workspace each time it launches, which is a good idea for E4 development as often the new files aren't copied over or stale files can be left behind.

Go to the **Run | Run Configurations...** menu, select the `com.packtpub.e4.application` configuration. On the **Main** tab there is an option to **Clear**:

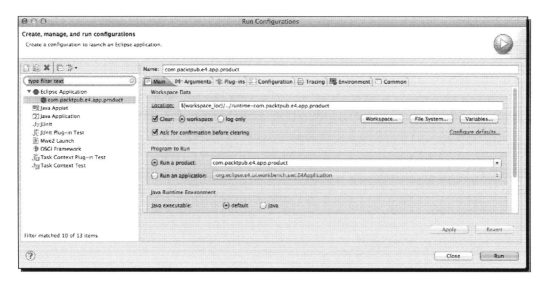

13. Leave the option to **Ask for confirmation before clearing** selected to be prompted with a dialog each time the product is run, or deselected to delete the contents of the runtime workspace each time.

14. If still not shown, put a breakpoint in the `@PostConstruct` method to verify that it is being called. If not, check `@javax.annotation.PostConstruct` annotation is on the method, that the right class name in the `e4xmi` file, and that everything is saved before launching. Another approach is to delete the launch configuration and launch a new one via the product launch as before.

## What just happened?

Eclipse 4 applications are modeled with an `e4xmi` file, which defines both visual and non-visual contents. At runtime, an Eclipse 4 application is booted with `org.eclipse.e4.ui.workbench.swt.E4Application`, which reads the file specified in the product's `applicationXMI` property. The default name created by the wizard is `Application.e4xmi`, but this can be replaced if necessary.

 Other renderers exist, such as e(fx)clipse's implementation built on JavaFX.

Parts in E4 are the equivalent of views/editors in Eclipse 3.x. The structure of viewable content in the default E4 application is:

1. Application, which contains
2. (Trimmed) windows, which contains
3. Perspective stacks, which contains
4. Perspectives, which contains
5. PartSashContainer, which contains
6. Part stacks, which contains
7. Parts

In addition, Trimmed Windows can also contain Menus and Menu Items. Menu Items are covered later in this chapter.

In the default application, the window uses a Trimmed Window, which means it can have toolbars such as the save and open tools. (These are shown as **Handled Tool Item** or **Direct** in the application editor.) Each element can have a control which allows parts to be mixed and matched; for example, it's not mandatory for a Window to use any perspectives at all; they can just contain controls if desired.

The `Hello` part was created and added into the application by adding it to the model. At runtime, the class is instantiated, followed by an invocation of the method annotated with `@PostConstruct`. Any required arguments are injected in automatically, which are obtained from the runtime context which is akin to a `HashMap` of services by class name. Finally, the `@Focus` call is invoked when the part gets the focus; it should delegate that call to the key widget within the part.

Note, that since the hook between the application model and the code is the pointer in the **Class URI** reference to the fully qualified class name, when renaming Java class names or packages, it's important to select the option that allows the fully qualified name to be replaced in other files, as otherwise links between the application model and the parts may be broken.

It may be necessary to clear the workspace when starting. This is because the application model is not only used for an initial starting point of the application; it's also used to model the runtime of the application as well. Any changes to the model (creating new views, resizing the parts) updates the runtime model. When the application shuts down normally, the updated state of the model is saved and used for subsequent launches. As a result, a newly launched application with the same workspace will show the state of the workspace at the last time it shut down, not any new state that may have been added at development time.

# Time for action – styling the UI with CSS

The user interface for Eclipse 4 is styled with CSS. Although this is loosely based on the CSS syntax used in browsers, the content that can be used is interpreted by the Eclipse 4 runtime. CSS stylesheets are composed of selectors and style rules. A selector can be one of a widget name (for example, `Button`), a model class name (for example, `.MPartStack`) or an identifier (for example, `#PerspectiveSwitcher`).

**1.** The default Eclipse 4 application generated by the wizard with sample content will have an empty CSS file called `css/default.css`. Open this file, and add the following rule:

```
Shell {
   background-color: blue;
}
```

**2.** Run the application, and the background of the window (`Shell`) will be shown in blue.

**3.** Basic CSS color names are supported, but hex values can also be used. Modify the `default.css` file as follows:

```
Shell {
   background-color: #00FF00;
}
```

**4.** Run the application, and the background color will be shown in green.

**5.** It's possible to support vertical gradients in colors by specifying more than one color in the list. Modify the `default.css` as follows:

```
Shell {
   background-color: yellow blue;
}
```

**6.** Run the application, and the background will be a gradient from yellow to blue.

**7.** The colors split at the 50 percent mark by default, but it is possible to specify where the break occurs as a percentage. Using 25 percent makes the switch to blue happen at the top quarter of the screen—conversely, using 75 percent makes the switch to blue happen at the bottom quarter of the screen. Modify the `default.css` as follows:

```
Shell {
   background-color: yellow blue 25%;
}
```

**8.** Run the application, and the background will be a gradient from yellow to blue but with the split nearer the top.

**9.** If more than two colors are specified, then multiple gradient points are specified. This creates a rainbow-style effect. Modify the `default.css` as follows:

```
Shell {
   background-color: red orange yellow green blue indigo violet
                     15%    30%    45%   60%  75%     90%;
}
```

**10.** Run the application, and the background will be rainbow style:

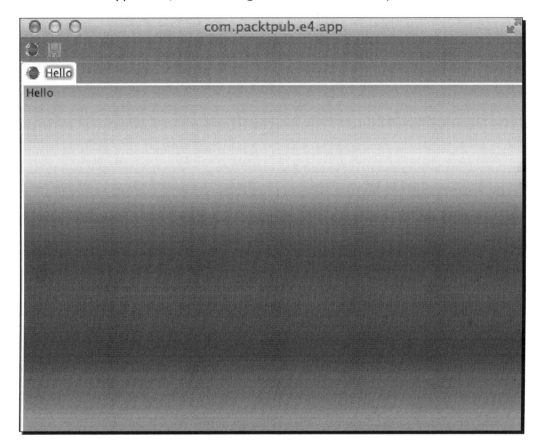

**11.** In addition to using Java class names as selectors, IDs and CSS classes can also be used. For example, to target the Hello part, its ID can be used. The default one will be `com.packtpub.e4.application.part.0` if it is not explicitly specified at creation.

Go to the **Part** in the application viewer to see the ID. To translate it to CSS, use the # selector and replace . with – in the name. To place the rainbow only on that specific part, use this rule instead:

```
#com-packtpub-e4-application-part-0 {
    background-color: red orange yellow green blue indigo violet
                      15%     30%    45%   60%  75%    90%;
}
```

> The Eclipse 4.2 tools may show this as an error in the CSS file, but this is a bug in the CSS editor and not in the CSS rule itself running the application, and the rainbow part should now be targeted to just the Hello part.

12. Another way of coloring each part is to use the pseudo class .MPart, which allows a rule to be targeted to all parts in the UI:

```
.MPart {
    background-color: red orange yellow green blue indigo violet
                      15%     30%    45%   60%  75%    90%;
}
```

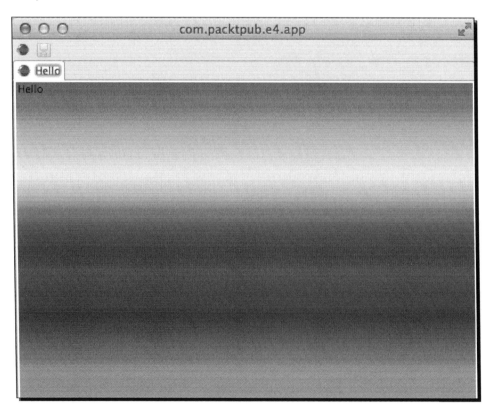

# What just happened?

The `default.css` file, created with the application wizard, was modified to explore how to style properties declaratively. Although loosely based on the CSS specification, some differences are apparent. Style selectors can be:

- Widget (SWT) class names, like `Button`, `Label`, and `Shell`
- CSS class names like `.MPart`, `.MPartStack`, and `.MTrimmedWindow`
- CSS IDs like `#IDEWindow`, `#org-eclipse-jdt-ui-MembersViewMStack`, and `#left`

There is also a "pseudo selector" which can be used. These apply to certain subsets of the classes:

- `Shell:active` used for applying styles to the active `Shell`
- `Button:checked` used if a `Button` is checked
- `:selected` used if a tab folder/item is selected

In addition, CSS selectors can be combined. For example, to have the same rules applied to `.MPart` and an `.MPartStack`, use `.MPart, .MPartStack` as a selector. The comma represents "either".

Dependencies can be combined; `.MPart Label` will apply to `Label` elements which are contained (anywhere) inside an `.MPart`.

To restrict it to direct descendants, use `Shell > Label`. This will apply only to those `Label` elements which are immediately inside a `Shell`, but not those `Label` elements which exist in `Container` instances in the `Shell`.

In addition to `background-color`, other CSS properties can be used, such as:

- `alignment`: Used for `Buttons` (for example, `up`) or `Label` (for example `left`/`right`/`center`)
- `border-visible`: Is `true` if the border should be shown for `CTabFolder`
- `background-image`: An image referenced as a URL `url('platform:/plugin/com.packtpub.e4.application/icons/icon.gif')`
- `color`: As with `background-color`; names or hex values
- `font`: Used to specify font name (for example, `Courier New`) and size (for example, `128px`)
- `font-family`: The font name (for example, `Courier New`)
- `font-size`: The font size (for example, `128px`)

- `font-adjust`: The font size adjustment, not supported in 4.2 (CSS3 name is `font-size-adjust`, so this may change)

- `font-stretch`: The font stretch size, not supported in 4.2

- `font-style`: Can be `italic`, or `bold`

- `font-variant`: The font variant, not supported in 4.2 (`normal`, `small-caps`, and `inherit`)

- `font-weight`: The font weight, not supported in 4.2 (`normal`, `bold`, `bolder`, `lighter`, and `inherit`)—use `font-style` instead

- `margin`: The space (in pixels) around the content (`-top`, `-bottom`, `-left`, and `-right`)

- `maximized`: If the widget is maximized or not

- `minimized`: If the widget is minimized or not

- `padding`: The space (in pixels) between elements (`-top`, `-bottom`, `-left`, and `-right`)

- `text-align`: Can be `left`, `right`, or `center`

- `text-transform`: Can be `capitalize`, `uppercase`, or `lowercase`

There are also some Eclipse-specific properties as well:

- `eclipse-perspective-keyline-color`: The color of perspective lines.

- `swt-background-mode`: The background of the composite to be `none`, `default`, or `force`, corresponding to the Java call `Composite.setBackgroundMode(INHERIT_NONE/DEFAULT/FORCE)`. This ensures the background of the children either override or inherit their parent's background.

- `swt-corner-radius`: The size (in pixels) of the corner radius.

- `swt-inner-keyline-color`: The color of the inside line of the tabs, drawn by the CTabRenderer (see `swt-tab-renderer`).

- `swt-keyline-color`: The keyline color.

- `swt-maximize-visible`: Is `true` or `false` if the maximize icon is shown.

- `swt-maximized`: Is `true` or `false` if the view is maximized (used as a selector)

- `swt-minimize-visible`: Is `true` or `false` if the minimize icon is shown.

- `swt-minimized`: Is `true` or `false` if the view is minimized (used as a selector).

- `swt-mru-visible`: Is `true` (for "Indigo-like" tab behavior) or `false` (default).

- `swt-outer-keyline-color`: The color of the outside line of the tabs, drawn by the CTabRenderer (see `swt-tab-renderer`)

- ◆ `swt-selected-tabs-background`: The background color of selected tabs.
- ◆ `swt-selected-tab-fill`: The fill color of the selected tab.
- ◆ `swt-show-close`: Is `true` or `false` if the close icon is shown.
- ◆ `swt-shadow-visible`: Is `true` or `false` if the shadow is visible.
- ◆ `swt-shadow-color`: The color of shadows, if visible.
- ◆ `swt-simple`: Is `true` (for "new style" tabs) or `false` (for "old style" tabs, default).
- ◆ `swt-tab-outline`: Is `true` or `false` if the tab should have an outline.
- ◆ `swt-tab-renderer`: Is `null` for classic style, or a class URL like `url('bundleclass://org.eclipse.e4.ui.workbench.renderers.swt/org.eclipse.e4.ui.workbench.renderers.swt.CTabRendering')`.
- ◆ `swt-tab-height`: Height, in pixels, of the tabs.
- ◆ `swt-text-align`: Can be `left`, `right`, `up`, `down`, `center`, `lead`, or `trail`.
- ◆ `swt-unselected-close-visible`: Is `true` or `false` if the close icon is shown on unselected tabs.
- ◆ `swt-unselected-tabs-color`: The color of the unselected tabs.
- ◆ `swt-unselected-image-visible`: Is `true` or `false` if the image is shown on unselected tabs.

The reference to the `default.css` file is specified in the `plugin.xml`; the product property `applicationCSS` points to the top-level CSS file. It can also be overridden with command line arguments `-applicationCSS` and `-applicationCSSResources`, both of which use a URL for identifying the location of the main CSS file and its associated resources.

## Have a go hero – using the theme manager

Eclipse 4 ships with a "theme manager" which can be used to swap between themes (in essence, separate CSS files). The theme manager is available for inclusion in E4 based applications by adding the `org.eclipse.e4.ui.css.swt` plug-in as a dependency to the application, and by adding one or more `org.eclipse.e4.ui.css.swt.theme` extension points.

To switch between different themes, create a handler that has an `org.eclipse.e4.ui.css.swt.theme.IThemeEngine` injected, and invoke `engine.setTheme(id, persist)`, where `id` is the reference to the theme defined in the extension point, and `persist` is a `boolean` denoting whether the theme switch should be saved and used by default in the next launch.

# Using services and contexts

An IDE is more than a collection of its component parts, and the Eclipse 4 framework allows these to coordinate and communicate with each other.

In prior releases of Eclipse, the `Platform` (or `PlatformUI`) object would act as an oracle of the known services in the runtime infrastructure, as well as providing hooks for accessing those services, for example:

```
IExtensionRegistry registry = Platform.getExtensionRegistry();
IWorkbench workbench = PlatformUI.getWorkbench();
```

Although this provides a programmatic way of making the services available, it has two key disadvantages:

♦ The provider of the interface is tightly coupled with the bundle containing the accessor, even if they are unrelated

♦ Introducing new services requires a code change to a core object, and has disadvantages in being introduced to existing systems

The goal of E4 is to decouple service providers and service consumers through the use of **OSGi services**. These are contributed to the runtime, and can be looked up via interface name using either standard OSGi mechanisms, or through E4 injection. Although that is the general trend, some platform services accessed by the `IServiceLocator` aren't backed by OSGi services.

## Time for action – adding logging

The OSGi platform defines a `LogService` which allows messages to be logged to a central collector. In the E4 platform, an instance of `LogService` is available as part of the platform, routing error messages through to the console.

**1.** Open the `Hello` class and add a `private` field `LogService log`.

**2.** Add an `@Inject` annotation above the `LogService` field.

**3.** In the `create()` method, add a call to the `log` service.

**4.** The `Hello` class will look like:

```
import javax.inject.Inject;
import org.osgi.service.log.LogService;
public class Hello {
   @Inject
   private LogService log;
   @PostConstruct
   public void create(Composite parent) {
```

```
      label = new Label(parent, SWT.NONE);
      label.setText("Hello");
      log.log(LogService.LOG_ERROR,"Hello");
    }
  }
```

**5.** Run the application, and a log message will be printed out to the console of the host Eclipse:

```
!ENTRY org.eclipse.e4.ui.workbench 4 0 2013-01-24 23:15:51.543
!MESSAGE Hello
```

## *What just happened?*

The E4 runtime infrastructure injected the reference into the class when it was constructed. The instance was obtained from the E4 context, which looks through a hierarchy of contexts until it can find an instance which matches the class type. At the root of the context tree, the list of OSGi services is consulted.

If a `LogService` cannot be found in the context, the part will fail to be created with an error message:

```
!ENTRY org.eclipse.e4.ui.workbench 4 0 2013-01-24 23:19:04.328
!MESSAGE Unable to create class 'com.pactpub.e4.app.parts.Hello'
 from bundle '29'
!STACK 0
org.eclipse.e4.core.di.InjectionException: Unable to process
  "Hello.log": no actual value was found for the argument "LogService"
   at org.eclipse.e4.core.internal.di.InjectorImpl.
      reportUnresolvedArgument(InjectorImpl.java:394)
```

To mark the service as optional (that is it can be `null`), annotate it with `@Optional`:

```
import org.eclipse.e4.core.di.annotations.Optional;
public class Hello {
  @Inject @Optional
  private LogService log;
  @PostConstruct
  public void create(Composite parent) {
    if (log != null) {
      log.log(LogService.LOG_ERROR, "Hello");
    }
  }
```

Remember that `@Optional` annotated fields or parameters have to be guarded against the possibility of being `null`.

If a service arrives after instantiation, the service will be injected into the part.

# Time for action – getting the window

In an Eclipse 3.x application, the main window is typically accessed via a static accessor like `Display.getDisplay()` or `workbench.getWorkbenchWindows()`. Both of these assume there is a way of getting to this global list in the first place, often through tightly coupled code references. In addition to OSGi services, E4 can also be used to inject references to GUI components. However, rather than accessing the GUI components directly, models are used instead. As a result, components in E4 tend to start with M (for Model) – such as `MPart`, `MWindow`, and `MPerspective`.

1. To obtain the reference to the window, add a field `MWindow` window to the `Hello` class, along with an `@Inject` annotation.

2. Modify the `create()` method so that the label of the text is taken from the window's title (label). The class will look like:

```
import org.eclipse.e4.ui.model.application.ui.basic.MWindow;
public class Hello {
  @Inject
  private MWindow window;
  @PostConstruct
  public void create(Composite parent) {
    Label label = new Label(parent, SWT.NONE);
    label.setText(window.getLabel());
  }
}
```

3. Run the application, and the name of the label should be the name of the window, which is `com.packtpub.e4.application`.

4. Open the `Application.e4xmi` file, and go to **Applications | Windows | Trimmed Window** which is where the label is defined. Modify the label to `Hello E4` and save the file.

5. Run the application, and the name of the label and window should be `Hello E4`.

6. Go back to the `Application.e4xmi` file, select the **Trimmed Window** node and do **Edit | Copy**. Select the **Windows** node and do **Edit | Paste**. This will create a duplicate node for the **Trimmed Window**. Modify the label to `Other E4` and save the file.

7. Run the application, and two windows should be displayed. The first will contain a label "Hello E4" while the other will contain **Other E4**.

8. Finally, modify the **Other E4** part to be invisible by unchecking the **Visible** checkbox on the **Trimmed Window**.

## What just happened?

A reference to the enclosing `MWindow` was acquired, using the same mechanism as for the OSGi `LogService`. However, while the `LogService` is a global instance, the `MWindow` is local to the currently selected part.

The lookup strategy for objects follows a hierarchical set of contexts, which are hash table like structures that contain named objects. These are represented with the `MContext` interface, which is implemented by:

- ◆ `MApplication`
- ◆ `MWindow`
- ◆ `MPerspective`
- ◆ `MPart`
- ◆ `MPopupMenu`

The context search starts at the most specific element, and works its way up to the top level. If they aren't found in the `MApplication`, the OSGi services are consulted.

Each of these are organized into a hierarchy with `IEclipseContext`, which maintains parent/child relationships between them. The lookup automatically follows the chain if an object cannot be located in the current context.

In the last example, having two separate windows means that two contexts are used, and so although the code is identical between the two, one has the "Hello E4" window model injected, while the other has the "Other E4" window model injected.

## Time for action – obtaining the selection

The current selection can be obtained through the selection service with a listener, similar to Eclipse 3.x. However, the `ISelectionService` in Eclipse 3.x has been replaced with an almost identical `ESelectionService` in Eclipse 4.x. (Other than the minor lack of JavaDoc and change of package name, the only significant difference between the two is that there is no `add/removePostSelection` methods.)

1. Create a class called `Rainbow` in the `com.packtpub.e4.application.parts` package. Add a `static final` array of strings with colors of the rainbow.

2. Add a `create()` method, along with a `@PostConstruct` annotation, that takes a `Composite` parent. Inside, create a `ListViewer` and set the input to the array of rainbow colors. The class will look like:

```
public class Rainbow {
  private static final Object[] rainbow = { "Red", "Orange",
    "Yellow", "Green", "Blue", "Indigo", "Violet" };
```

```
@PostConstruct
public void create(Composite parent) {
  ListViewer lv = new ListViewer(parent, SWT.NONE);
  lv.setContentProvider(new ArrayContentProvider());
  lv.setInput(rainbow);
 }
}
```

3. Open the `Application.e4xmi` and go to **Application | Windows | Trimmed Window | Controls | Perspective Stack | Perspective | Controls | Part Stash Container | Part Stack**. Right-click on the **Part Stack** and choose **Add child** followed by **Part**. Set the label as `Rainbow` and find the `Rainbow` class with the **Find** button, or by using the `bundleclass` URI `bundleclass://com.packtpub. e4.application/com.pactpub.e4.app.parts.Rainbow`.

4. Run the application, and two tabs should be shown. Next to the **Hello** tab, the **Rainbow** tab will be shown, containing the rainbow colors in a list.

5. To synchronize the selection between the two tabs, add a field of type `ESelectionService` called `selectionService`, along with an `@Inject` annotation. In the `create()` method, add an anonymous `ISelectionChangedListener` to the `ListViewer`, such that if a selection event is received, the selection is reflected in the `selectionService`. The implementation will look like:

```
@Inject
private ESelectionService selectionService;
@PostConstruct
public void create(Composite parent) {
  ListViewer lv = new ListViewer(parent, SWT.NONE);
  lv.setContentProvider(new ArrayContentProvider());
  lv.addSelectionChangedListener(new ISelectionChangedListener() {
    @Override
    public void selectionChanged(SelectionChangedEvent event) {
      selectionService.setSelection(event.getSelection());
    }
  });
  ...
}
```

6. When a selection is made on the `ListViewer`, it will send a selection event to the platform's selection service. To determine what objects are selected, the `Hello` part can register for changes in the selection, and use that to display the text in the label. Add a `setSelection()` method on the `Hello` class as follows:

```
@Inject @Optional
public void setSelection(
```

```
  @Named(IServiceConstants.ACTIVE_SELECTION)
  Object selection) {
  if (selection != null) {
    label.setText(selection.toString());
  }
}
```

**7.** Run the application, switch to the **Rainbow** part, and select the **Red** color from the list. Switch back to the **Hello** part and it should show `[Red]` in the label.

## What just happened?

The list viewer is similar to the previous example. Here, a simple array of `String` values is being used, backed with an `ArrayContentProvider`. By creating a new part, it is possible to switch between the tabs to see the effect of changing the selection.

In order to hook up the viewer's selection with the platform's selection, the viewer's `selectionChanged` event needs to be delegated to the platform. To do that, the `ESelectionService` needs to be injected.

The E4 context contains a set of name/value pairs (like a `HashMap`), and one of these is used to track the current selection. When the selection changes, the new value is set into the context, and this triggers the method calls on the corresponding parts.

Because there may not be a selection when the part is created, it is necessary to annotate it with `@Optional`. If a method is marked with `@Optional` then it won't be called at all; if a parameter is marked as `@Optional` then the method will be called, but with a `null` parameter.

In general, for methods that receive events, mark them as `@Optional` so that they are not called at creation time.

E4 can automatically inject the active selection as it changes. The context contains an object with a key of `IServiceConstants.ACTIVE_SELECTION` (which has the value `org.eclipse.ui.selection`), which can be injected as a `@Named` parameter in a method call. Since there may not be a selection, the `@Optional` annotation must be used, as otherwise exceptions will be reported when the part is created.

# Time for action – dealing with events

There's a more generic way of passing information between components in Eclipse 4, using the OSGi `EventAdmin` service. This is a message bus, like JMS, but operates in memory. There is also an Eclipse-specific `EventBroker`, which provides a slightly simpler API to send messages.

**1.** Add the following bundles as dependencies to the `com.packtpub.e4.application` project, by double-clicking on the project's `META-INF/MANIFEST.MF` file and going to the **Dependencies** tab:

   - `org.eclipse.osgi.services`
   - `org.eclipse.e4.core.services`
   - `org.eclipse.e4.core.di.extensions`

**2.** Open the `Rainbow` class and obtain an instance of `EventBroker` through injection.

**3.** Modify the `selectionChanged()` method, so that instead of setting a selection, it uses the `EventBroker` to `post()` the color asynchronously to the `rainbow/colour` topic.

```
public void selectionChanged(SelectionChangedEvent event) {
  selectionService.setSelection(event.getSelection());
  IStructuredSelection sel = (IStructuredSelection)
   event.getSelection();
  Object colour = sel.getFirstElement();
  broker.post("rainbow/colour",colour);
}
```

**4.** Open the `Hello` class, and add a new method `receiveEvent()`. It should be annotated with `@Inject` and `@Optional`. The parameter should be defined with an annotation `@EventTopic("rainbow/colour")` to pick up the data from the event. It will look like:

```
@Inject
@Optional
public void receiveEvent(
 @EventTopic("rainbow/colour") String data) {
  label.setText(data);
}
```

**5.** Run the application, and switch to the **Rainbow** tab. Select an item in the list, and go back to the **Hello** tab. Nothing will be displayed. Open the Console view in the host Eclipse, and an error will be visible:

```
!MESSAGE Exception while dispatching event
  org.osgi.service.event.Event [topic=rainbow/colour] to handler
```

```
   org.eclipse.e4.core.di.internal.extensions.
      EventObjectSupplier$DIEventHandler@1a91782f
!STACK 0
org.eclipse.e4.core.di.InjectionException:
   org.eclipse.swt.SWTException: Invalid thread access at
org.eclipse.e4.core.internal.di.MethodRequestor.
      execute(MethodRequestor.java:63)
```

**6.** This happens because the dispatched event runs on a non-UI thread by default.
There are two ways of solving this problem; either re-dispatch the call to the
UI thread, or use @UIEventTopic instead of @EventTopic. Modify the
receiveEvent() as follows:

```
public void receiveEvent(
  @EventTopic("rainbow/colour") String data) {
  @UIEventTopic("rainbow/colour") String data) {
    label.setText(data);
}
```

**7.** Run the application, go to the **Rainbow** tab and select a color. Switch back to the
**Hello** tab and the text of the label will be updated appropriately.

## What just happened?

Events allow components to communicate in a highly decoupled mechanism. Using events to
pass data means that the only shared context is the name of the topic.

The OSGi EventAdmin service is a key component and will always be available in current
Eclipse 3.x and E4 applications, since much of the lower-level implementations are based
on events. Either the Eclipse EventBroker wrapper or the EventAdmin can be used,
depending on personal preferences. However, if the code is to be used in other OSGi
systems, building directly on top of the EventAdmin will give the greatest portability.

The Event object is either created automatically using EventBroker or can be created
manually. Each Event has an associated topic, which is a String identifier that allows
producers and consumers to coordinate with each other.

```
Map<String, Object> properties = new HashMap<String,Object>();
properties.put("message","Hello World");
properties.put(IEventBroker.DATA,"E4 Data Object");
eventAdmin.postEvent(new Event("topic/name",properties));
```

Note, that if the object passed in is a Map or Dictionary, it gets passed to the EventAdmin
as is. To pass a Map and receive it using the E4 tools, another Map, must be created and
passed in with the IEventBroker.DATA key. Alternatively, the EventAdmin service can be
used directly.

The `Event` can be posted synchronously (that is on the same thread as the delivery agent) or asynchronously (on a non-background thread).

◆ Synchronously, using `sendEvent()` or `send()`

◆ Asynchronously, using `postEvent()` or `post()`

**Synchronous or Asynchronous?**

Generally using asynchronous delivery is recommended, since synchronous delivery will block the calling thread. When delivering events from the UI asynchronous delivery should always be used, since it is not possible to place any bounds on how long the event receivers may take to execute.

To receive an event, a listener needs to be registered with the topic. This can be done via the OSGi `EventAdmin` service, or with the `@EventTopic` and `@UIEventTopic` annotations on a method marked with `@Inject @Optional`.

If an `Event` needs to be processed on the UI thread, it should not be sent synchronously from the UI thread. Doing so invites delays and blocking the UI, since it is possible for other listeners to pick up on the event and do excessive computation on an unnecessary thread. Instead, send it from a non-UI thread, and in the event hander, delegate it to the UI thread or consume it via the `@UIEventTopic` annotation.

The topic name is specified in the annotation (or via the subscription in the `EventHandler` interface). Topic names can be any string, but are typically separated with / characters. This is because the OSGi specification allows for subscription to both topics by exact match and to partial matches. The subscription `topic/*` will pick up both `topic/name` and `topic/another/example`. Note that it is not a regular expression; the topics are explicitly delimited by the / character, and /* means "and everything below". So `topic/n*e` won't match anything, and nor will `topic/*/example`.

To be more selective about the topics subscribed, use the `EventAdmin EVENT_FILTER` to specify an LDAP-style query. Subscribe to the highest level that makes sense (such as `topic/*`) and then use an LDAP filter to refine it further, using `event.filter` with `(event.topic=topic/n*e)`.

Currently, the annotations cannot be used to apply an LDAP filter, but it's possible to register an `EventHandler` interface which supplies this property.

Finally, it is conventional for the topic name to be constructed from the same kind of reverse domain names used for bundles, with . replaced with / for example `com/packtpub/e4/app/`.

# Time for action – calculating values on demand

The Eclipse context can supply not only services but also dynamically calculated values. These are supplied via an interface `IContextFuction`. By registering a service with that class name, and a key name with the `service.context.key` it is possible to create a value upon request.

**1.** Create a class called `RandomFunction` which extends `ContextFunction` and which returns a random value:

```
package com.packtpub.e4.application;
import org.eclipse.e4.core.contexts.IContextFunction;
import org.eclipse.e4.core.contexts.IEclipseContext;
public final class RandomFunction extends ContextFunction {
  @Override
  public Object compute(final IEclipseContext context) {
    return Math.random();
  }
}
```

**2.** To allow E4 to recognize the function, register an instance with the OSGi runtime. This could be done within the `Activator`, but currently a bug prevents this from happening. Instead, register it using declarative services. Create a file called `random.xml` in a folder called `OSGI-INF` with the following content:

```
<?xml version="1.0" encoding="UTF-8"?>
<scr:component xmlns:scr="http://www.osgi.org/xmlns/scr/v1.1.0"
 name="math.random">
  <implementation
    class="com.packtpub.e4.application.RandomFunction"/>
  <service>
    <provide
      interface="org.eclipse.e4.core.contexts.IContextFunction"/>
  </service>
  <property name="service.context.key" type="String"
  value="math.random"/>
</scr:component>
```

**3.** Add the `OSGI-INF` folder to the `build.properties`, to ensure that it gets added when the bundle is built:

```
bin.includes = OSGI-INF/,\
               META-INF/,\
```

**4.** To allow DS to load and create the component, add this header into `META-INF/MANIFEST.MF`:

```
Service-Component: OSGI-INF/*.xml
```

**5.** Finally, inject this value into the application. In the `Hello` part, add the following:

```
@Inject
@Named("math.random")
private Object random;
@PostConstruct
public void create(Composite parent) {
  label = new Label(parent, SWT.NONE);
  label.setText(window.getLabel() + " " + random);
}
```

**6.** Run the application, and this time, the **Hello** tab starts out with a random value appended to the window's title text. Each time the application is started, a different value is calculated.

## What just happened?

The `IEclipseContext` can acquire calculated values as well as values inserted into the runtime. The calculation is done through a function, registered with the `IContextFunction` interface—though currently the only way to register it is with the declarative services model, as shown previously.

The implementation class should extend `ContextFunction`, as the interface `IContextFunction` is marked as `@NoImplement`. This allows additional methods to be added. In Eclipse 4.3, a new method was added to the interface `compute(IEclipseContext, String)` which was also added to the `ContextFunction` parent class.

The OSGi declarative services API allows a service to be created and made available to clients that need to use it. To register a service with DS, a service document is created (in the example this is `random.xml`), and it is referred to with the `Service-Component` header in the `MANIFEST.MF` file. When the plug-in is installed, the DS component notices this header, reads the service document, and then creates the class. This class then becomes available through the E4 context for inclusion in the injection of parts.

Note that the value of the calculated function is cached upon first calculation. So even if the code is changed to inject the value as a method parameter, only the first value calculated will be seen. Although the `IEclipseContext` has a method to remove the value, it doesn't necessarily trigger the removal from all contexts. The recommendation is to use an OSGi service for data that must be calculated each time.

# Time for action – using preferences

In addition to injecting in specific elements from the context, it is also possible to acquire preferences from the Eclipse preference store. Recall that preferences are stored in a hierarchical node structure, with each node having an identifier (conventionally the plug-in name) and a number of key/value pairs. An annotation @Preference allows these to be accessed easily.

1. Add a String greeting field to the Hello part. To obtain a preference, annotate it with @Inject and @Preference as follows:

```
@Inject
@Preference(nodePath="com.packtpub.e4.application",
  value="greeting")
private String greeting;
```

2. Modify the create() method to use this greeting value as the initial value for the Hello label.

```
@PostConstruct
public void create(Composite parent) {
    label = new Label(parent, SWT.NONE);
    label.setText(greeting+" "+window.getLabel()+" "+random);
```

3. Run the application, and the Hello label will show a null value for the greeting.

4. To set a preference value, an IEclipsePreferences object needs to be injected into the Hello part. Add a new field called prefs which is used to interact with the preferences store:

```
@Inject
@Preference(nodePath="com.packtpub.e4.application")
private IEclipsePreferences prefs;
```

>  If the preference's nodePath is not specified, a runtime error occurs.

5. Modify the receiveEvent() method created previously and set the value of the color as the greeting:

```
@Inject
@Optional
public void receiveEvent(
 @UIEventTopic("rainbow/colour") String data) {
  label.setText(data);
  prefs.put("greeting", "I like " + data);
  prefs.sync();
}
```

**6.** Now run the application, go to the **Rainbow** tab and select a color. Switch back to the **Hello** tab and verify that the event was received. Now, close down the application and re-open the application; the persisted greeting should be visible (provided that the workspace is not being cleaned upon each launch).

**7.** Changes to the preference value gets injected dynamically into the part, but as it stands there is no notification when an injected field value has been changed. To be notified when a new value is set, the preference can be injected as an annotated @Preference parameter on an @Optional method:

```
@Inject
@Optional
void setText(@Preference(nodePath="com.packtpub.e4.application",
  value="greeting") String text) {
  if (text != null && label != null && !label.isDisposed()) {
    // NB Run in UI thread!
    label.setText(text);
  }
}
```

**8.** Now, if the preference is set, the label's text will be updated automatically. However, the preference invocation is not necessarily on the UI thread, so the call should be delegated appropriately. It may also be the case that this method is called during startup or as the runtime is closing down, in which case, the setting of any UI components need to be guarded against either being null or being disposed.

## What just happened?

Acquiring preferences with E4 injection makes it trivial to obtain and set preference values. Using a single preference value is the easiest way to get individual values; however, if the preferences need to be mutated then a reference to the IEclipsePreferences store is required.

If the user interface needs to react to changes in the preference, the preference value should be injected via a setter. When the preference value changes, the setter is invoked and it can update the UI.

Note that the preference value setter may be invoked on any thread; if the UI needs to be updated then this should be done via the UI thread. How to do this is covered in the next section.

# Time for action – interacting with the UI

Sometimes it is necessary to write code to run in the UI thread, but when called back via a handler it's not always clear if the method is in the UI thread or not. In Eclipse 3.x there is a `Display.getDefault().syncExec()` for running `Runnables` inside the UI thread, or `.asyncExec()` for a non-UI thread. Eclipse 4 introduces the `UISynchronize` class, which is an abstract mechanism for executing code on the UI thread. (It's like an interface for `Display`, except that `Display` doesn't implement it and it's not an interface.) This provides `syncExec()` and `asyncExec()` methods which can be used to schedule `Runnable` events. If a long calculation needs to update the UI after concluding, using `UISynchronize` allows the UI update to be scheduled on the right thread.

1. Create a new `Button` as a field in the `Hello` part, and attach a selection listener such that when it is pressed, it invokes `setEnabled(false)` on itself. At the same time, schedule a `Job` to run after one second that invokes `setEnabled(true)` again:

```
private Button button;
@PostConstruct
public void create(Composite parent) {
  button = new Button(parent, SWT.PUSH);
  button.setText("Do not push");
  button.addSelectionListener(new SelectionListener() {
  @Override
  public void widgetSelected(SelectionEvent e) {
    button.setEnabled(false);
    new Job("Button Pusher") {
      @Override
      protected IStatus run(IProgressMonitor monitor) {
        button.setEnabled(true);
        return Status.OK_STATUS;
      }
      }.schedule(1000);
  }
  @Override
  public void widgetDefaultSelected(SelectionEvent e) {
  }
  });
  ...
}
```

**2.** When the application runs and the button is pushed, the button will be disabled (grayed out) immediately. One second later, an exception will be logged to the console with an "Invalid thread access" message:

```
!MESSAGE An internal error occurred during: "Button Pusher".
!STACK 0
org.eclipse.swt.SWTException: Invalid thread access
  at org.eclipse.swt.SWT.error(SWT.java:4361)
```

**3.** The error occurs because the `setEnabled()` call must be made on the UI thread. Although `Display.getDefault().syncExec()` can be used to do this, E4 provides an annotation-based way of doing the same thing. Inject an instance of the `UISynchronize` into the `Hello` part:

```
@Inject
private UISynchronize ui;
```

**4.** Modify the `Job` implementation in the `create()` method as follows:

```
protected IStatus run(IProgressMonitor monitor) {
  ui.asyncExec(new Runnable() {
    @Override
    public void run() {
      button.setEnabled(true);
    }
  });
  return Status.OK_STATUS;
}
```

**5.** Now run the application and press the button. It will be disabled for one second, and then re-enabled afterwards.

## What just happened?

Using `UISynchronize` provides a way to interact with the UI thread safely. Another way of achieving this would be to use a `UIJob`.

One advantage of using `UISynchronize` is that it is not necessarily tied down to SWT. E4 provides the option of having different part renderers, which could allow for future runtimes based on HTML or Swing, or JavaFX such as e(fx)clipse.

When building plug-ins that will be shared between E4 and Eclipse 3.x systems, continue to use `Display.getDefault()` or `Display.getCurrent()` in order to schedule UI updates, as the `UISynchronize` class is not present in earlier releases.

# Using Commands, Handlers, and MenuItems

The command and handlers in Eclipse 4 work the same way as in Eclipse 3. A command represents a generic operation, and the handler is the code that implements the operation. However, the implementation for the handler takes advantage of E4's annotations, instead of a custom subclass.

## Time for action – wiring a menu to a command with a handler

As with Eclipse 3.x, a command has an identifier and an associated `Handler` class, which can be bound to Menus. Unlike Eclipse 3.x, it is not specified in the `plugin.xml` file; instead, it is specified in the `Application.e4xmi` file.

1.  Open the `Application.e4xmi` file in the `com.packtpub.e4.application` project.

2.  Navigate to the **Application | Commands** node in the tree, and click on **Add child** to add a new command:

    □   **ID:** `com.packtpub.e4.application.command.hello`

    □   **Name:** `helloCommand`

    □   **Description:** `Says Hello`

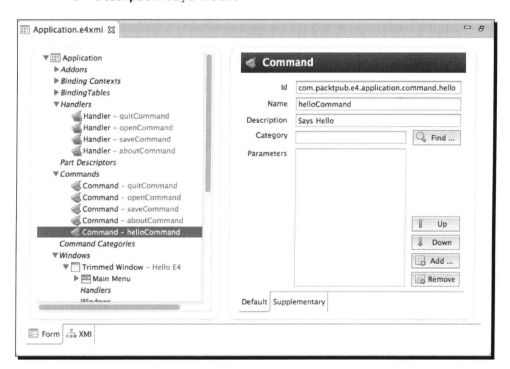

**3.** Create a `HelloHandler` class in the `com.packtpub.e4.application.handlers` package. It doesn't need to have any specific superclass or method implementation. Instead, create a method called `hello()` which takes no arguments, and prints a message to `System.out`. The method needs the `@Execute` annotation:

```
package com.packtpub.e4.application.handlers;
import org.eclipse.e4.core.di.annotations.Execute;
public class HelloHandler {
  @Execute
  public void hello() {
    System.out.println("Hello World");
  }
}
```

**4.** The handler needs to be defined in the `Application.e4xmi`. Navigate to the **Application | Handlers** node in the tree, and right-click and **Add child** to add a new handler. Fill in the details as follows:

- **ID**: `com.packtpub.e4.application.handler.hello`

- **Command**: `helloCommand – com.packtpub.e4.application.command.hello`

- **Class URI**: `bundleclass://com.packtpub.e4.application/com.packtpub.e4.application.handlers.HelloHandler`

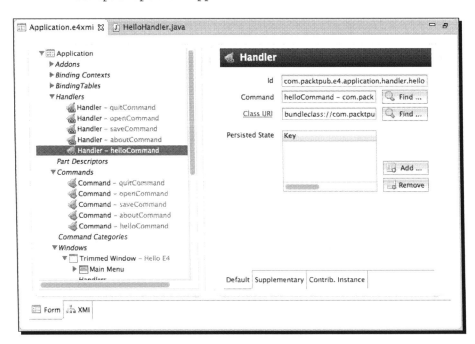

**5.** Finally, to associate the handler with a menu, go into the **Application | Windows | Trimmed Window | Main Menu | File** and click on **Add child** to add a new **Handled MenuItem**. This can also be done by right-clicking on the **Menu – File** node and choosing **Add child | Handled MenuItem**. Add it as follows:

- ❑ **ID**: `com.packtpub.e4.application.handledmenuitem.hello`
- ❑ **Label**: `Hello`
- ❑ **Tooltip**: `Says Hello World`
- ❑ **Command**: `helloCommand - com.packtpub.e4.application.command.hello`

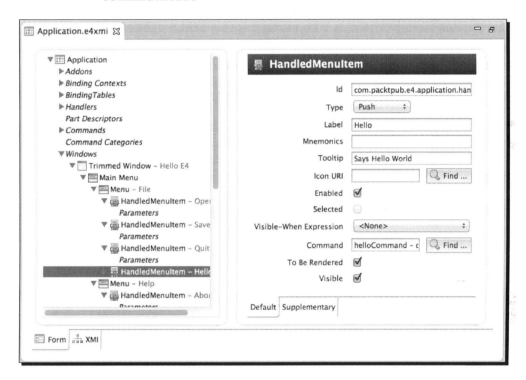

**6.** Save the `Application.e4xmi` and run the application. Go to the **File** menu, and click on **Hello** from the menu item to display **Hello World** in the Console view of the host Eclipse.

## *What just happened?*

The `HelloHandler` class provides a simple message output and an entry point annotated with `@Execute`. The handler can also report whether it can be executed through a `boolean` returning method annotated with `@CanExecute`, but this defaults to `true` if a handler is always valid.

A command is a generic ID that can be associated with one or more handlers and with one or more UI elements, such as `MenuItems`, `Buttons`, or programmatic execution. The `helloCommand` is associated by default to the `HelloHandler`.

Finally, the command is associated with the **File | Hello** menu item so that it can be invoked.

## Time for action – passing command parameters

Displaying a message to `System.out` shows that the command works, but what if the command needed to pick up a local state? Fortunately, the `@Named` and `@Inject` annotations allow objects to be injected into the method when it is called.

1. Modify the `hello()` method so that instead of printing a message to `System.out`, it opens a dialog window, using the active shell:

```
public void hello(@Named(IServiceConstants.ACTIVE_SHELL) Shell s){
  MessageDialog.openInformation(s, "Hello World",
    "Welcome to Eclipse 4 technology");
}
```

2. Other arguments can be passed in from the context, managed by the `IEclipseContext` interface. For example, using the `math.random` function from earlier, a value could be injected into the handler like this:

```
public void hello(@Named(IServiceConstants.ACTIVE_SHELL) Shell s,
  @Named("math.random") double value) {
```

3. If the same handler is being used for different functions (for example, **Paste** and **Paste Special**) they can be disambiguated by passing in a hard-coded value in the command. Modify the `helloCommand` to add a parameter, by opening the `Application.e4xmi` and navigating to the **Application | Commands | helloCommand**, right-click and go to **Add child | Command Parameter** to add a command parameter:

   - **ID:** `com.packtpub.e4.application.commandparameter.hello.value`
   - **Name:** `hello.value`
   - **Optional:** Ensure that **Optional** is selected

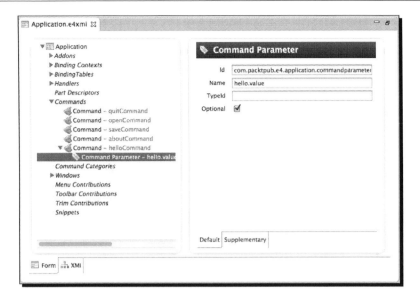

4. To pass a value into the command, go to the `Application.e4xmi` and navigate to **Application | Windows | Main Menu | Menu (File) | HandledMenuItem (Hello) | Parameters**. Right-click and go to **Add child | Parameter** to create a parameter:

   ❏ **ID**: `com.packtpub.e4.application.parameter.hello.value`

   ❏ **Name**: `com.packtpub.e4.application.commandparameter.hello.value`

   ❏ **Value**: `Hello World Parameter`

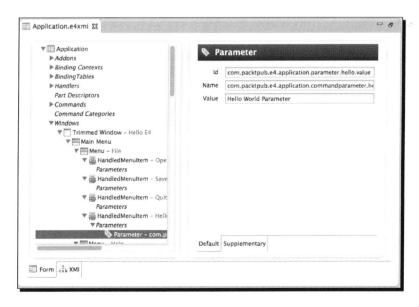

**5.** Finally, modify the command handler so that it receives the value encoded with the handler:

```
public void hello(@Named(IServiceConstants.ACTIVE_SHELL) Shell s,
  @Optional
  @Named(
    "com.packtpub.e4.application.commandparameter.hello.value")
  String hello)
  @Named("math.random") double value) {
    MessageDialog.openInformation(s, "Hello World", hello+value);
  }
}
```

**6.** Run the application, and go to the **File | Hello** menu. The parameter will be passed in to the handler

## What just happened?

Any values can be injected into the method when it is invoked, provided that they are available in the context when the handler is called. These can be taken from standard constants (such as those in `IServiceConstants`) or be custom values injected at runtime. Other values include:

◆ `ACTIVE_WINDOW`: The currently displayed window

◆ `ACTIVE_PART`: The currently selected part

◆ `ACTIVE_SELECTION`: The current selection

If the values are one of a set of values, they can be encoded in the menu or other command invocation. They can also be set via code which calls `IEclipseContext.set()` with an appropriate value.

## Time for action – creating a direct menu and keybindings

Although using commands and handlers provides a generic way for reusing content, it is possible to provide a shorter route to implementing menus with a Direct MenuItem. The difference between this and a Handled MenuItem is that Direct just contains a reference to the `@Executable` class.

**1.** To add a new direct menu item, open the `Application.e4xmi` file and navigate to the **Application | Windows | Trimmed Window | Main Menu | Menu (File)**. Right-click on the menu and choose **Add child | Direct MenuItem**. In the dialog shown, fill in the details, including the class URI link to the `HelloHandler`, defined previously:

  ❑ **ID**: `com.packtpub.e4.application.directmenuitem.hello`

  ❑ **Label**: `Direct Hello`

□ **Class URI**: `bundleclass://com.packtpub.e4.application/`
`com.packtpub.e4.application.handlers.HelloHandler`

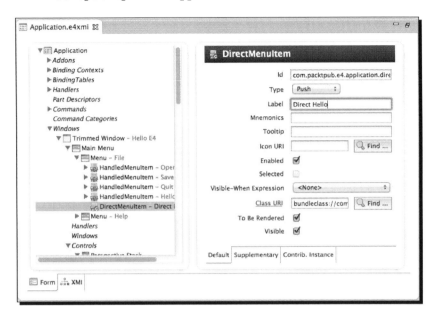

2. Run the application, choose **File | Direct Hello** to show the same message as before.

3. Keys can be bound to commands in an application, and can be enabled in one of the several UI contexts. By default, these include **In Dialogs and Windows**, **In Dialogs**, and **In Windows**; additional contexts can be created. To set a keybinding to the menu, open the `Application.e4xmi` and navigate to the **Application | BindingTables | BindingTable – In Dialog and Windows**. Right-click on the binding table and **Add child | KeyBinding**. Fill in the fields as follows:

   □ **ID**: leave blank

   □ **Sequence**: `M1+L`

❑ **Command:** `helloCommand - com.packtpub.e4.application. command.hello`

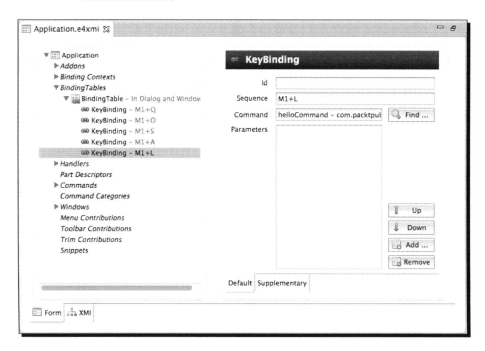

**4.** Run the application, and press M1 + *L* (*Cmd* + *L* on OS X, *Alt* + *L* on Windows/Linux). The Hello command will be run.

## What just happened?

A Direct MenuItem is a way of hooking up a menu item directly to an executable method in a very simple way, without needing to have a separate command and handler defined. For application-wide operations, such as quitting the application, using a Direct MenuItem may be appropriate.

However, if the command needs to be handled in a different context then it is more appropriate to define a handler which can be replaced in different scopes.

Unlike a Handled MenuItem, the Direct MenuItem cannot have command parameters associated with it. Nor can a Direct MenuItem have a keybinding assigned.

To associate a keybinding with a command, an associated context must be selected. This is typically the **In Dialogs and Windows**, although other contexts can be selected as well (such as **In Dialogs** and **In Windows**). These are represented as the **Binding Table** in the `Application.e4xmi` node.

The sequence can be a single character, or it can be a sequence of characters. The meta characters (M1, M2, M3, M4, and so on) are defined in the `org.eclipse.ui.bindings` extension point.

- ◆ M1 is the *Cmd* key on OS X and *Ctrl* on Windows
- ◆ M2 is *Shift* on all platforms
- ◆ M3 is *Alt* on all platforms
- ◆ M4 is *Ctrl* on OS X

When the binding is invoked, it will execute the command specified in the list. As a command, it can have associated parameters like the Handled MenuItems.

## Time for action – creating a pop-up menu and a view menu

Pop-up and view menus are defined declaratively in the `Application.e4xmi` file. These are specific to a part, so the option is defined underneath the part declaration.

*1.* Open the `Application.e4xmi` file.

*2.* Navigate to **Application | Windows | Trimmed Window | Controls | Perspective Stack | Perspective | Controls | PartSashContainer | Part Stack | Part (Hello) | Menus**.

*3.* Right-click on the **Menus** node and go to **Add child | Popup Menu**. Now right-click on the **Popup Menu** and do **Add child | HandledMenuItem**. This is exactly the same as for other menus; fill in the details as follows:

   ❏ **Label:** `Hello`

□ **Command:** `helloCommand - com.packtpub.e4.application.command.hello`

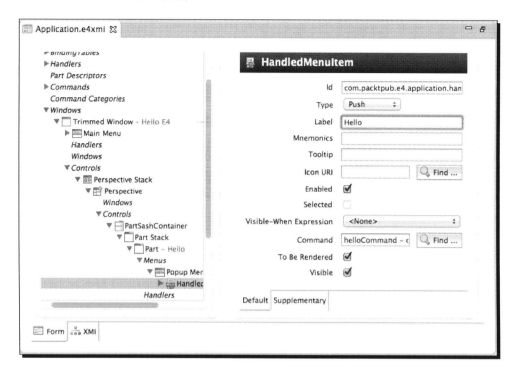

4. Right-click on the **Menus** node again, and go to **Add child | View Menu**. Give the menu a label **View Menu** and right-click to **Add child | Handled MenuItem**. Use the same label and command as for the pop-up menu.

5. Run the application. On the top-right, there will be a triangular drop-down icon which should contain the view menu. However, the pop-up menu won't be triggered, because the SWT component has to be bound to the pop-up menu through its ID.

**6.** Go to **Popup Menu** and set the ID to `com.packtpub.e4.application.` `popupmenu.hello`:

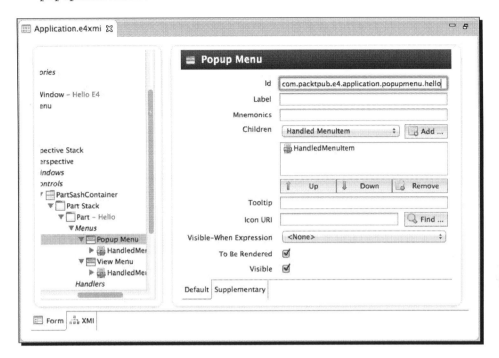

**7.** Add the `org.eclipse.e4.ui.workbench.swt` dependency to the dependencies tab of the `plugin.xml` editor.

**8.** Add a line to the `Hello` class' `create()` method, that registers the context menu with the ID specified. To do this, a new parameter `EMenuService menu` needs to be passed, from which `registerContextMenu()` can be called:

```
public void create(Composite parent, EMenuService menu) {
    menu.registerContextMenu(parent,
        "com.packtpub.e4.application.popupmenu.hello");
```

**9.** Run the application, and right-click on the Hello label or elsewhere in the Hello part. The pop-up menu should be shown, and the Hello command can be run.

## What just happened?

The pop-up menu can be associated with a part, but it doesn't get shown by default. Instead, it has to be registered with a SWT widget. The pop-up menu can be for the entire part's component, or it can be just for specific components in the part.

The `EMenuService` is the interface to the E4 menus. It gets injected into the creation of the widget and provides the detector to listen to the mouse and keyboard events that trigger the pop-up menu.

Adding a **View Menu** is exactly the same as a **Popup Menu**, except that no additional code is required to make it happen.

# Creating custom injectable classes

The injection framework in E4 allows custom injectable classes and services. In addition to registering OSGi services, POJOs can be defined and instantiated on demand.

The rules for allowing a type to be instantiated automatically are:

♦ It must be a non-`abstract` class.

♦ It must have a non-`private` default constructor.

♦ It must be annotated with `@Creatable`.

## Time for action – creating a simple service

POJOs can be instantiated and made available in the E4 context, such that they can be injected into other classes or created on demand. This allows an application to be built in a flexible manner without tight coupling between services.

*1.* Create a class in the `com.packtpub.e4.application` package called `StringService` with a `@Creatable` annotation, and a `process()` method that takes a `String` and returns an upper-case version:

```
import org.eclipse.e4.core.di.annotations.Creatable;
@Creatable
public class SimpleService {
  public String process(String string) {
    return string.toUpperCase();
  }
}
```

*2.* Add an injectable instance of `StringService` to the `Rainbow` class:

```
@Inject
private StringService stringService;
```

*3.* Use the injected service to process the string color choice before posting the event to the event broker:

```
public void selectionChanged(SelectionChangedEvent event) {
  IStructuredSelection sel = (IStructuredSelection)
```

```
    event.getSelection();
  Object colour = sel.getFirstElement();
  broker.post("rainbow/colour",
    stringService.process(colour.toString()));
}
```

**4.** Run the application. Go to the **Rainbow** part and select a color; switch back to the **Hello** part, and the color should be shown, but in uppercase.

## What just happened?

By denoting a POJO with `@Creatable`, when the dependency injection in E4 needs to satisfy a type it knows that it can create an instance of the class to satisfy the injection demand. It will invoke the default constructor and assign the result to the injected field.

Note that the resulting instance is not stored in the context; as a result, if additional instances are required (either in a separate field in the same part, or in an alternative part) the dependency injection will create new instances for each injection.

Generally, the use of injectable POJOs in this way should be restricted to stateless services. If the service needs a state that should be shared by multiple callers, register an OSGi service instead, or use a singleton service injected in the context.

## Time for action – injecting subtypes

Although creating a POJO can be an efficient way of creating simple classes, it can be limiting to have a concrete class definition scattered through the class definitions. It is a better design to use either an abstract class or an interface as the service type.

**1.** Create a new interface in the `com.packtpub.e4.application` package, called `IStringService`. Define the `process()` method as abstract:

```
public interface IStringService {
  public abstract String process(String string);
}
```

**2.** Modify the reference in the `Rainbow` class to refer to the `IStringService` interface instead of the `StringService` class:

```
@Inject
private IStringService stringService;
```

**3.** Run the application, switch to the **Rainbow** tab, and a dependency injection fault will be shown in the host Eclipse instance's Console view:

```
org.eclipse.e4.core.di.InjectionException:
  Unable to process "Rainbow.stringService":
   no actual value was found for the argument "IStringService".
```

**4.** Although the runtime knows that the `StringService` is a `@Creatable` instance, it doesn't look for subtypes of an interface by default. To inject an alternative type, modify the `Activator` and add the following:

```
public class Activator implements BundleActivator {
  public void start(BundleContext bundleContext) throws Exception{
    Activator.context = bundleContext;
    InjectorFactory.getDefault().
     addBinding(IStringService.class).
      implementedBy(StringService.class);
  }
}
```

**5.** Run the application and the part should be created correctly.

## What just happened?

Using an interface for the service type is best practice, since it further decouples the use of the service with its implementation. In order for the dependency injection framework to provide an instance of an abstract type (whether an interface or abstract class, or even a concrete class without a `@Creatable` annotation) a binding needs to be created for the injector.

The binding created above tells the `InjectorFactory` to create an instance of `StringService` when an `IStringService` is required.

## Have a go hero – using the tools bridge

Although Eclipse 3.x parts can run in an Eclipse 4 IDE, to take advantage of the E4 model the code has to be implemented as a POJO such that it can be registered with a model. To fit an E4 POJO into an Eclipse 3.x IDE, the E4 bridge has to be used. Install the "Eclipse E4 Tools Bridge for 3.x" from the E4 update site, which provides the compatibility views.

Now, create a class called `HelloView` which extends `DIViewPart<Hello>` and passes the instance of `Hello.class` to the superclass' constructor. Register the `HelloView` in the `plugin.xml` as would be the case with Eclipse 3.x views, and the part is now visible either as a standalone part in Eclipse 4 or as a wrapped view in Eclipse 3.x.

## Pop quiz – understanding E4

Q1. What is the application model, and what is it used for?

Q2. What is the different between a part and a view?

Q3. Are extension points still used in Eclipse 4?

Q4. How can Eclipse 4 parts be styled?

Q5. What is the Eclipse 4 context?

Q6. What annotations are used by Eclipse 4, and what are their purpose?

Q7. How are preferences accessed in Eclipse 4?

Q8. How can messages be sent and received on the event bus?

Q9. How is the selection accessed in Eclipse 4?

# Summary

Eclipse 4 is a new way of building Eclipse applications, and provides a number of features that make creating parts (views/editors), as well as obtaining service references and communication between parts much easier. If you are building Eclipse-based RCP applications, then there is no reason not to jump on the Eclipse 4 framework to take advantage of its features.

If you are building plug-ins that will run on both Eclipse 3.x and Eclipse 4, then you have to consider backward compatibility requirements before you can make the switch. One way of supporting both is to use the workbench compatibility plug-in (which is what Eclipse 4.x uses if you download the SDK or one of the EPP packages) and continue to use the Eclipse 3.x APIs. However, this means the code cannot take advantage of the Eclipse 4.x mechanisms. Another approach is to write Eclipse 4 based plug-ins, and then wrap them in a reverse compatibility layer. Such a layer is provided in the "Eclipse E4 Tools Bridge for 3.x" feature, which is available from the E4 tools update site. This provides classes `DIViewPart`, `DISaveableViewPart`, and `DIEditorPart`, which can be used to provide an adapter for an E4 part in an Eclipse 3.x view extension point.

In the next chapter, we'll look at how to create features and update sites that allows the plug-ins written so far to be served and installed into other Eclipse applications.

# 8
# Creating Features, Update Sites, Applications, and Products

*Eclipse is much more than just an application; its plug-in architecture allows additional functionality to be installed. Plug-ins can be grouped into features, and both can be hosted on an update site. These allow functionality to be installed into an existing application, but it's also possible to build your own applications and products.*

In this chapter, we shall:

- ◆ Create a feature that combines plug-ins
- ◆ Generate an update site containing features and plug-ins
- ◆ Categorize the update site
- ◆ Create an application
- ◆ Create and export a product

## Grouping plug-ins with features

Although functionality is provided in Eclipse through the use of plug-ins, typically individual plug-ins aren't installed separately. Historically, the Eclipse platform only dealt with features, a means of grouping a number of plug-ins together. Although the P2 update system (used in Eclipse since 3.5) is capable of installing plug-ins separately, almost all functionality used in Eclipse runtimes is installed through features.

## Time for action – creating a feature

A feature project is used in Eclipse to create, test, and export features. Features are used to group many plug-ins together into a coherent unit. For example, the JDT feature consists of 26 separate plug-ins. Features are also used in the construction of update sites, which are covered later in this chapter.

**1.** Create a feature project by going to **File | New | Project...** and then selecting **Feature Project**.

**2.** Name the project `com.packtpub.e4.feature` and this will be used as the default name for the **Feature ID**. As with plug-ins, they are named in reverse domain name format, though typically they end with `feature` to distinguish them from the plug-in that they represent. The version number defaults to `1.0.0.qualifier`. The feature name is used as the text name which is shown to the user when it's installed, and will default to the last segment of the the project name.

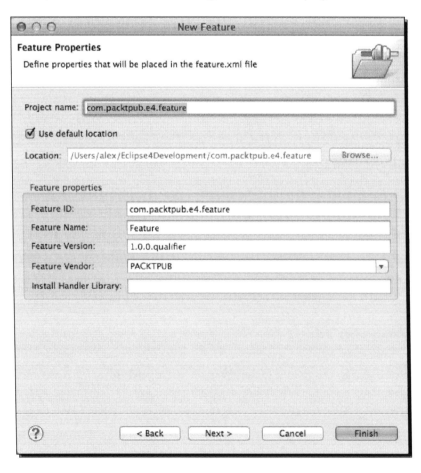

**3.** Click on **Next** and it will prompt for plug-ins to be chosen. Choose `com.packtpub.e4.clock.ui` from the list.

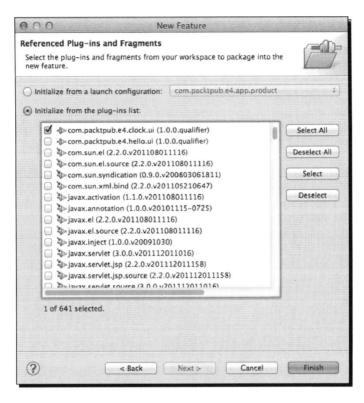

**4.** Click on **Finish** to create the feature project.

**5.** Double-click on the `feature.xml` file to open it in an editor, go to the **Plug-ins** tab, and verify that the clock plug-in has been added as part of the feature.

**6.** Add additional information such as feature descriptions, copyright notices, and license agreements via the **Information** tab.

## *What just happened?*

A feature project called `com.packtpub.e4.feature` was created with a `feature.xml` file. The information specified in the dialog can be seen in this file, and changed later if necessary.

```
<feature id="com.packtpub.e4.feature"
  label="Feature"
  version="1.0.0.qualifier"
  provider-name="PACKTPUB">
  <plugin id="com.packtpub.e4.clock.ui"
```

```
        download-size="0"
        install-size="0"
        version="0.0.0"
        unpack="false"/>
  </feature>
```

The feature ID must be globally unique, as this is the identifier Eclipse and P2 will use for installation. The feature version follows the same format as plug-in versions; `major.minor.micro.qualifier`, where:

- ◆ Increments of major versions indicate backward incompatible changes
- ◆ Increments of minor versions indicate new functionality with backward compatibility
- ◆ Increments of micro versions indicate no new functionality other than bug fixes

The qualifier can be any textual value. The special keyword `qualifier` is used by Eclipse to substitute the build number, which if not specified is formed from the date and timestamp.

The plug-in listed here is the one chosen from the wizard. It will default to `0.0.0`—but when the feature is published, it will choose the highest version available and then replace the version string for the plug-in.

There may also be other elements in the `feature.xml` file, such as `license`, `description`, and `copyright`. These are optional, but if present, will be displayed in the update dialog when installing.

## Time for action – exporting a feature

Once a feature has been created and has one or more plug-ins added, they can be exported from the workbench. An exported feature can be installed into other Eclipse instances, as the next section will demonstrate. Note that exporting a feature also builds and exports all the associated plug-ins as well.

1. To export a plug-in, go to **File | Export | Deployable features**. This will launch a dialog with the option to select any features in the workspace.

2. Choose the `com.packtpub.e4.feature` and give a suitable directory location.

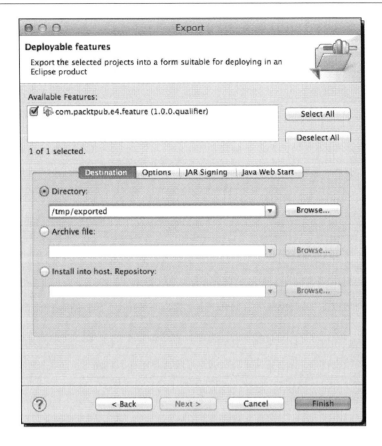

3.  Click on **Finish** and the feature and all of its plug-ins will be exported.

4.  Open the destination location in a file explorer and see the files created:

    □  `artifacts.jar`

    □  `content.jar`

    □  `features/com.packtpub.e4.feature_1.0.0.201305070958.jar`

    □  `plugins/com.packtpub.e4.clock.ui_1.0.0.201305070958.jar`

## *What just happened?*

The **File | Export | Deployable features** did a number of steps under the covers. First, it compiled the referenced plug-ins into their own JARs. It then zipped up the contents of the feature project, and finally moved them both into the directory under the `features` and `plugins` subdirectories.

When a feature is exported, the associated plug-ins are built, and so problems in exporting are often caused by problems compiling the plug-ins.

To debug problems with plug-in compilation, check the `build.properties` file. This is used to control the ant-based build that PDE uses under the covers. Sometimes, PDE will flag warnings or errors in this file, especially if the source or compilation folders are moved or renamed after creating a project.

A `build.properties` file looks similar to the following:

```
source.. = src/
output.. = bin/
bin.includes = plugin.xml,\
               META-INF/,\
               .,\
               icons/
```

If there are any problems, verify that these correspond to paths in the plug-in's directory. The `source..` is actually a reference to the current directory. If there are multiple JARs being created, then this will read `source.ajar` and `source.anotherjar`. The source directive is used if plug-ins have source exported; classes and other compiled output comes from the `output` property. If the output directory is renamed (for example `target/classes`) then ensure the `output..` property is updated in the `build.properties` file.

If there are non-Java assets that need to be exported, they must be explicitly listed in this file. If a directory (such as `icons/`) is included, then this path will be re-created in the plug-in's JAR structure when it is created. Individual assets underneath the `icons/` folder do not need to be explicitly listed.

**Oracle Java 1.7 on OSX**

Exporting a feature on OSX with Oracle's Java 1.7 may give an error such as, `/Library/Java/JavaVirtualMachines/.../Contents/Home/Classes does not exist`. To fix this, go into the `Home` directory mentioned in the error, and run `sudo ln -s jre/lib Classes` to re-create it.

## Time for action – installing a feature

Now that the feature has been exported, it can be installed into Eclipse. Either the current Eclipse instance can be used for this, or a new instance of Eclipse can be created by running the `eclipse` executable with a different workspace. (On OS X double-clicking on the `Eclipse.app` will show the current Eclipse instance again; to run a second instance on OSX, open up the application in the terminal and run `eclipse` from the home of the application folder.)

***1.*** To install the feature into Eclipse, go to **Help | Install New Software...**.

**2.** In the dialog that appears, type in the directory's URL in the **work with** box. If the feature was exported into `/tmp/exported`, **then put** `file:///tmp/exported` into the **work with** field. If it was exported on Windows, say to `c:\temp\exported` then use a URL such as `file:///c:/temp/exported`. **Note** that on Windows the directory slashes are reversed in the URL.

**3.** After the URL has been put in, hit *Enter*. The message may say **no categorized items**—but deselect the checkbox at the bottom **Group items by category** and the feature should appear:

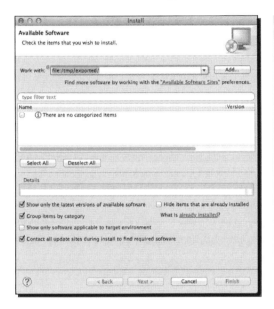 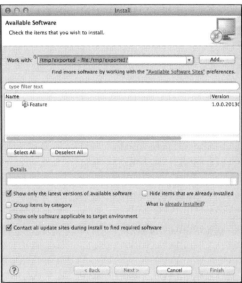

**4.** Select the checkbox next to the feature and click on **Finish** to install the feature and associated plug-in to the Eclipse workspace.

**5.** Restart Eclipse to complete the install.

**6.** Verify that the various Clock views are available by going to **Window | Show View | Other | Timekeeping**.

## What just happened?

The feature exported from the earlier step was imported from the same location. Unless the feature is categorized, it won't show up on the list of things to install. Deselecting the **Group items by category** checkbox allows all features to be shown, not just categorized ones.

The **Feature** name here is derived from the default value in the `feature.xml` file; it can be replaced with a more appropriate value if desired.

If the Eclipse instance isn't showing changes (for example, because the feature or plug-in has been modified), go to the preferences and find **Install/Update | Available Software Sites** and click on the exported repository. The **Reload** button on the right-hand side will be enabled, and clicking on that will refresh from disk the contents of the repository.

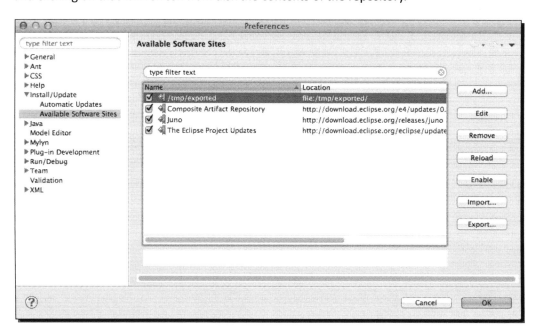

Once the repository is reloaded, go back into the **Help | Install New Software** and the update should be seen. If it is not, verify that the version ends with `.qualifier` on the end of the features' and plug-ins' version number. Without a monotonically increasing version number, Eclipse gets confused and cannot detect that the plug-in or feature has been changed and so refuses to re-install it. Check also that the exported version of the plug-in and feature ends with a more recent date, or remove the contents of the exported folder, export, and then reload.

## Time for action – categorizing the update site

The **Group items by category** mechanism allows a small subset of features to be shown in the list, grouped by category. Eclipse is a highly modular application, and a regular install is likely to include over 400 features and over 600 plug-ins. A one-dimensional list of all of the features will take up a significant amount of UI space and would not provide the best user experience; and in any case, many of the features are subsets of the core functionality (Mylyn alone will install over 150 features depending on what combinations are selected in the install).

This categorization works by providing a `category.xml` file (also known as `site.xml`) which defines a category and a collection of features (from Eclipse 4.3 onwards, plug-ins as well as features). When the **Group items by category** checkbox is selected, only the groups and features defined in the `category.xml` file are shown, and the rest of the features and plug-ins are hidden. These are usually done via a separate **Update Site Project**.

*1.* Create a new project called `com.packtpub.e4.update` as an **Update Site Project**. This will create a new project with a `site.xml` file. (If it is renamed from `site.xml` to `category.xml` it will fail; so don't do that.)

*2.* Double-click on the `site.xml` file and it will open an editor.

*3.* Click on the **New Category** button and enter the following:

  ❑ **ID:** `com.packtpub.e4.category`

  ❑ **Name:** `PacktPub Example E4 Category`

  ❑ **Description:** `Contains features for the PacktPub E4 book by Alex Blewitt`

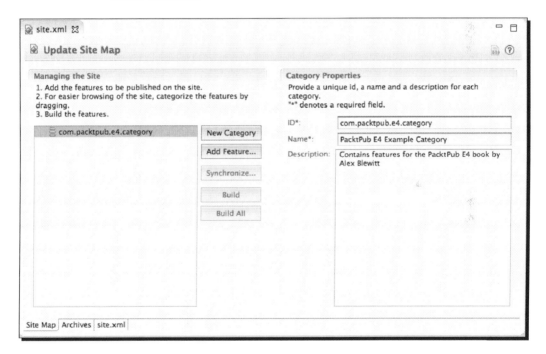

*4.* Ensure that the `com.packtpub.e4.category` is selected, and click on the **Add Feature** button.

**5.** Select the `com.packtpub.e4.feature` from the pop-up menu, and this will add it to the highlighted category:

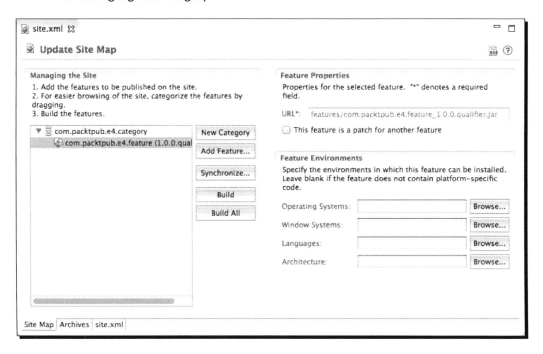

**6.** Click on the **Build All** button, and an update site will be materialized into the project folder:

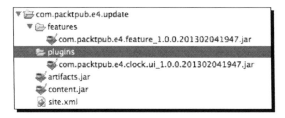

**7.** Finally, check that the categories are set up correctly by going into **Help | Install New Software** and placing the path to the workspace in use.

**8.** Ensure the **Group items by category** checkbox is selected, and the category containing the feature should be seen:

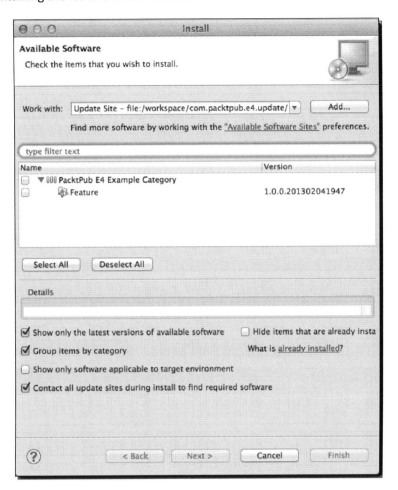

## *What just happened?*

The `site.xml` file is not required by modern Eclipse runtimes, but the `artifacts.jar` and `content.jar` contain XML files required by P2 to perform installation. These contain a list of all of the features and plug-ins, and what constraints are required for their installation (such as the packages a bundle exports or imports).

P2 generates a categorization from either a `site.xml` or `category.xml` file. These are essentially the same, but the update site has a nicer UI for editing and generating the content required.

```
<site>
  <feature id="com.packtpub.e4.feature" version="1.0.0.qualifier"
   url="features/com.packtpub.e4.feature_1.0.0.qualifier.jar">
    <category name="com.packtpub.e4.category"/>
  </feature>
  <category-def name="com.packtpub.e4.category"
   label="PacktPub E4 Example Category">
    <description>
      Contains features for the PacktPub E4 book by Alex Blewitt
    </description>
  </category-def>
</site>
```

This file contains a list of features (which themselves contain plug-ins) and can be used to generate an update site, which is a `features` and `plugins` directory along with the top-level content. If the `artifacts.jar` or `content.jar` is missing (and there is no `site.xml` file), Eclipse will be unable to install content from the repository.

>  The ability to load content from a repository only containing a `site.xml` has been removed from Eclipse 4.3 onwards.

When the update site is built, it will replace the `.qualifier` with a build identifier, which is derived and then composed of the year/month/day/time. It is possible to override this with a different value if desired.

The `artifacts.jar` and `content.jar` files are ZIP files which contain a single `xml` file. This `xml` file is put in a JAR solely for compression; it can be served (though less efficiently) as `artifacts.xml` or `content.xml` as well.

This update site can be transferred to host onto a remote server to allow installation into other Eclipse instances. Eclipse supports HTTP as well as FTP by default, although it can be extended to allow other protocols.

Generally, only top-level features should be exposed in the update site. These may include other features or plug-ins, but only the top-level features are shown in the update site and in the installed list in Eclipse via **Help | About | Installation Details**.

# Time for action – depending on other features

If a feature needs functionality provided by another feature, it can be declared via the
`feature.xml` file of the feature itself. For example, installing the E4 feature may depend
on some runtime components provided by JGit, so installing the JGit feature will mean that
everything required is present. To add JGit as a dependency to the E4 feature:

1. Edit the `feature.xml` file and go to the **Dependencies** tab.

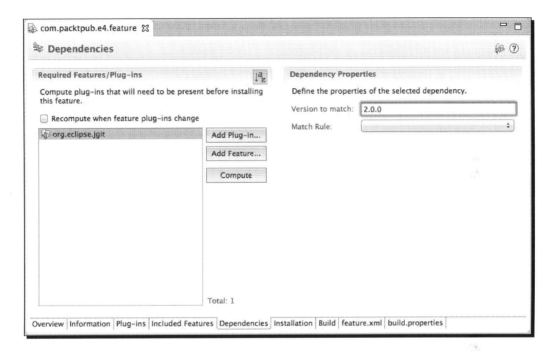

2. Click on **Add Feature** and select `org.eclipse.jgit` from the list. It will fill in a
   version range using the exact version specified in the plug-in; invariably it is better
   to substitute that with a lower-bound version number since that will allow the
   feature to be installed with a dependency that is slightly lower. This will result in a
   `feature.xml` file that looks similar to the following:

```
<feature id="com.packtpub.e4.feature" label="Feature"
  version="1.0.0.qualifier" provider-name="PACKTPUB">
  <requires>
    <import feature="org.eclipse.jgit" version="2.0.0"/>
  </requires>
  <plugin id="com.packtpub.e4.clock.ui"
    download-size="0"
    install-size="0"
```

```
        version="0.0.0"
        unpack="false"/>
<feature/>
```

**3.** Run the **Build All** again. The `features/` directory will contain just the `com.packtpub.e4.feature`, and the `plugins/` directory will contain just the `com.packtpub.e4.clock.ui` plug-in.

**4.** Install the feature again (or do **Help | Check for Updates** if the directory has already been added). This time, as well as installing the E4 feature, it should prompt to install JGit as well, which it will get from the standard Eclipse update sites.

## What just happened?

By adding a dependency on another feature, when it is installed into a running Eclipse platform it requires that the other feature be present. If the **Consult all update sites** checkbox is selected, and if the feature is not installed and cannot be found from the current update site, other update sites will be consulted to acquire the missing feature.

Note that the JGit feature will not be present in the exported site. This is generally desirable since it is unnecessary to duplicate features that are available elsewhere. However, if this is desired then remove the dependency from the **Dependency** tab and add it to the **Included features** tab. This will result in the `requires` dependency being changed to an `includes` dependency in the `feature.xml` file.

## Time for action – branding features

Features generally don't show up in the **About** dialog of Eclipse, as there is only space for a handful of features to appear there. Only top-level features which have branding information associated with them are shown in the dialog.

**1.** Go to **Help | About** (on OS X, this is under **Eclipse | About Eclipse**) and there will be a number of icons present, consisting of the top-level branded features that have been installed. These features have an associated branding plug-in which contains a file called `about.ini` that supplies the information:

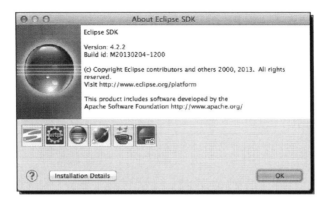

**2.** First, set up an association between the feature and its branding plug-in, by re-using the com.packtpub.e4.clock.ui plug-in from before. Open the feature.xml file, go to the **Overview** tab and add the name of the branding plug-in as com. packtpub.e4.clock.ui:

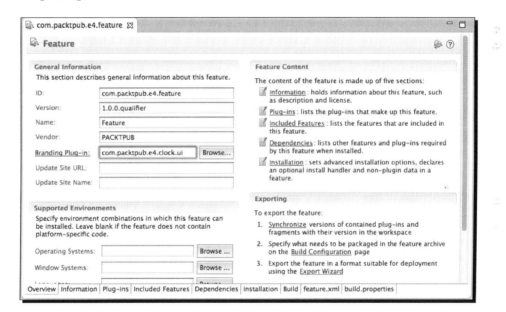

**3.** Now, create a file in the `com.packtpub.e4.clock.ui` plug-in called `about.ini` with the following content:

```
featureImage=icons/sample.gif
aboutText=\
Clock UI plug-in\n\
\n\
Example of how to use plug-ins to modularise applications\n
```

**4.** Build the update site, and install the plug-in into Eclipse. After restarting, go to the **Help | About** menu. Unfortunately, the about text won't be present. That's because despite the `about.ini` file being part of the plug-in, Eclipse doesn't bundle it into the plug-in's JAR. There is another change which is required in the `build.properties` file in the `com.packtpub.e4.clock.ui` plug-in to include the `about.ini` file explicitly:

```
bin.includes = plugin.xml,\
  META-INF/,\
  .,\
  icons/,\
  about.ini,\
  ...
```

**5.** Export the update site and the plug-in JAR will now have the `about.ini` included.

**6.** Reload the update site from the **Window | Preferences | Install/Update | Available Update Sites** window and by doing a **Reload** on the exported repository.

**7.** Run **Help | Check for Updates** to pick up the changes, and restart Eclipse.

**8.** Go into the **About** screen to show the generic icon used by the feature:

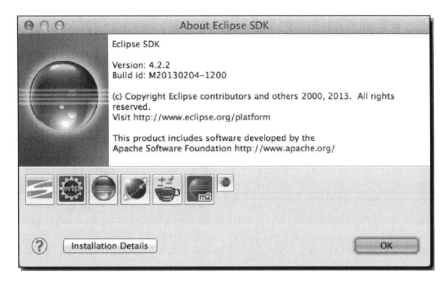

## What just happened?

A feature is associated with a branding plug-in, which contains a section of text and an icon. This feature branding consists of an `about.ini` file, which is included in the associated branding plug-in, and optionally a 32 x 32 icon.

The icon generated by the same wizard is 16 x 16, so it shows up as a quarter of the size of other icons in this list. A feature icon should be 32 x 32 size, otherwise the inconsistent size will be seen. Supplying a 32 x 32 feature icon is left as an exercise for the reader.

### Have a go hero – publishing the content remotely

Since update sites can be served on websites, upload the update content to a remote web server and install it from there. Alternatively, use a web server such as Apache or those built into the operating system to serve the content via a local web server.

# Building applications and products

An Eclipse runtime consists of groups of features which are themselves groups of plug-ins. The application that they all live within is referred to as the product. A product has top-level branding, dictates what the name of the application is, and coordinates what platforms the code will run on, including ensuring that any necessary operating system specific functionality is present. In the previous chapter, a product based on E4 was created; but products work in the same way for both Eclipse 3.x and Eclipse 4.x.

## Time for action – creating a headless application

A product hands the runtime off to an application, which can be thought of as a custom Eclipse `Runnable` class. This is the main entry point to the application which is responsible for setting up and tearing down the content of the application.

***1.*** Create a new plug-in, called `com.packtpub.e4.headless.application`. Ensure that the **This plug-in will make contributions to the UI** checkbox is deselected and **Would you like to create a rich client application** is set to **No**:

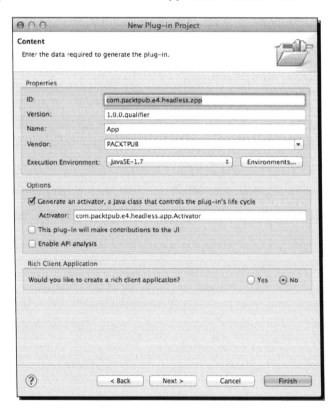

2. Click on **Finish** and the project will be created.

3. Open the project and select **Plug-in Tools | Open Manifest** and go to the **Extensions** tab. This is where Eclipse keeps its list of extensions to the system, and where an application is defined.

4. Click on **Add** and then type `applications` into the box. Ensure the **Show only extension points from the required plug-ins** checkbox is deselected. Choose the `org.eclipse.core.runtime.applications` extension point:

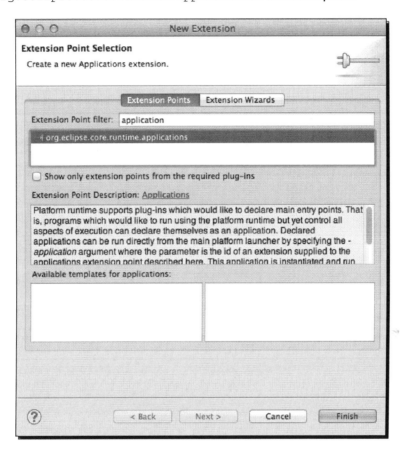

**5.** When **Finish** is selected, a dialog may ask if the plug-in should add the dependency `org.eclipse.equinox.app`. If so, say **Yes** to this:

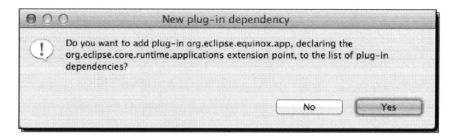

**6.** The editor will switch to a tree-based view. Right-click on **(application)** and choose **New | run** to create a new application reference:

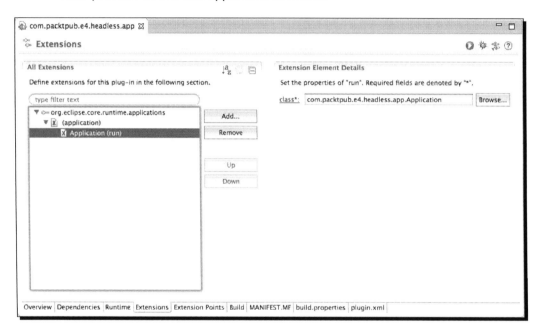

**7.** Use `com.packtpub.e4.headless.application.Application` as the class name and click on the underlined **class*:** link on the left to open a new class wizard, which pre-fills the class name and supplies the `IApplication` interface:

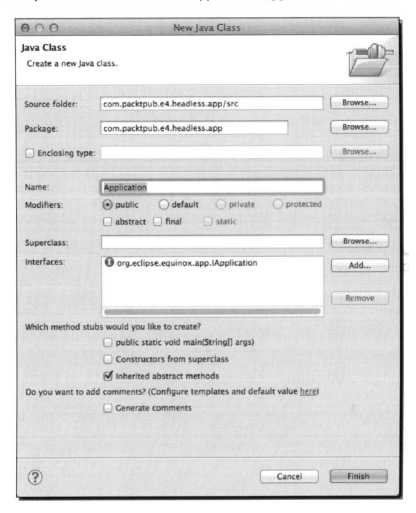

**8.** Implement the class as follows:

```
public class Application implements IApplication {
  public Object start(IApplicationContext c) throws Exception {
    System.out.println("Headless Application");
    return null;
  }
  public void stop() {
  }
}
```

**9.** Run the application, by going to the **Extensions** tab of the manifest and clicking on the play button at the top right, or via the **Launch an Eclipse application** hyperlink. **Headless Application** will be displayed to the Console view.

## What just happened?

Creating an application requires an extension point and a class that implements the IApplication interface. Using the wizard, an application was created and the start method was implemented with a simple display message.

When play is clicked, Eclipse will create a new launch configuration which points to an application:

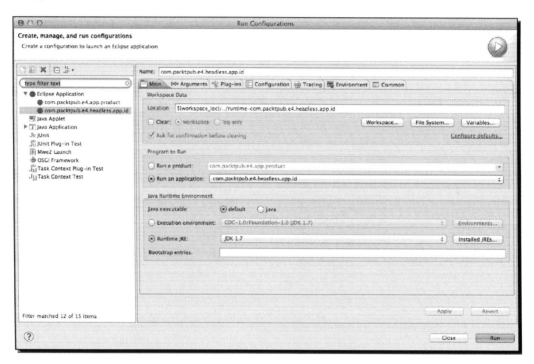

This references the automatically generated ID of the application from the `plugin.xml`. When Eclipse starts the runtime, it will bring up the runtime environment and then hand runtime control over to the application instance. At the end of the start method's execution, the application will terminate.

# Time for action – creating a product

An Eclipse product is a branding and a reference to an application. The product also has control over what features or plug-ins will be available, and whether those plug-ins will be started or not (and if so, in what order).

*Chapter 7, Understanding the Eclipse 4 Model* created a product to bootstrap the E4 application (provided by the `org.eclipse.e4.ui.workbench.swt.E4Application` class) but this section will create a product that binds to the headless application created previously to demonstrate how the linkage works.

*1.* Use **File | New | Other | Plug-in Development | Product Configuration** to bring up the product wizard.

*2.* Select the `com.packtpub.e4.headless.application` project and put `headless` as the filename.

*3.* Leave **Create a configuration file with the basic settings** selected.

*4.* Click on **Finish** and it will open up `headless.product` in an editor.

*5.* Fill in the details as follows:

  ❑ **ID:** `com.packtpub.e4.headless.application.product`

  ❑ **Version:** `1.0.0`

  ❑ **Name:** `Headless Product`

*6.* Click on **New** on the right of the product definition section, which will launch a dialog to create a product. Fill in the dialog as follows:

  ❑ **Defining plug-in:** `com.packtpub.e4.headless.application`

  ❑ **Product ID:** `product`

❑ **Application:** `com.packtpub.e4.headless.application.id`

 It may say `id1`, `id2`, and so on. This comes from the `plugin.xml` file in the previous step.

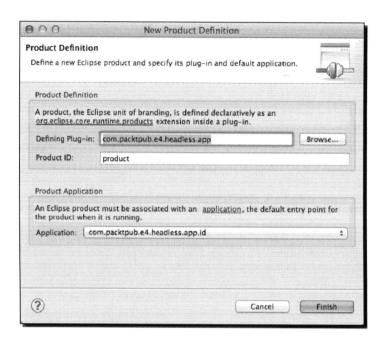

7. Click on **Run** on the top-right corner of the product to launch the product:

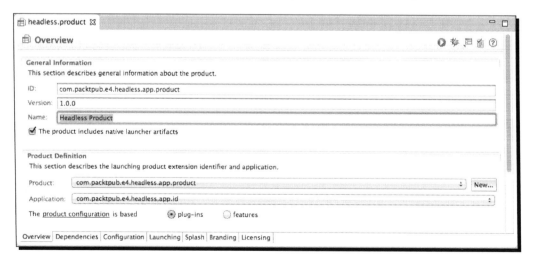

**8.** There will be an error reported `java.lang.ClassNotFoundException: org.eclipse.core.runtime.adaptor.EclipseStarter` because the runtime can't find the required plug-ins. Switch to the **Dependencies** tab, and add:

- `com.packtpub.e4.headless.application`
- `org.eclipse.core.runtime`

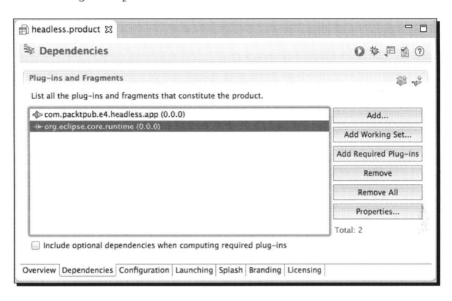

**9.** Click on **Add Required Plug-ins** and the rest of the dependencies will be added:

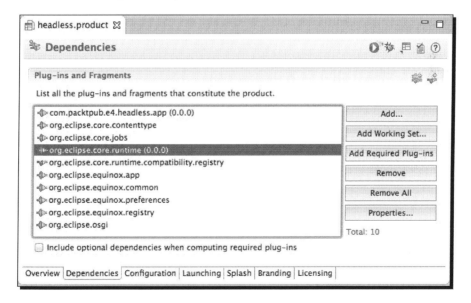

**10.** Run the product and the same **Headless Application** should be displayed as before.

**11.** Export the product, either via **File | Export | Plug-in Development | Eclipse Product**, or via the **Export** button at the top of the product editor, to a local directory.

**12.** From the directory where the product was exported, run `eclipse` to see the message being printed. On Windows, run `eclipsec.exe` to see the output. On OS X, run `Eclipse.app/Contents/MacOS/eclipse`.

## What just happened?

Using and running a product may not seem that different from running an application, but the key difference between the two is that an application is a start point and one which can be installed into an existing Eclipse runtime, whereas a product is a standalone system that can be run independently.

A product defines the look and feel of the application's launch icons, specifies what will be bundled, and how it is launched. The product then hands over control to an application, which executes the runtime code.

The editor is a GUI for the product file, which is an XML file that will look similar to the following:

```xml
<?xml version="1.0" encoding="UTF-8"?>
<?pde version="3.5"?>
<product name="Headless Product"
    uid="com.packtpub.e4.headless.application.product"
    id="com.packtpub.e4.headless.application.product"
    application="com.packtpub.e4.headless.application.id"
    version="1.0.0"
    useFeatures="false" includeLaunchers="true">
    <configIni use="default"/>
    <launcherArgs>
        <vmArgsMac>-XstartOnFirstThread
            -Dorg.eclipse.swt.internal.carbon.smallFonts</vmArgsMac>
    </launcherArgs>
    <launcher>
        <solaris/>
        <win useIco="false">
            <bmp/>
        </win>
    </launcher>
    <vm/>
    <plugins>
        <plugin id="com.packtpub.e4.headless.application"/>
        <plugin id="org.eclipse.core.contenttype"/>
        <plugin id="org.eclipse.core.jobs"/>
```

```
        <plugin id="org.eclipse.core.runtime"/>
        <plugin id="org.eclipse.core.runtime.compatibility.registry"
            fragment="true"/>
        <plugin id="org.eclipse.equinox.app"/>
        <plugin id="org.eclipse.equinox.common"/>
        <plugin id="org.eclipse.equinox.preferences"/>
        <plugin id="org.eclipse.equinox.registry"/>
        <plugin id="org.eclipse.osgi"/>
    </plugins>
</product>
```

## Have a go hero – creating a product based on features

The product created previously specified an exact set of plug-ins that are needed to run the code. Many Eclipse applications are based on features, and products can also be defined by features as well.

Move the plug-in dependencies from the product to a feature, and then have the product depend on the feature instead. That way, when the feature is updated, it can be done externally to the product definition.

## Pop Quiz – understanding features, applications, and products

Q1. What is the keyword used in the version number that gets replaced by the timestamp?

Q2. What files get generated in an update site build?

Q3. What is the name of the file that allows an update site to be categorized?

Q4. What is the difference between feature "requires" and "includes"?

Q5. What is the difference between an application and a product?

Q6. What is an application's entry point?

# Summary

In this chapter, we covered how to create features and update sites, which allows plug-ins to be exported and installed into different Eclipse instances. The contents of the update site can be published to a web server and registered with the Eclipse marketplace to gain wide visibility. We also covered how to create applications and products which can be used to export top-level applications.

In the next chapter, we will look at how to write automated tests for Eclipse plug-ins.

# 9
# Automated Testing of Plug-ins

*JUnit is the testing framework of choice for Eclipse applications, and can be used to run either pure Java tests or plug-in tests. If user interfaces need to be exercised, SWTBot provides a facade onto the underling Eclipse application, and can be used to drive menus, dialogs and views.*

In this chapter, we will do the following:

- ◆ Create a JUnit test running as pure Java code
- ◆ Create a JUnit test running as a plug-in
- ◆ Write a UI test using SWTBot
- ◆ Interrogate views and work with dialogs
- ◆ Wait for a condition to occur before continuing

## Using JUnit for automated testing

One of the original automated unit testing frameworks, JUnit has been in use at Eclipse for over a decade. Eclipse's quality can be partly attributed to the set of automated unit tests that exercise both UI and non-UI (headless) components.

JUnit works by creating a **test case** with one or more tests, which usually correspond to a class or methods respectively. Conventionally, test classes end with `Test`, but this is not a requirement. Multiple test cases can be aggregated into **test suites**, although implicitly a project becomes its own test suite.

## Time for action – writing a simple JUnit test case

This section explains how to write and run a simple JUnit case in Eclipse.

1. Create a new Java project called `com.packtpub.e4.junit.example`.

2. Create a class called `MathUtil` in `com.packtpub.e4.junit.example`.

3. Create a `public static` method called `isOdd()` that takes an int value, and returns a `boolean` value if it is an odd number (using `value % 2 == 1`).

4. Create a new class called `MathUtilTest` in the package `com.packtpub.e4.junit.example`.

5. Create a method called `testOdd()` with an annotation `@Test`, which is how JUnit 4 signifies that this method is a test case.

6. Click on the quick-fix saying `Add JUnit 4 library to the build path`, or edit the build path manually to point to Eclipse's `plugins/org.junit_4.*.jar` file.

7. Implement the `testOdd()` method as follows:

   ```
   assertTrue(MathUtil.isOdd(3));
   assertFalse(MathUtil.isOdd(4));
   ```

8. Add a `static import` to `org.junit.Assert.*` to fix the compile-time errors.

9. Right-click on the project and go to **Run As | JUnit Test**, and the JUnit test view should be shown with a green test result:

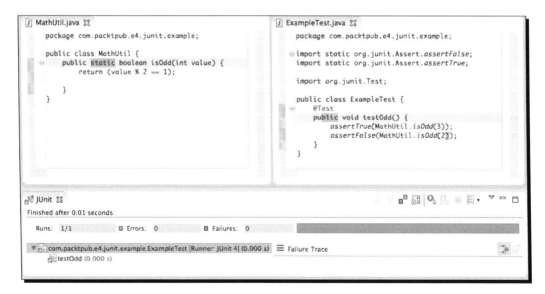

**10.** Verify that the test works, by modifying the `isOdd()` method to return `false` and re-run it—a red-colored test-failure text should be seen instead.

## What just happened?

The example project demonstrated how JUnit tests are written and executed in Eclipse. The example works for both OSGi and non-OSGi projects, provided JUnit can be resolved and executed accordingly.

Remember to annotate the test methods with `@Test`, otherwise they won't run. It can sometimes be helpful to write a method that knowingly fails at first, and then run the tests, just to confirm it's actually being run. There's nothing more useless than a green test bar with tests that are never run, but would fail when they are run.

It is also possible to re-run tests from the JUnit view; the green play button allows all tests to be re-run, while the one with a red cross allows just the tests that have failed to be re-executed (shown as disabled in the previous example).

## Time for action – writing a plug-in test

Although Java projects and Java plug-in projects both use Java and JUnit to execute, plug-ins typically need to have access to them (provided by the runtime platform), which is only available if running in an OSGi or Eclipse environment.

**1.** Create a new plug-in project called `com.packtpub.e4.junit.plugin`.

**2.** Create a new JUnit test called `PlatformTest` in the `com.packtpub.e4.junit.plugin` package.

**3.** Create a method called `testPlatform()`, which asserts that the `Platform` is running:

```
@Test
public void test() {
  assertTrue(Platform.isRunning());
}
```

**4.** Click on the quick-fix to add `org.junit` to the required bundles.

  ❑ Alternatively, open up the project's manifest by right-clicking on it and going to **Plug-in Tools | Open Manifest**.

  ❑ Go to the **Dependencies** tab and click on **Add**, and select **org.junit** from the dialog.

  ❑ Ensure that `org.eclipse.core.runtime` is also added as a dependency.

**5.** Run the test by right-clicking on the project and going to **Run As | JUnit Test**. You will see the error message `fail` (with an assertion error).

**6.** Run the test as a plug-in, by right-clicking on the project and going to **Run As | JUnit Plug-in Test**. You will see the test pass.

## What just happened?

Although the test code is exactly the same, the way in which the tests are run is slightly different. In the first instance, it uses the standard JUnit test runner, which executes the code in a standalone JVM. Since this doesn't have the full Eclipse runtime inside, the test fails.

The plug-in test is launched in a different way: a new Eclipse instance is created, the plug-in is exported and installed into the runtime, the various OSGi services that are needed to power Eclipse are brought up, and then the test runner executes the plugin in place.

As a result, running a plug-in test can add latency to the test process, because the platform has to be booted first. Sometimes, quick-tests are run as standalone Java tests, while integration tests run in the context of a full plug-in environment.

Code sections that depend on OSGi and Platform services need to be run as plug-in tests.

# Using SWTBot for user interface testing

SWTBot is an automated testing framework that allows the Eclipse user interface and SWT applications to be tested in place. Although writing tests and exercising the models behind an application can be essential, sometimes it is necessary to test the interaction of the user interface itself.

## Time for action – writing an SWTBot test

The first step is to install SWTBot from the Eclipse update site. These examples were tested with Version 2.1.0, downloaded from `http://download.eclipse.org/technology/ swtbot/releases/latest/`. Note that Eclipse Kepler (4.3) requires SWTBot 2.1.1 or above.

**1.** Go to **Help | Install New Software** and enter the SWTBot update site.

**2.** Select everything except the GEF feature:

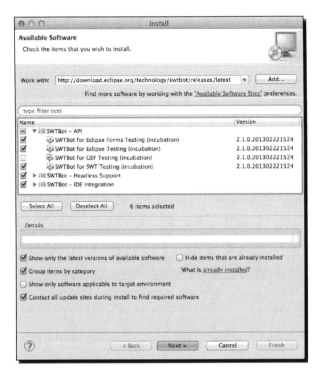

**3.** Click on **Next** to install SWTBot.

**4.** Restart Eclipse, when prompted.

**5.** Add the following bundle dependencies to the plug-in manifest for the com.
packtpub.e4.junit.plugin project:

- org.eclipse.swtbot.junit4_x

- org.eclipse.swtbot.forms.finder

- org.eclipse.swtbot.eclipse.finder

- org.eclipse.ui

**6.** Create a class called UITest in the com.packtpub.e4.junit.plugin package.

**7.** Add a class annotation @RunWith(SWTBotJunit4ClassRunner.class).

**8.** Create a method called testUI() with an annotation @Test.

**9.** Inside the testUI() method, create an instance of SWTWorkbenchBot.

**10.** Iterate through the bot's `shells()` method and assert that the one that is visible has a title `Java - Eclipse SDK` (this is the title of the Eclipse window, and may be different in your case). Here's what the code looks like:

```
package com.packtpub.e4.junit.plugin;
import static org.junit.Assert.assertEquals;
import org.eclipse.swtbot.eclipse.finder.SWTWorkbenchBot;
import org.eclipse.swtbot.swt.finder.junit.SWTBotJunit4ClassRunner;
import org.eclipse.swtbot.swt.finder.widgets.SWTBotShell;
import org.junit.Test;
import org.junit.runner.RunWith;
@RunWith(SWTBotJunit4ClassRunner.class)
public class UITest {
  @Test
  public void testUI() {
    SWTWorkbenchBot bot = new SWTWorkbenchBot();
    SWTBotShell[] shells = bot.shells();
    for (int i = 0; i < shells.length; i++) {
      if (shells[i].isVisible()) {
        assertEquals("Java - Eclipse SDK", shells[i].getText());
      }
    }
  }
}
```

**11.** Run the test by right-clicking on the project and going to **Run As | SWTBot Test**.

**12.** Verify that the JUnit tests have passed.

## What just happened?

SWTBot is a UI testing mechanism that allows the state of the user interface to be driven programmatically. In this test, a new `SWTWorkbenchBot` was created to interact with the Eclipse workbench. (For pure SWT applications, there is the `SWTBot` class.)

The bot iterates through the available shells once the workspace has been opened. Although more than one shell is returned in the list, only one of them is visible. The shell's title can be obtained through the `getText()` method, which returns `Java - Eclipse SDK` if the Eclipse SDK package opens on the Java perspective by default—but this value may differ depending on what perspective and which Eclipse package is being used. Substitute it as necessary for the title shown in the dialog if the test fails on this specific comparison.

This application is similar to an Eclipse product launch; combinations of plug-ins, start-up properties, and product or application choices can be made via the **Run** or **Debug** configurations menu. As with ordinary JUnit tests, the launch can be invoked in Debug mode and breakpoints can be set.

# Time for action – working with menus

Note that SWTBot works on a non-UI thread by default, so as to avoid a deadlock with modal dialogs and other user interface actions. If the tests need to interact with specific SWT widgets, it is necessary to invoke a runnable via the UI thread.

To make this easier, the SWTBot framework has several helper methods that can provide a facade of the workspace, including the ability to click on buttons and displaying menus.

1. Create a new test method called `createProject()` in the `UITest` class with a `@Test` annotation.

2. Create a new `SWTWorkbenchBot` instance.

3. Use the bot's `menu()` method to navigate to **File | Project...**, and perform a `click()`.

4. Use the bot's `shell()` method to get the newly opened shell with a title **New Project**. Activate the shell to ensure that it has focus.

5. Use the bot's `tree()` method to find a tree in the shell and expand the **General** node, and finally select **Project**.

6. Invoke the `Next >` button with a `click()` method. Note the space between `Next` and the `>` symbol.

7. Find the label titled **Project name:** and set its text to `SWTBot Test Project`.

8. Click on the **Finish** button.

9. The code will look like the following block:

```
@Test
public void createProject() {
    SWTWorkbenchBot bot = new SWTWorkbenchBot();
    bot.menu("File").menu("Project...").click();
    SWTBotShell shell = bot.shell("New Project");
    shell.activate();
    bot.tree().expandNode("General").select("Project");
    bot.button("Next >").click();
    bot.textWithLabel("Project name:").
       setText("SWTBot Test Project");
    bot.button("Finish").click();
}
```

10. Run the test as a **SWTBot Test**, and verify `createProject()` success.

# What just happened?

After creating the workspace bot, go to **File | Project....** Since this opens up a new dialog, a handle needs to be acquired to point to the newly created shell.

To do this, a new SWTBotShell is created, which is a handle to the displayed shell. The title is used as a key to find a given shell. If one is not currently visible, it polls (every 500 milliseconds by default) until one is found or the default timeout period (5 seconds) ends when a WidgetNotFoundException is thrown.

The activate() method waits until the dialog has focus. To navigate through a dialog, methods such as tree() and textWithLabel() allow specific elements to be pulled out from the UI, with exceptions being raised if these are not found. If there is only one element of a particular type, then simple accessors like tree() may be sufficient; if not, there are xxxWithLabel() and xxxWithId() accessors that can find a specific element in a particular section.

To set an ID on an object so that it can be found using the withId() method, call widget. setData(SWTBotPreferences.DEFAULT_KEY,"theWidgetId").

When objects are accessed, they aren't directly the underlying SWT widgets. Instead, they are wrappers, much like SWTWorkspaceBot is a wrapper for the workspace. Although the code is calling setText() on what looks like a label, the code is in fact running on a non-UI thread. It posts a runnable to the UI thread, with an instruction to set the text; all of this is done "under the covers" by SWTBot.

One thing that's immediately obvious from this is that when using labels, the tests are highly specific to the localization of the product. The tests will fail if the application is run in a different language, for example. They are also implicitly tied to the structure of the application—if the UI changes significantly then it may be necessary to re-write or update the tests.

## Have a go hero – using resources

Automated testing exercises code paths, but it is often necessary to verify that not only has the user interface reacted in the right way, but also that the side effects have happened correctly.

In this case, to find out if a project has been created, use the ResourcesPlugin (from the org.eclipse.core.resources bundle) to get the workspace, from which the root will provide a means of accessing an IProject object. Use the exists() method of the project to determine that the project has been successfully created.

Amend the createProject() method to verify that the project does not exist at the start of the method, and does exist at the end of the method.

Note that the `getProject()` method of `IWorkspaceRoot` will return a non-null value regardless of whether the project exists or not.

# Working with SWTBot

There are some techniques that help us while writing SWTBot tests, such as organizing the test code and hiding the welcome screen at the start, which otherwise might distort the test run.

## Time for action – hiding the welcome screen

When Eclipse starts, it typically displays a welcome page. Since this often gets in the way of automated user testing, it is useful to close this at startup.

1.  In the `createProject()` method, within a `try` block obtain a view with the title `Welcome`.

2.  Invoke the `close()` method.

3.  The code will change to look like this:

```
SWTWorkbenchBot bot = new SWTWorkbenchBot();
try {
  bot.viewByTitle("Welcome").close();
}
catch (WidgetNotFoundException e) {
  // ignore
}
```

4.  Run the test—the welcome screen should be closed before the test is run.

## What just happened?

Upon startup, the IDE will show a welcome screen. This is shown in a view with a `Welcome` title.

Using the `viewByTitle()` accessor, the SWTBot wrapper view can be accessed. If the view doesn't exist then an exception will be thrown for a safety check; catch any `WidgetNotFoundException` since not finding the welcome screen is not a failure.

Having found the welcome page, invoking the `close()` method will close the view.

# Time for action – avoiding SWTBot runtime errors

As more test methods are added, the runtime may start throwing spurious errors. This is because the order of the tests may cause changes, and the ones that ran previously may modify the state of the workbench. This can be mitigated by moving the common setup and tear-down routines to a single place:

**1.** Create a `static` method `beforeClass()`.

**2.** Add the annotation `@BeforeClass` from the `org.junit` package.

**3.** Move references to create a `SWTWorkbenchBot` to the `static` method, and save the value in a `static` field.

**4.** The code looks like this:

```
private static SWTWorkbenchBot bot;
@BeforeClass
public static void beforeClass() {
  bot = new SWTWorkbenchBot();
  try {
    bot.viewByTitle("Welcome").close();
  } catch (WidgetNotFoundException e) {
    // ignore
  }
}
```

**5.** Run the tests and ensure that they pass appropriately.

## What just happened?

The JUnit annotation `@BeforeClass` allows a single `static` method to be executed prior to any of the tests running in the class. This is used to create an instance of `SWTWorkbenchBot`, which is then used by all other tests in the class. This is also an opportune location to close the Welcome view, if it is shown, so that all other tests can assume that the window has been cleaned up.

Do not call `bot.resetWorkbench()`, otherwise subsequent tests will fail in the test cases.

# Working with views

As with menus and dialogs, views that have been created can be interrogated with SWTBot as well.

# Time for action – showing views

To show other views, the same mechanism is followed in the UI tests, as a user would do; by going to **Window | Show View | Other**.

**1.** Create a new method, `testTimeZoneView()`, with a `@Test` annotation.

**2.** From the bot, open the **Other** dialog by going to **Window | Show View**.

**3.** Get the shell with the title **Show View** and activate it.

**4.** Expand the **Timekeeping** node and select the **Time Zone View** node (the view created in *Chapter 2, Creating Views with SWT*).

**5.** Click on the **OK** button to have the view shown.

**6.** Use the `bot.viewByTitle()` method to acquire a reference to the view.

**7.** Assert that the view is not `null`.

**8.** The code looks like this:

```
@Test
public void testTimeZoneView() {
    bot.menu("Window").menu("Show View").menu("Other...").click();
    SWTBotShell shell = bot.shell("Show View");
    shell.activate();
    bot.tree().expandNode("Timekeeping").select("Time Zone View");
    bot.button("OK").click();
    SWTBotView timeZoneView = bot.viewByTitle("Time Zone View");
    assertNotNull(timeZoneView);
}
```

**9.** Run the tests and ensure that they were successful.

## What just happened?

Using the built-in Eclipse mechanism to switch views, the bot navigated to the **Time Zone View** menu inside **Window | Show View | Other | Timekeeping** to bring the view to the screen.

Once shown, the `viewByTitle()` method of the bot can be used to get a reference to the widget; verify that it is not `null`.

Being able to select a view programmatically is such a common occurrence that it can help to have a utility method to open a view on demand.

# Time for action – interrogating views

Having been able to acquire a reference to the view, the next step is to deal with specific user-interface components. For standard controls such as `Button` and `Text` labels, the bot provides standard methods. To get hold of other components, the widget hierarchy will have to be interrogated directly.

**1.** In the `testTimeZoneView()` method, get the `Widget` from the returned `SWTBotView`.

**2.** Create a `Matcher` that is based on `widgetsOfType(CTabItem.class)`.

**3.** Use `bot.widgets()` to search for a list of `CTabItem` instances in the view's widget.

**4.** Ensure that 18 elements are returned. Check the running application to verify how many tabs there are in the time zone view; there may be more or less, depending on how many timezones your computer has.

**5.** The code looks like this:

```
SWTBotView timeZoneView = bot.viewByTitle("Time Zone View");
assertNotNull(timeZoneView);
Widget widget = timeZoneView.getWidget();
org.hamcrest.Matcher<CTabItem> matcher =
  WidgetMatcherFactory.widgetOfType(CTabItem.class);
final java.util.List<? extends CTabItem> ctabs =
  bot.widgets(matcher,widget);
assertEquals(18,ctabs.size());
```

**6.** Run the tests and ensure that they are successful.

## What just happened?

It is possible to write code to walk the user interface tree directly. However, because the widgets have to be interrogated on the UI thread, care has to be taken to find the children.

SWTBot provides a generic `Matcher` mechanism, which is a predicate that can return `true` if a certain condition occurs. The `Matcher` provided by `widgetOfType()` matches items that have a certain class type; similarly many other matchers can be instantiated with the `withXxx()` calls, such as `withLabel()` and `withId()`. Matchers can be combined with the `allOf()` and `anyOf()` methods, by providing AND/OR logic respectively.

The `widgets()` call walks through the tree recursively to find all widgets that match a particular specification. A single-argument version finds all elements from the active shell; the two-argument version allows a specific parent to be searched, which in this case is the `TimeZoneView` itself.

Finally, the size of the list is compared with the number of time-zone groups, which in this case is 18.

# Interacting with the UI

While interrogating the user interface, care needs to be taken as to which thread is used to access the UI. This section will show how to obtain values and wait for asynchronous results that are to be delivered by the workbench.

## Time for action – getting values from the UI

Note that if the test tries to access a property from the returned widget, there may be an invalid thread-access error. For example, `ctabs.get(0).getText()` will result in an `Invalid thread access` SWT error.

To perform tests on widgets, the code has to be run in the UI thread. Either the `Display.getDefault().syncExec()` or the equivalent `Synchronizer` class can be used, but SWTBot has a general interface called `StringResult`, which is like a `Runnable` method that can return a `String` value through `syncExec()` on the bot.

1. In the last `testTimeZone()` method of the `UITest` class, create a new `StringResult` and pass it to `UIThreadRunnable.syncExec()`.

2. In the `run()` method, get the first `cTabItem` and return its text value.

3. After the `Runnable` method has been run, assert that the value is `Africa`.

4. The code looks like this:

```
String tabText = UIThreadRunnable.syncExec(new StringResult() {
  @Override
  public String run() {
    return ctabs.get(0).getText();
  }
});
assertEquals("Africa", tabText);
```

5. Run the tests and ensure they are successful.

## What just happened?

To interact with widgets, code must be run on the UI thread. To run code on the UI thread in SWT, it needs to be wrapped into a `Runnable`, which needs to be posted to the display (or `Synchronizer`) and executed there.

Using a `syncExec()` means that the result is guaranteed to be available for testing. If an `asyncExec()` operation is used, the result may not be available by the time the following assert operation runs.

To pass a value back from the UI thread to a non-UI thread, the result has to be stored in a variable. This has to be either a field on the class or a value in a final array. The `StringResult` of the `SWTBot` package wraps this up effectively in the `UIThreadRunnable`, in which an `ArrayList` is created to hold the single element.

Java 8 will make this significantly easier in that it will allow for lambda methods to be executed. At the time of writing, the syntax of Java 8 was not finalized.

# Time for action – waiting for a condition

Typically, an action may require a result to happen in the user interface before testing can continue. Since SWTBot can run much faster than a human can, waiting for a result of an action may be necessary. To demonstrate this, create a Java project with a single source file and then use the conditions to wait until the class file is compiled.

1. Create a new method called `createJavaProject()` in the `UITest` class.

2. Use the `bot` to create a new Java project by copying the `createProject()` method as a template.

3. Add `org.eclipse.core.resources` as a dependency to the plug-in.

4. Add a method `getProject()`, which returns an `IProject` from `ResourcesPlugin.getWorkspace().getRoot().getProject()`.

5. Use the `getProject()` with the test project to get the `src` folder .

6. If the folder does not exist, create it.

7. Get the file called `Test.java` from `src`.

8. Create it with the contents from the `"class {}".getBytes()` bytes as a `ByteArrayInputStream`.

9. Use the `bot.waitUntil()` call to pass in a new anonymous subclass of `DefaultCondition`.

10. In the `test()` method of the condition, return if the project's `bin` folder has a file called `Test.class`.

11. In the `getFailureMessage()` of the condition, return a suitable message.

12. The code looks like the following snippet:

```
@Test
public void createJavaProject() throws Exception {
    String projectName = "SWTBot Java Project";
```

```
bot.menu("File").menu("Project...").click();
SWTBotShell shell = bot.shell("New Project");
shell.activate();
bot.tree().expandNode("Java").select("Java Project");
bot.button("Next >").click();
bot.textWithLabel("Project name:").setText(projectName);
bot.button("Finish").click();
final IProject project = getProject(projectName);
assertTrue(project.exists());
final IFolder src = project.getFolder("src");
final IFolder bin = project.getFolder("bin");
if (!src.exists()) {
  src.create(true, true, null);
}
IFile test = src.getFile("Test.java");
test.create(new ByteArrayInputStream(
  "class Test{}".getBytes()), true, null);
bot.waitUntil(new DefaultCondition() {
  @Override
  public boolean test() throws Exception {
    return project.getFolder("bin").
      getFile("Test.class").exists();
    }
  public String getFailureMessage() {
    return "File bin/Test.class was not created";
  }
});
assertTrue(bin.getFile("Test.class").exists());
}
```

**13.** Run the test and verify that it was successful.

**14.** Comment out the waitUntil() call and verify that the test fails.

## What just happened?

When the Test.java file is created in the project, an event is fired that runs the Java compiler. This in turn results in the creation of both the bin folder, as well as the Test.class file that is being tested. However, both of these operations occur on different threads, and so while the test is running, if it needs to act on the generated file, it must wait until that file is created.

Although this example could have been implemented outside of SWTBot, it provides a simple way to block the execution until a particular condition occurs. This can be useful if the user interface is running some kind of long-running action and the code needs to wait until a certain dialog message is shown, or something that can be determined programmatically (such as the file's existence, as in this case).

Other types of conditionals and tests are possible as well; there is a `waitWhile()`, which is similar to the bot's `waitUntil()` but has the opposite behavior.

Note that when the wait condition is commented out, the test fails, because the test execution thread will hit the assertion before the Java compiler has been run.

One advantage of using the wait code in SWTBot is that if the condition doesn't occur within a given timeout then an exception is generated and the test will fail. Since the same wait condition is used elsewhere in SWTBot, the delay is configurable and can be changed externally.

## Have a go hero – driving the New Class wizard

Instead of using the source file as a text file, use SWTBot to open the **New Class** wizard by going to the **File** menu. Pass in the name of the project, the package, and the class; the source and class files should be created in the background. This is how integration tests (that show the application working from a user's perspective) can be implemented, instead of having a set of tests that show only the underlying libraries at work.

## Pop quiz – understanding SWTBot

Q1. What is the name of the JUnit test runner that is required for SWTBot?

Q2. How are views shown with SWTBot?

Q3. How do you get the text value of a field in a dialog?

Q4. What is a `Matcher` and when is it to be used?

Q5. How can values from the UI be returned to the user without having to worry about thread interaction?

Q6. When some asynchronous events are happening in the background, how can the test wait (without blocking the test) until a particular condition occurs?

# Summary

Being able to test code automatically is a key part of creating quality software. Whether the tests exercise the underlying models or the user interface—or ideally a combination of both—more tests help to highlight problems that occur when changes happen to the underlying framework, or when dependencies change and introduce unwanted side-effects.

The final chapter will show how to integrate everything to an automated build.

# 10

# Automated Builds with Tycho

*The final part of the puzzle is how to build plug-ins automatically. Most plug-ins are now built with Tycho, a Maven plugin infrastructure for building Eclipse plug-ins.*

In this chapter, we will do the following:

- Automate a plug-in build
- Automate a feature build
- Create an update site
- Execute UI and non-UI tests
- Sign the plug-ins
- Learn how to publish the update site

## Using Maven to build Eclipse plug-ins with Tycho

Maven is an automated build tool that builds using a declarative file called `pom.xml` that tells it how and what to build. Maven projects have a group, an artifact, and a version, all of which help in identifying them in repositories such as the Central repository, and also a packaging type that tells Maven what it is trying to build. The default is `jar` since the widest use of Maven is for building Java archives; for Tycho, we need to use a variety of other types.

Maven Tycho is a set of plug-ins that allow the building of Eclipse plug-ins. Tycho requires at least Maven 3.0 to work; the instructions in this chapter have been tested against Maven 3.0.5 and Tycho 0.18.0.

# Time for action – installing Maven

In this section, we will install and use Maven to build a simple Java project to ensure that the tool is configured appropriately. The first time it runs, it will cache many JAR files from the Central repository into a folder `${user.home}/.m2/repository`; for subsequent runs it will be much faster.

1. Go to `http://maven.apache.org/` and download the **Maven 3.0.5.zip** package (for Windows) or **Maven 3.0.5.tgz** (for Mac OS X/Linux).

2. Unzip/untar the package and install Maven at a convenient directory, referred to in these instructions as `MAVEN_HOME`.

3. Either add `MAVEN_HOME/bin` to the `PATH` environment variable or specify the full path to the Maven executable JAR. Run `mvn --version` and if all works well, a version message should be printed out.

4. To create a new Maven project, run `mvn archetype:generate`

   `-DarchetypeGroupId=org.apache.maven.archetypes`

   `-DarchetypeArtifactId=maven-archetype-quickstart`

   `-DarchetypeVersion=1.1`

5. When prompted for the `groupId`, enter `com.packtpub.e4`.

6. When prompted for the `artifactId`, enter `com.packtpub.e4.tycho`.

7. When prompted for the version and package, hit *Enter* to take the defaults of `1.0-SNAPSHOT` and `com.packtpub.e4` respectively.

8. Finally, hit *Enter* to create the project:
   ```
   Define value for property 'groupId': : com.packtpub.e4
   Define value for property 'artifactId': : com.packtpub.e4.tycho
   Define value for property 'version':  1.0-SNAPSHOT: :
   Define value for property 'package':  com.packtpub.e4: :
   Confirm properties configuration:
   groupId: com.packtpub.e4
   artifactId: com.packtpub.e4.tycho
   version: 1.0-SNAPSHOT
   package: com.packtpub.e4
    Y: : Y
   ```

9. Change into the `com.packtpub.e4.tycho` directory created and run `mvn package` to run the tests and create the package:
   ```
   [INFO] Scanning for projects
   [INFO]
   ```

```
[INFO] Building com.packtpub.e4.tycho 1.0-SNAPSHOT
[INFO]


 T E S T S

Running com.packtpub.e4.AppTest
Tests run: 1, Failures: 0, Errors: 0, Skipped: 0, Time elapsed:
0.009 sec


Results :

Tests run: 1, Failures: 0, Errors: 0, Skipped: 0

[INFO]
[INFO] Building jar: com.packtpub.e4.tycho-1.0-SNAPSHOT.jar
[INFO]
[INFO] BUILD SUCCESS
[INFO]
[INFO] Total time: 1.977s
[INFO] Final Memory: 15M/136M
```

## *What just happened?*

The Maven launcher knows how to connect to the Central repository and download additional plug-ins. When it is launched for the first time, it will download a set of plug-ins, which in turn have dependencies on other JAR files that will be resolved automatically prior to project building.

Fortunately, these are cached in the local Maven repository (`~/.m2/repository` by default), so this is done only once. The repository can be cleaned or removed; the next time Maven runs, it will download any needed plug-ins again.

When `mvn archetype:generate` is executed, a sample Java project is created. This creates a `pom.xml` file with the `groupId`, `artifactId`, and `version` given, and sets it up for a Java project.

When `mvn package` is executed, the operation depends on the packaging type of the project. This will be `jar` if not specified, and the default package operation for `jar` is to run the `compile`, then the `run` test, and finally create the JAR file of the package.

The `maven quickstart` plugin is a useful way of creating a `pom.xml` file with known good values, and a way of verifying connectivity to the outside before moving ahead with the Eclipse-specific Tycho builds. If there's a problem with these steps, check the troubleshooting guides at `http://maven.apache.org/users/` for assistance.

# Time for action – building with Tycho

Now that Maven is installed, it's time to build a plug-in with Tycho. Tycho is a set of plug-ins for Maven 3 that emulates the older PDE build used by Eclipse. The Eclipse platform has moved to building with Tycho and Maven 3 under the name Common Build Infrastructure (http://wiki.eclipse.org/CBI).

**1.** Change into the com.packtpub.e4.clock.ui project created in *Chapter 2, Creating Views with SWT*. (If you don't have this project, see the book's GitHub repository for sample code.)

**2.** Create a file called pom.xml at the root of the project, with the following empty contents:

```xml
<?xml version="1.0" encoding="UTF-8"?>
<project xsi:schemaLocation="http://maven.apache.org/
   POM/4.0.0 http://maven.apache.org/xsd/maven-4.0.0.xsd"
   xmlns="http://maven.apache.org/POM/4.0.0"
   xmlns:xsi="http://www.w3.org/2001/XMLSchema-instance">
   <modelVersion>4.0.0</modelVersion>
</project>
```

This can be copied from the pom.xml file generated in the previous section, since every pom.xml has this same signature.

**3.** Give the project a unique groupId, artifactId, and version, by placing the following after the modelVersion tag:

```xml
<groupId>com.packtpub.e4</groupId>
<artifactId>com.packtpub.e4.clock.ui</artifactId>
<version>1.0.0-SNAPSHOT</version>
```

The version here has to match the one in the plugin.xml file, with .qualifier replaced with -SNAPSHOT.

The artifactId has to be the name of the fully qualified plug-in name (the Bundle-SymbolicName in the MANIFEST.MF file)

**4.** Define the packaging type to be eclipse-plugin:

```xml
<packaging>eclipse-plugin</packaging>
```

**5.** If the build is now run with mvn package, an error message, Unknown packaging: eclipse-plugin, will be displayed. To fix this, add Tycho as a build plugin:

```xml
<build>
  <plugins>
    <plugin>
```

```
            <groupId>org.eclipse.tycho</groupId>
            <artifactId>tycho-maven-plugin</artifactId>
            <version>0.18.0</version>
            <extensions>true</extensions>
          </plugin>
        </plugins>
      </build>
```

**6.** Run the build again. This time it will complain of an "unsatisfiable" build error:

```
[ERROR] Internal error: java.lang.RuntimeException:
  "No solution found because the problem is unsatisfiable.":
  ["Unable to satisfy dependency from
  com.packtpub.e4.clock.ui 1.0.0.qualifier to bundle
  org.eclipse.ui 0.0.0."] -> [Help 1]
```

**7.** Add the `juno` (or `kepler`, `luna`) release repository:

```
<repositories>
  <repository>
    <id>juno</id>
    <layout>p2</layout>
    <url>http://download.eclipse.org/releases/juno</url>
  </repository>
  <!-- repository>
    <id>kepler</id>
    <layout>p2</layout>
    <url>http://download.eclipse.org/releases/kepler</url>
  </repository -->
  <!-- repository>
    <id>luna</id>
    <layout>p2</layout>
    <url>http://download.eclipse.org/releases/luna</url>
  </repository -->
</repositories>
```

**8.** Now run `mvn clean package` and the plug-in should be built.

## What just happened?

All Maven projects have a `pom.xml` file that controls their build process, and Eclipse plug-ins are no different. The header for a `pom.xml` file doesn't change, and so generally this is copied from an existing one (or auto-generated by tools) rather than being typed in by hand.

Each Maven `pom.xml` file needs to have a unique `groupId` / `artifactId` / `version`. For `eclipse-plugin` projects, the name of the `artifactId` must be the same as the `Bundle-SymbolicName` in `MANIFEST.MF`, otherwise an error is thrown:

```
[ERROR] Failed to execute goal
    org.eclipse.tycho:tycho-packaging-plugin:0.18.0:validate-id
    (default-validate-id) on project com.packtpub.e4.clock.uix:
    The Maven artifactId (currently: "com.packtpub.e4.clock.uix")
    must be the same as the bundle symbolic name
    (currently: "com.packtpub.e4.clock.ui") -> [Help 1]
```

The same is true for the version in the `pom.xml` file, which must match the version in `MANIFEST.MF`. Without this, the build will fail with a different error:

```
[ERROR] Failed to execute goal
    org.eclipse.tycho:tycho-packaging-plugin:0.18.0:validate-version
    (default-validate-version) on project com.packtpub.e4.clock.ui:
    Unqualified OSGi version 1.0.0.qualifier must match unqualified
    Maven version 1.0.1-SNAPSHOT for SNAPSHOT builds -> [Help 1]
```

Tycho knows how to build Eclipse plug-ins by setting the packaging type to `eclipse-plugin`. However, in order for Maven to know about the `eclipse-plugin` type, Tycho has to be defined as a Maven plugin for the build. Importantly, it needs to be defined as an extension, otherwise it doesn't contribute to the packaging type:

```xml
<plugin>
  <groupId>org.eclipse.tycho</groupId>
  <artifactId>tycho-maven-plugin</artifactId>
  <version>0.18.0</version>
  <extensions>true</extensions>
</plugin>
```

Although it's possible to hard-code the version of the Tycho plug-in like this, it's conventional to replace it with a property instead. We will replace the version number with a property when we create the parent project later.

Finally, an Eclipse repository was added to `pom.xml` so that the build could resolve any additional plug-ins and features. This needs to be defined as a `p2` repository type, to distinguish it from the `default` type, which stores Maven artifacts.

Note that it is best practice to not put repositories in `pom.xml` files in general. Instead, this can be extracted to a `settings.xml` file. This allows the same project to be built against different versions of Eclipse in the future without changing the source, or to run against a closer mirror of the same. A settings file can be passed to Maven with `mvn -s /path/to/settings.xml` that allows the plug-in's dependencies to be varied over time without mutating the `pom.xml` file.

## Have a go hero – using target platforms

Although it is possible to build an Eclipse-based application by pointing to a repository, this does not provide reproducibility of the build. For example, a build might be run against the `Kepler` release repository in July 2013 when Kepler is released as 4.3.0, and the same build can be run again in December 2013 when Kepler 4.3.1 is released. The results of these two builds will be different, even if no source code changes have occurred in the meantime.

A target platform can be defined in Eclipse by going to the **Target Platform** preferences page by navigating to **Window | Preferences | Plug-in Development**. Create a new target definition, consisting of the Base RCP, and then click on **Share** to allow the `.target` file to be saved on the filing system. A corresponding `eclipse-target-definition` packaging type can be used to define a GAV co-ordinate for the `.target` file, and when combined with the `target-platform-configuration` plug-in, it can be specified to build just against those components. See the Tycho documentation or the book's GitHub repository for more examples.

# Building features and update sites with Tycho

The process for building features and update sites is similar to that for plug-ins, but with different packaging types. However, it's common for features and plug-ins to be built in the same Maven build, which requires a little reorganization of the projects. These are typically organized into a "parent" project and then into several "child" projects.

## Time for action – creating a parent project

It's common for the parent and child projects to be located outside the workspace. For historic reasons, Eclipse doesn't deal well with nested projects in the workspace. It's also common for the parent project to host all the Tycho configuration information, which makes setting up the child projects a lot easier.

1. Create a `General` project by navigating to **File | New | Project | General | Project**.
2. Unselect **use default location**.
3. Put in a location that is outside the Eclipse workspace.
4. Name the project `com.packtpub.e4.parent`.
5. Click on **Finish**.
6. Create a new file `pom.xml` in the root of the project.
7. Copy the content of the plug-in's `pom.xml` file to the parent, but change the `artifactId` to `com.packtpub.e4.parent` and the `packaging` to `pom`.

**8.** Create a `properties` element in the `pom.xml` file. Inside, create two child tags: `tycho-version` (which has the content `0.18.0`) and `eclipse` (with the value `http://download.eclipse.org/releases/juno`).

**9.** Modify the reference to `0.18.0` in the existing `Tycho` plugin and replace it with `${tycho-version}`.

**10.** Modify the reference to `http://download.eclipse.org/releases/juno` in the existing repositories URL and replace it with `${eclipse}`.

**11.** Move the `com.packtpub.e4.clock.ui` plug-in underneath the parent project.

**12.** Add a `modules` element to the `pom.xml` file, and underneath a `module` element with the value `com.packtpub.e4.clock.ui`.

**13.** The parent `pom.xml` should look like:

```xml
<?xml version="1.0" encoding="UTF-8"?>
<project xsi:schemaLocation="http://maven.apache.org/
  POM/4.0.0 http://maven.apache.org/xsd/maven-4.0.0.xsd"
  xmlns="http://maven.apache.org/POM/4.0.0"
  xmlns:xsi="http://www.w3.org/2001/XMLSchema-instance">
  <modelVersion>4.0.0</modelVersion>
  <groupId>com.packtpub.e4</groupId>
  <artifactId>com.packtpub.e4.parent</artifactId>
  <version>1.0.0-SNAPSHOT</version>
  <packaging>pom</packaging>
  <properties>
    <tycho-version>0.18.0</tycho-version>
    <eclipse>http://download.eclipse.org/releases/
      juno</eclipse>
  </properties>
  <modules>
    <module>com.packtpub.e4.clock.ui</module>
  </modules>
  <build>
    <plugins>
      <plugin>
        <groupId>org.eclipse.tycho</groupId>
        <artifactId>tycho-maven-plugin</artifactId>
        <version>${tycho-version}</version>
        <extensions>true</extensions>
      </plugin>
    </plugins>
  </build>
  <repositories>
    <repository>
      <id>juno</id>
```

```
        <layout>p2</layout>
        <url>${eclipse}</url>
      </repository>
    </repositories>
  </project>
```

14. Modify the `com.packtpub.e4.clock.ui/pom.xml` file and add a parent element with a `groupId`, `artifactId`, and `version` that are the same as the parent. It is also possible to remove the `version` and `groupId` from the child `pom.xml` file, as it will default to the parent's `groupId` and `version`, if not specified:

```
<parent>
  <groupId>com.packtpub.e4</groupId>
  <artifactId>com.packtpub.e4.parent</artifactId>
  <version>1.0.0-SNAPSHOT</version>
</parent>
```

15. Remove the `plugins` and `repositories` elements from the `pom.xml` file of `com.packtpub.e4.clock.ui`.

16. Now, change into the parent project and run `mvn clean package`. The parent will be built, which in turn builds all the modules in the list:

```
[INFO] Reactor Summary:
[INFO]
[INFO] com.packtpub.e4.parent ............ SUCCESS [0.049s]
[INFO] com.packtpub.e4.clock.ui .......... SUCCESS [1.866s]
[INFO]
[INFO] BUILD SUCCESS
```

## What just happened?

Each plug-in is its own Eclipse project, and therefore its own Maven project. To build a set of projects together, there needs to be a parent `pom.xml` file, which acts as an aggregator.

At build time, Maven calculates the order in which projects need to be built, and then arranges the build steps accordingly.

The other benefit provided by a parent `pom.xml` is the ability to specify standard build plug-ins and configuration information. In this case, the parent specifies the link with Tycho and its versions. This simplifies the implementation of the other plug-ins and features that lie underneath the parent project.

# Time for action – building a feature

Features can be built in the same way as plug-ins, although this time the packaging type is
`eclipse-feature`.

1.  Move the `com.packtpub.e4.feature` project underneath the `com.packtpub.e4.parent` project.

2.  Add the line `<module>com.packtpub.e4.feature</module>` to the parent
    `pom.xml` file.

3.  Copy the `pom.xml` file from the `clock` plugin to the `feature` project.

4.  Modify the packaging to `<packaging>eclipse-feature</packaging>`.

5.  Change the `artifactId` to `com.packtpub.e4.feature`.

6.  The resulting `pom.xml` file will look like:

```
<?xml version="1.0" encoding="UTF-8"?>
<project xsi:schemaLocation="http://maven.apache.org/
  POM/4.0.0 http://maven.apache.org/xsd/maven-
  4.0.0.xsd" xmlns="http://maven.apache.org/POM/4.0.0"
  xmlns:xsi="http://www.w3.org/2001/XMLSchema-instance">
    <modelVersion>4.0.0</modelVersion>
    <parent>
      <groupId>com.packtpub.e4</groupId>
      <artifactId>com.packtpub.e4.parent</artifactId>
      <version>1.0.0-SNAPSHOT</version>
    </parent>
    <groupId>com.packtpub.e4</groupId>
    <artifactId>com.packtpub.e4.feature</artifactId>
    <!-- version>1.0.0-SNAPSHOT</version -->
  <packaging>eclipse-feature</packaging>
</project>
```

7.  Run `mvn clean package` from the parent and it should build both the plug-in and
    the feature:

```
[INFO] Reactor Summary:
[INFO]
[INFO] com.packtpub.e4.parent ................. SUCCESS
[0.070s]
[INFO] com.packtpub.e4.clock.ui ............... SUCCESS
[1.872s]
[INFO] com.packtpub.e4.feature ............... SUCCESS
[0.080s]
[INFO] BUILD SUCCESS
```

## What just happened?

By adding the feature into the list of modules, the feature is built at the same time as everything else. The version of the plug-in built earlier is used to compose the feature contents. If the plug-in wasn't listed as part of the Maven build modules and it couldn't be resolved from a remote repository, then the build would fail.

The child module will inherit the `groupId` and `version` of the parent project, if specified. As a result, the version can be commented out (or removed), which makes managing the versions easier.

At present, the feature and plug-in are built but cannot be easily installed into an existing Eclipse instance. The assumption is that the plug-ins and features can be tested using PDE directly in Eclipse, and that, therefore, there's no need to directly install a plug-in or feature from the result of a build.

It's necessary to define an additional module—an update site—that will allow the plugin to be installed or hosted.

## Time for action – building an update site

The update site created in *Chapter 8, Creating Features, Update Sites, Applications, and Products*, is used to provide a standard hosting mechanism for Eclipse plug-ins and features. This can be built automatically with Tycho as well.

1.  Move the `com.packtpub.e4.update` project underneath the `com.packtpub.e4.parent` project.

2.  Add the line `<module>com.packtpub.e4.update</module>` to the parent `pom.xml` file.

3.  Copy the `pom.xml` file from the `clock` plugin to the `update` project.

4.  Modify the packaging to `<packaging>eclipse-repository</packaging>`.

5.  Change the `artifactId` to `com.packtpub.e4.update`.

6.  The resulting `pom.xml` file will look like this:

```
<?xml version="1.0" encoding="UTF-8"?>
<project xsi:schemaLocation="http://maven.apache.org/
    POM/4.0.0 http://maven.apache.org/xsd/maven-
    4.0.0.xsd" xmlns="http://maven.apache.org/POM/4.0.0"
    xmlns:xsi="http://www.w3.org/2001/XMLSchema-instance">
  <modelVersion>4.0.0</modelVersion>
  <parent>
    <groupId>com.packtpub.e4</groupId>
    <artifactId>com.packtpub.e4.parent</artifactId>
    <version>1.0.0-SNAPSHOT</version>
```

```
        </parent>
        <groupId>com.packtpub.e4</groupId>
        <artifactId>com.packtpub.e4.update</artifactId>
        <!-- version>1.0.0-SNAPSHOT</version -->
        <packaging>eclipse-repository</packaging>
    </project>
```

**7.** Rename the `site.xml` file to `category.xml`. (This is an entirely pointless change required by p2 since the files are identical in format.)

**8.** Verify that the `category.xml` file does not contain a `url` attribute and that the `version` attribute is `0.0.0`, otherwise the message `Unable to satisfy dependencies` may be seen.

```
<feature id="com.packtpub.e4.feature" version="0.0.0">
```

**9.** Run `mvn package` from the parent project and it should now build the update site as well:

```
[INFO] Reactor Summary:
[INFO]
[INFO] com.packtpub.e4.parent ................. SUCCESS [0.048s]
[INFO] com.packtpub.e4.clock.ui ............... SUCCESS [1.416s]
[INFO] com.packtpub.e4.feature ............... SUCCESS [0.074s]
[INFO] com.packtpub.e4.update ................. SUCCESS [2.727s]
[INFO] BUILD SUCCESS
```

**10.** In Eclipse, install the update site by going to **Help | Install New Software** and typing `file:///path/to/com.packtpub.e4.parent/com.packtpub.e4.update/target/repository` into the **work with** field, and installing the feature shown there.

## What just happened?

Creating an update site is no different from creating a plug-in or feature project. There is a `pom.xml` file that defines the name of the update site itself, and it uses or detects the file called `category.xml` to generate the update site.

The `category.xml` file is functionally equivalent to the `site.xml` file created previously, and is a name change introduced by p2 some four or five releases ago. However, the update site project still generates it using the old name, so it may be necessary to rename it from `site.xml` to `category.xml` in order to be built with Tycho. (There is an `eclipse-update-site` packaging type that uses the `site.xml` file as-is, but this is deprecated and may be removed in future versions.)

As with the Eclipse update project, when the update site is built, the versions of the features and plug-ins in the `category.xml` file are replaced with the versions of the features and plug-ins just built.

## Time for action – building a product

A product (a branded Eclipse application, or one that is launched from `eclipse -application` from the command line) can also be built with Tycho using the `eclipse-repository` packaging type. To do this, the app project needs to be built with Tycho and made available in the feature, and a new project for the product needs to be created.

*1.* Move the `com.packtpub.e4.application` project under the `com.packtpub.e4.parent` project.

*2.* Add the line `<module>com.packtpub.e4.application</module>` to the parent `pom.xml` file.

*3.* Copy the `pom.xml` file from the `clock` plugin to the `application` project.

*4.* Change the `artifactId` to `com.packtpub.e4.application`.

*5.* The resulting `pom.xml` file will look like this:

```
<?xml version="1.0" encoding="UTF-8"?>
  <project
    xsi:schemaLocation="http://maven.apache.org/POM/4.0.0
      http://maven.apache.org/xsd/maven-4.0.0.xsd"
    xmlns="http://maven.apache.org/POM/4.0.0"
    xmlns:xsi="http://www.w3.org/2001/XMLSchema-instance">
  <modelVersion>4.0.0</modelVersion>
  <parent>
    <groupId>com.packtpub.e4</groupId>
    <artifactId>com.packtpub.e4.parent</artifactId>
    <version>1.0.0-SNAPSHOT</version>
  </parent>
  <groupId>com.packtpub.e4</groupId>
  <artifactId>com.packtpub.e4.application</artifactId>
  <!-- version>1.0.0-SNAPSHOT</version -->
  <packaging>eclipse-plugin</packaging>
</project>
```

*6.* Modify `com.packtpub.e4.feature/feature.xml` to add the reference to the application plug-in:

```
<feature>
  ...
  <pluginid="com.packtpub.e4.application" download-
    size="0" install-size="0" version="0.0.0"
    unpack="false"/>
</feature>
```

7. Run `mvn clean package` from the parent, and the build should complete with the application plug-in.

8. Now, create an additional project as a Java plug-in project, called `com.packtpub.e4.product`. Move the `com.packtpub.e4.application.product` file from the `com.packtpub.e4.application` project into the product project.

9. Copy `com.packtpub.e4.application/pom.xml` into the `com.packtpub.e4.product` project, and modify the `artifactId` to be `com.packtpub.e4.product`. Change the `packaging` type to `eclipse-repository`.

10. Add the product to the parent by adding the module to the `pom.xml` file with `<module>com.packtpub.e4.product</module>`.

11. Run `mvn clean package` from the parent, and it will complain with an error:

```
[ERROR] Failed to execute goal
  org.eclipse.tycho:tycho-p2-publisher-
  plugin:0.18.0:publish-products
  (default-publish-products) on project
  com.packtpub.e4.application:
   The product file com.packtpub.e4.application.product does
   not contain the mandatory attribute 'uid' -> [Help 1]
```

12. Edit the `com.packtpub.e4.application/com.packtpub.e4.application.product` and add `uid` as a copy of the `id` attribute.

13. Switch to a feature-based build (if not already done so) and depend on the `org.eclipse.rcp` and `com.packtpub.e4.feature` features, removing the plugins element:

```
<product name="com.packtpub.e4.application"
 uid="com.packtpub.e4.application.product"
 id="com.packtpub.e4.application.product"
 application="org.eclipse.e4.ui.workbench.swt.E4Application"
 version="1.0.0.qualifier"
 useFeatures="true"
 includeLaunchers="true">
  <features>
    <feature id="com.packtpub.e4.feature" version="0.0.0"/>
    <feature id="org.eclipse.rcp" version="0.0.0"/>
  </features>
  <plugins/>
  ...
</product>
```

14. Run `mvn package` from the parent again, and the build should succeed. The `com.packtpub.e4.product/target/repository` now contains the product for the target platform you're running on.

**15.** To build for more than one platform, add the following to either the product's
pom.xml file, or the parent pom.xml:

```xml
<plugin>
  <groupId>org.eclipse.tycho</groupId>
  <artifactId>target-platform-configuration</artifactId>
  <version>${tycho-version}</version>
  <configuration>
    <environments>
      <environment>
        <os>win32</os>
        <ws>win32</ws>
        <arch>x86_64</arch> <!--arch>x86</arch-->
      </environment>
      <environment>
        <os>linux</os>
        <ws>gtk</ws>
        <arch>x86_64</arch> <!--arch>x86</arch-->
      </environment>
      <environment>
        <os>macosx</os>
        <ws>cocoa</ws>
        <arch>x86_64</arch> <!--arch>x86</arch-->
      </environment>
    </environments>
  </configuration>
</plugin>
```

**16.** Now, run the build and a product per OS should be built. The example builds for
Windows, Linux and OS X on a 64-bit architecture; to build for the 32-bit versions,
duplicate the environment block and use `<arch>x86</arch>` instead.

**17.** To materialize the products, and not just provide a p2 repository for them, add the
materialize-products goal to the com.packtpub.e4.application/pom.
xml file:

```xml
<build>
  <plugins>
    <plugin>
      <groupId>org.eclipse.tycho</groupId>
      <artifactId>tycho-p2-director-plugin</artifactId>
      <version>${tycho-version}</version>
      <configuration>
        <formats>
          <win32>zip</win32>
          <linux>tar.gz</linux>
          <macosx>tar.gz</macosx>
        </formats>
      </configuration>
      <executions>
```

```
          <execution>
            <id>materialize-products</id>
            <goals>
              <goal>materialize-products</goal>
            </goals>
          </execution>
          <execution>
            <id>archive-products</id>
            <goals>
              <goal>archive-products</goal>
            </goals>
          </execution>
        </executions>
      </plugin>
    </plugins>
</build>
```

18. Run the build from the parent with `mvn clean package` and the build will create `com.packtpub.e4.application/target/products/os/ws/arch`, as well as creating archives (ZIP files) of them.

19. When running the product that is generated, an error may be seen (or can be seen running `eclipse -consoleLog`):

```
java.lang.IllegalStateException: Unable to acquire
 application service.
Ensure that the org.eclipse.core.runtime bundle is
 resolved and started (see config.ini).
```

20. This is an Eclipse product error. In essence, Eclipse products need to have a number of plugins started at boot time in order to run `eclipse -application`. Add this to the `com.packtpub.e4.application.product` file:

```
<configurations>
    <plugin id="org.eclipse.core.runtime"
     autoStart="true" startLevel="4"/>
    <plugin id="org.eclipse.equinox.common"
     autoStart="true" startLevel="2"/>
    <plugin id="org.eclipse.equinox.ds"
     autoStart="true" startLevel="2"/>
    <!-- for 'dropins' directory support -->
    <!-- plugin id="org.eclipse.equinox.p2.reconciler.dropins"
     autoStart="true" startLevel="4"/ -->
    <plugin id="org.eclipse.equinox.simpleconfigurator"
     autoStart="true" startLevel="1"/>
    <!-- disable old update manager -->
    <property name="org.eclipse.update.reconcile" value="false"/>
    <!-- for 'new' update manager support -->
    <!-- plugin id="org.eclipse.update.configurator"
     autoStart="true" startLevel="4"/ -->
</configurations>
```

**21.** Run `mvn clean package` and try running the product again. This time it should succeed.

## What just happened?

Eclipse applications are built and made available as a `p2` repository or as archived downloads. The `p2` repository allows the product to be updated using the standard update mechanisms; this is how updates from 4.2.0 to 4.2.1 to 4.2.2 occur. The archives are used to provide direct download links, as are found at `http://download.eclipse.org` for the standard packages.

For RCP-based applications, it is easier to build on the RCP feature, which provides the necessary platform-specific fragments for SWT and file-systems. Although building a product based on plug-ins is possible, almost all RCP and SDK applications are built upon either the RCP feature or the IDE feature respectively.

For Eclipse to launch successfully, a number of plug-ins need to be started when the application starts. This is controlled using the `config.ini` file, which in turn is read by `simpleconfigurator`, so this needs to be started at the started at the launch of the runtime. In addition to this, the `E4` platform requires **Declarative Services** (**DS**) to be installed and started, as well as the runtime bundle.

By decomposing the projects into a feature, and then having the same feature used for both the SWTBot and product definitions, it becomes the de-facto place for adding new content. Then these changes to the feature are automatically visible in the product, the automated tests, and in the update site.

## Have a go hero – depending on Maven components

Sometimes, it is necessary to depend on components that have been built by ordinary Maven jobs. Although it's not possible to mix and match Tycho and ordinary Maven reactor builds in the same build, it is possible to allow Tycho to resolve Maven components as part of the target platform.

Since ordinary Maven dependencies are represented by the `<dependencies>` tag, it is possible to define additional dependencies that can be consumed or used by Tycho builds. Normally Tycho won't use this information, but to allow Tycho to resolve those and make them available as OSGi bundles for the purposes of the Eclipse build, modify the configuration for `target-platform-configuration` and add the line `<pomDependencies>consider</pomDependencies>` to the `<configuration>` element.

Note that only OSGi bundles are added to the dependencies list; others are silently ignored.

# Testing and releasing

The final step of an Eclipse build is to ensure that all the automated tests are run, and that all the versions that need to be bumped for the release stage are done prior to the code being published.

## Time for action – running automated tests

Although a plug-in's code-based tests (those under `src/test/java`) will be run automatically as part of a Maven build, very often it is necessary to test them in a running Eclipse application. The previous chapter covered creating automated UI tests; now they will be run as part of the automated build.

1. Move the `com.packtpub.e4.junit.plugin` project underneath the `com.packtpub.e4.parent` project.

2. Add the line `<module>com.packtpub.e4.junit.plugin</module>` to the parent `pom.xml` file.

3. Add the `SWTBot` repository to the parent `pom.xml` file:

   ```
   <properties>
     <swtbot>http://download.eclipse.org/technology
        /swtbot/releases/latest</swtbot>
   </properties>
   ...
   <repositories>
     <repository>
       <id>swtbot</id>
       <layout>p2</layout>
       <url>${swtbot}</url>
     </repository>
   </repositories>
   ```

    For Kepler (4.3), SWTBot must be version 2.1.1 or higher.

4. Copy the `pom.xml` file from the `clock` plugin to the `junit.plugin` project.

5. Modify the packaging to `<packaging>eclipse-test-plugin</packaging>`.

6. Change the `artifactId` to `com.packtpub.e4.junit.plugin`.

**7.** To run the Tycho tests, add the following as a build plugin:

```
<build>
  <sourceDirectory>src</sourceDirectory>
  <plugins>
    <plugin>
      <groupId>org.eclipse.tycho</groupId>
      <artifactId>tycho-surefire-plugin</artifactId>
      <version>${tycho-version}</version>
      <configuration>
        <useUIHarness>true</useUIHarness>
        <useUIThread>false</useUIThread>
        <product>org.eclipse.sdk.ide</product>
        <application>org.eclipse.ui.ide.workbench</application>
      </configuration>
    </plugin>
  </plugins>
</build>
```

**8.** Now, running `mvn integration-test` should run the tests when not run on OS X. If run on an OS X, a line must be added to the configuration for JVM:

```
<configuration>
  <useUIHarness>true</useUIHarness>
  <useUIThread>false</useUIThread>
  <argLine>-XstartOnFirstThread</argLine>

  ...
</configuration>
```

Although the tests run, they fail, because the SWTBot environment is giving the bare minimum dependencies required for the JUnit plug-in. In this case, it doesn't even include the clock plug-in developed earlier. To fix this, a dependency needs to be added to the `pom.xml` file so that the runtime can instantiate the correct workspace, including both the clock plug-in and the Eclipse SDK—since the tests rely on the workbench for the **Open View** command and the JDT for the Java project:

```
<configuration>
  <useUIHarness>true</useUIHarness>
  <useUIThread>false</useUIThread>
  <dependencies>
    <dependency>
      <type>p2-installable-unit</type>
      <groupId>com.packtpub.e4</groupId>
      <artifactId>com.packtpub.e4.clock.ui</artifactId>
    </dependency>
    <dependency>
      <type>p2-installable-unit</type>
```

```
            <artifactId>org.eclipse.sdk.feature.group</artifactId>
        </dependency>
    </dependencies>
    ...
</configuration>
```

**9.** Finally, run `mvn integration-test` and the tests should run and pass.

## What just happened?

The `tycho-surefire-plugin` allows SWTBot applications to be launched. The tests are executed and then a return value indicates whether or not they were successful to be passed back to the Maven build process.

Although it may seem that specifying the product or application will also bring in the necessary dependencies, that isn't the case. When the SWTBot test is run, it appears to pay no attention to the application or product when considering dependencies. As a result, these have to be added manually to the `pom.xml` file so that SWTBot sets up the right environment for the tests to run.

The SWTBot tests written previously also had an implicit dependency on the SDK, from asserting the title of the workbench window to expecting the **Show View** menu to be present. These are examples of loosely coupled dependencies—they aren't code related, but to run, they do require the environment to be pre-seeded with the necessary plug-ins and features.

Normally, if applications or features are being developed then these can be used to add the required dependencies instead of using individual plug-ins. In the example, the `clock.ui` plugin was added explicitly and the `org.eclipse.sdk.feature` was added as well. Note that the naming convention for the p2 feature's installable units is to add the suffix `.feature.group` to the end of the name; so the `clock.ui` plug-in dependency could be replaced with `com.packtpub.e4.feature.feature.group` as a dependency instead.

Using features for dependencies makes it easier to maintain, as the test project can depend only on the feature, and the feature can depend on the necessary plug-ins. If a dependency needs to be added, it need only be added to the feature and it will apply to both the update site, as well as runtime and test projects.

Finally, it is possible to determine whether or not a build is running on a Mac box dynamically, and switch in a value for the `-XstartOnFirstThread` argument. This can be achieved by setting a property using profiles which are automatically selected based on the operating system:

```
<profiles>
  <profile>
```

```
      <id>OSX</id>
      <activation>
        <os>
          <family>mac</family>
        </os>
      </activation>
      <properties>
        <swtbot.args>-Xmx1024m -XstartOnFirstThread</swtbot.args>
      </properties>
    </profile>
    <profile>
      <id>NotOSX</id>
      <activation>
        <os>
          <family>!mac</family>
        </os>
      </activation>
      <properties>
        <swtbot.args>-Xmx1024m</swtbot.args>
      </properties>
    </profile>
  </profiles>
```

The OSX profile is automatically enabled for the mac family builds, and the NotOSX profile is automatically enabled for any non-mac family builds (with the negation character ! at the start of the family name).

## Time for action – changing the version numbers

When a new version of the project is released, the plug-in and feature numbers need to be updated. This can be done manually, or by modifying the pom.xml file and MANIFEST.MF version numbers, or by running a tool to do this.

1. From the parent directory, run the following (all on one line):

   ```
   mvn org.eclipse.tycho:tycho-versions-plugin:set-version
     -DnewVersion=1.2.3-SNAPSHOT
   ```

2. The output should say SUCCESS for the parent and SKIPPED for the others:

   ```
   [INFO] Reactor Summary:
   [INFO]
   [INFO] com.packtpub.e4.parent ................. SUCCESS [5.569s]
   [INFO] com.packtpub.e4.clock.ui ............... SKIPPED
   [INFO] com.packtpub.e4.junit.plugin ........... SKIPPED
   [INFO] com.packtpub.e4.feature ................ SKIPPED
   [INFO] com.packtpub.e4.update ................. SKIPPED
   ```

**3.** Now, run a build to verify that the versions were updated correctly:

```
[INFO] Building com.packtpub.e4.parent 1.2.3-SNAPSHOT
[INFO] Building com.packtpub.e4.clock.ui 1.2.3-SNAPSHOT
[INFO] Building com.packtpub.e4.junit.plugin 1.2.3-SNAPSHOT
[INFO] Building com.packtpub.e4.feature 1.2.3-SNAPSHOT
[INFO] Building com.packtpub.e4.update 1.2.3-SNAPSHOT
[INFO] Reactor Summary:
[INFO]
[INFO] com.packtpub.e4.parent ........... SUCCESS [0.001s]
[INFO] com.packtpub.e4.clock.ui ........ SUCCESS [0.561s]
[INFO] com.packtpub.e4.junit.plugin ..... SUCCESS [0.176s]
[INFO] com.packtpub.e4.feature ......... SUCCESS [0.071s]
[INFO] com.packtpub.e4.update ........... SUCCESS [2.764s]
```

**4.** Finally, once the development is complete, build with a release version:

```
mvn org.eclipse.tycho:tycho-versions-plugin:set-version
  -DnewVersion=1.2.3.RELEASE
```

## What just happened?

The Tycho `set-versions` plugin is very similar to the Maven `version:set` plugin. However, Tycho makes changes for both `META-INF/MANIFEST.MF` (needed by Eclipse) and `pom.xml` (needed by Maven).

Development version numbers in Maven end in `-SNAPSHOT` to indicate that they are a mutable release, and there's special handling in Maven builds to get "the latest" snapshot build. For Eclipse builds, the equivalent special name is `.qualifier`, which is appended onto the end of the plug-in and feature builds.

For simple projects, where there is a single plug-in and feature, it can often make sense to have the two versions kept in sync. Sometimes, when there are two highly related plug-ins in the same feature (for example, JDT and JDT UI) then it can also make sense in keeping them in sync. For larger projects where a single build may have multiple modules, it can make sense to have different version numbers on a plug-in by plug-in basis.

The version numbers in OSGi and, therefore, Eclipse plug-ins follow **semantic versioning** (see `http://semver.org`), in which the version-number component consists of a `major` version, a `minor` version, and a `micro` version, as well as an optional `qualifier`. The `major`, `minor`, and `micro` versions default to `0` if not present, while the `qualifier` defaults to the empty string. Typically, the qualifier is used to encode either a build timestamp or a build revision identifier (such as that produced by `git describe` on modern version control systems). While the `major`/`minor`/`micro` versions are sorted numerically, the qualifier is sorted alphabetically.

Unfortunately, OSGi version numbers and Maven version numbers differ in agreement on what the "highest" value is. For Maven, the empty qualifier is the highest (that is, `1.2.3.build < 1.2.3`), whereas for OSGi it is the other way around (`1.2.3.build > 1.2.3`). As a result, organizations such as SpringSource have created a de-facto policy of using a qualifier of `RELEASE` to indicate the release build, (`1.2.3.build < 1.2.3.RELEASE`). They also use `M1`, `M2`, and `M3` for milestone releases and `RC1`, `RC2` for release candidates, since all of these are less than `RELEASE`. As a result, the progression for Eclipse build qualifiers tends to follow `-SNAPSHOT`, `M1`, `M2`, `RC1`, `RC2`, `RELEASE`.

## Have a go hero – enabling builds for other plug-ins

Apply the same `pom.xml` builds to allow the other plug-ins built in the other chapters as part of the automated build. This includes the headless application (the product can be moved into the same product) and the Minimark editor. The standalone JUnit test will need to be built as a `jar` instead of an `eclipse-plugin`, and examples are available at the Maven homepage or the book's GitHub repository.

# Signing update sites

When installing content into a repository, Eclipse will report whether the plug-ins are "signed" or not. Digital signatures ensure that the content of the plug-ins have not changed, and the identity of the signer can be verified.

## Time for action – creating a self-signed certificate

To sign content, a private key and a public key must be used. The private key is used for signing the content, and the public key is used for verifying that the content has not been modified. A key-pair can be created using the Java `keytool` utility on the command line.

1.  Run `keytool` to see a list of options, and to verify that it is on the path.
2.  Create a new key-pair by running the following code (all on one line):

    ```
    keytool -genkey
     -alias packtpub
     -keypass SayK3ys
     -keystore /path/to/keystore
     -storepass BarC0der
     -dname "cn=packtpub,ou=pub,o=packt"
    ```

3.  Verify that the key-pair was generated correctly:

    ```
    keytool -list -keystore /path/to/keystore -
      storepass BarC0der
    ```

**4.** Create a JAR file for testing purposes, by zipping the contents of the directory:

```
jar cf test.jar .
```

**5.** Sign the JAR file to verify that it works, by running the following command (all on one line):

```
jarsigner  -keypass SayK3ys -storepass BarC0der
 -keystore /path/to/keystore test.jar packtpub
```

**6.** Verify the JAR signature by running the following command:

```
jarsigner -verify test.jar
```

## *What just happened?*

The Java **keytool** program manages keys and certificates for Java programs wanting to sign content. Each entry in the keystore has an alias (to allow for ease of reference if there are many) and an associated key password and store password.

The **keystore** is created at the location given, protected with a store password `BarC0der`. To use any of the keys in the keystore, the store needs to be unlocked with this password first.

To use the private key, we need to give the key password, which is `SayK3ys`. Typically, the key passwords will be different from the store password. If multiple keys are present, it is good practice to have a different password for each one.

The distinguished name (`dname`) is an LDAP identifier for the "owner" of the key. This is represented as a series of `name=value` comma-separated pairs. At the minimum, they need a common name (`cn`) and then some kind of organizational identifier. In this case, the organizational unit (`ou`) is `pub` and the organization (`o`) is `packt`.

Another common way of representing ownership is to use the domain components (`dc`), so an alternative is to use something like `cn=pakcktpub, dc=packtpub, dc=com` where each element in the `packtpub.com` domain is split into its own `dc` element in the distinguished name. Note that the order of elements is significant.

The **jarsigner** tool is used to sign a JAR file and needs access to the store, the store's password, and the key's password. The alias can be supplied, in which case it will use that one—but if it is left out then it will use any matching key in the chain (which assumes that the passwords are unique for keys, as is best practice).

Finally, the jarsigner tool can also be used to verify whether a signature is correct or not using the `-verify` argument.

# Time for action – signing the plug-ins

Integrating signatures into a Tycho build is a matter of adding a plug-in to the build script. In addition, Java properties need to be passed in to provide access to the arguments required by the jarsigner tool.

*1.* Add the plug-in to the parent `pom.xml` file:

```
<plugin>
  <groupId>org.apache.maven.plugins</groupId>
  <artifactId>maven-jarsigner-plugin</artifactId>
  <version>1.2</version>
  <executions>
    <execution>
      <id>sign</id>
      <goals>
        <goal>sign</goal>
      </goals>
    </execution>
  </executions>
</plugin>
```

*2.* Run `mvn package` and an error is shown:

```
[ERROR] Failed to execute goal
   org.apache.maven.plugins:maven-jarsigner-
   plugin:1.2:sign (sign)
   on project com.packtpub.e4.parent:
   The parameters 'alias' for goal
   org.apache.maven.plugins:maven-jarsigner-plugin:1.2:sign
   are missing or invalid -> [Help 1]
```

*3.* Pass in the arguments required by `jarsigner`, which are supplied as Java system properties with a `jarsigner` prefix as follows (all on one line):

```
mvn package
   -Djarsigner.alias=packtpub
   -Djarsigner.keypass=SayK3ys
   -Djarsigner.storepass=BarC0der
   -Djarsigner.keystore=/path/to/keystore
```

*4.* If it is successful, the output should be as follows:

```
[INFO] --- maven-jarsigner-plugin:1.2:sign (sign) @
   com.packtpub.e4.clock.ui ---
[INFO] 1 archive(s) processed
[INFO] --- maven-jarsigner-plugin:1.2:sign (sign) @
   com.packtpub.e4.feature ---
```

```
[INFO] 1 archive(s) processed
[INFO] --- maven-jarsigner-plugin:1.2:sign (sign) @
  com.packtpub.e4.update ---
[INFO] 1 archive(s) processed
```

5. To run the sign step conditionally, a profile can be used. Move the sign plug-in from `build` to a separate top-level element `profiles` in `pom.xml`:

```xml
<profiles>
  <profile>
    <id>sign</id>
    <build>
      <plugins>
        <plugin>
          <groupId>org.apache.maven.plugins</groupId>
          <artifactId>maven-jarsigner-plugin</artifactId>
          ...
        </plugin>
      </plugins>
    </build>
  </profile>
</profiles>
```

6. Now run the build with `mvn package`, and verify that it runs without signing.

7. Run the build with signing enabled by running `mvn package -Psign` to enable the `sign` profile; it should ask for the alias, as before.

8. To automatically enable the sign profile whenever the `jarsigner.alias` property is provided, add the following to the profile:

```xml
<profile>
  <id>sign</id>
  <activation>
    <property>
      <name>jarsigner.alias</name>
    </property>
  </activation>
  <build>
    ...
  </build>
</profile>
```

9. Now, run the build as `mvn package -Djarstore.alias=packtpub ...` to verify that signing runs without needing to specify the `-Psign` argument.

## What just happened?

By adding the `maven-jarsigner-plugin` to the build, Maven signed any JAR file that was built (including the `content.jar` and `artifacts.jar` files, which don't really need to be signed). This is a standard pattern for building any signed Java content in Maven and isn't Tycho or Eclipse-specific.

The parameters to `jarsigner` are specified as system properties. The `-D` flag for Maven, like Java, is used to specify a system property on the command line. The `maven-jarsigner-plugin` reads its properties with a prefix of `jarsigner`, so the alias is passed as `jarsigner.alias` and the keystore as `jarsigner.store`.

Note that the location of the store needs to be specified as a full path, since the plug-in will run with different directories (specifically the "target" directory of the build). Attempting to use a relative path will fail.

## Time for action – serving an update site

Now that the update site has been developed, tested, and automatically built, the final stage is to upload the contents of the update site (under `com.packtpub.e4.update/target/repository`) and make it available on a website or ftp server so that others can install it. If Python 2.7 or higher is installed, run a simple web server as follows:

1. Change to the directory `com.packtpub.e4.update/target/repository`.

2. Run Python's `SimpleHTTPServer`:

   ```
   python -m SimpleHTTPServer 8080
   Serving HTTP on 0.0.0.0 port 8080 ...
   ```

3. Verify the update site by adding `http://localhost:8080/` as a remote update site in Eclipse.

If you don't have Python installed, then some operating systems have a means to serve web-based content already, or another web server can be used. OS X has Web Sharing where files in `~/Sites` are served from; Linux systems typically have Apache configured to allow per-user web sharing in `~/public_html`, and Microsoft Windows has IIS where the default location is `c:\intepub\wwwroot`. See the operating system's documentation for details.

## What just happened?

An update site is simply an HTTP server that serves the contents of the `content.jar` and `artifacts.jar` files, along with their `plugins` and `features` directories.

If Python 2.7 is installed, a module called `SimpleHTTPServer` exists that can be run from the `update/target/repository` directory to allow the update site to be installed from `http://localhost:8080/`. Uploading the contents of the repository to a remote website is left as an exercise for the reader. For Python 3, the command is `python3 -m http.server`.

Finally, once published to a publicly visible website, it's possible to register the location of the update site at the Eclipse marketplace at `http://marketplace.eclipse.org`, so that other Eclipse users can find the update site from the Marketplace client.

## Pop quiz – understanding automated builds and update sites

Q1. What is a GroupId, ArtifactId, and Version (GAV)?

Q2. What are the four types of packaging types needed to build plug-ins, features, products, and update sites?

Q3. How can the version numbers of plug-ins and features be updated in Maven?

Q4. Why and how are JAR files signed?

Q5. How can a simple HTTP server be run in Python?

Q6. Where are Eclipse features typically registered for others to find?

# Summary

This chapter concludes the creation of Eclipse plug-ins and features. Since the final step is building and making it available to others, the steps in this chapter focused on how to automate the builds with Tycho and then take the published update site and make it available for others.

# Pop Quiz Answers

## Chapter 1, Creating Your First Plug-in

### Pop quiz – Eclipse workspaces and plug-ins

| | |
|---|---|
| Q1 | An Eclipse workspace is the location where all the projects are stored. |
| Q2 | The naming convention for Eclipse plug-in projects is to use a reverse domain name prefix, such as com.packtpub. Additionally, UI projects typically have a UI in their name. |
| Q3 | The three key files in an Eclipse plug-in are META-INF/MANIFEST.MF, plugin.xml, and build.properties. |

### Pop quiz – launching Eclipse

| | |
|---|---|
| Q1 | 1. Quit the application by navigating to **File** \| **Exit**.<br>2. Use the **Stop** button from the Debug or Console views. |
| Q2 | Launch configurations are similar to precanned scripts, which can start up an application, set its working directory and environment, and run a class. |
| Q3 | Launch configurations are modified by navigating to the **Run** \| **Run Configurations...** or **Debug** \| **Debug Configurations...** menus. |

## Pop quiz – debugging

| Q1 | Navigate to the **Debug | Debug configurations** or **Debug | Debug As...** menus. |
|----|----|
| Q2 | Set step filters via the preferences menu to avoid certain package names. |
| Q3 | Breakpoints can be conditional, method entry/exit, enabled/disabled, or number of iterations. |
| Q4 | Set a breakpoint and set it after a hit count of 256. |
| Q5 | Use a conditional breakpoint and set `argument==null` as the condition. |
| Q6 | Inspecting an object means opening it up in the viewer so that the values of the object can be interrogated and expanded. |
| Q7 | The expression watches the window that allows arbitrary expressions to be set. |

# Chapter 2, Creating Views with SWT

## Pop quiz – understanding views

| Q1 | In the Eclipse 3.x model, views must be subclasses of `ViewPart`. In the Eclipse 4.x model, parts do not need to have an explicit superclass. |
|----|----|
| Q2 | In the Eclipse 3.x model, views are registered via an `org.eclipse.ui.views` extension point in the `plugin.xml` file. |
| Q3 | The two arguments that most SWT objects have are a `Composite` parent and an integer `flags` field. |
| Q4 | When a widget is disposed, it will have its native resources released to the operating system. Any subsequent actions will throw an SWTException with a `Widget is disposed` message. |
| Q5 | The `Canvas` has many drawing operations; to draw a circle, use `drawArc()` and specify a full orbit. |
| Q6 | To receive drawing events, a `PaintListener` must be created and associated with the control by using the `addPaintListener` method. |
| Q7 | UI updates not on the UI thread will generate an `SWTException` with an `Invalid thread access` error. |
| Q8 | To perform an update on a widget from a non-UI thread, use the `asyncExec()` or `syncExec()` methods from `Display` (3.x) or `UISynchronize` (4.x) to wrap a runnable that will run on the UI thread. |
| Q9 | `SWT.DEFAULT` is used to indicate default options in the flags parameter that is passed to the construction of an SWT widget. |
| Q10 | Create a `RowData` object with the given size, and associate it with each `Widget`. |

## Pop quiz – understanding resources

| Q1 | Resource leaks occur when an SWT resource is acquired from the OS, but then not returned to it via a `dispose()` method prior to the object being garbage collected. |
|----|----|
| Q2 | The different types of resources are `Color`, `Cursor`, `Font`, `GC`, `Image`, `Path`, `Pattern`, `Region`, `TextLayout`, and `Transform`. |
| Q3 | Run the Eclipse instance in tracing mode with `org.eclipse.ui/debug` and `org.eclipse.ui/trace/graphics` set, specified in a debug file and launched with `-debug`. |
| Q4 | Use the displayed data to get the object's arrays, and iterate through them. |
| Q5 | The right way is to register a dispose listener with the view, and the wrong way is to override the dispose method. |

## Pop quiz – understanding widgets

| Q1 | Use the `setFocus()` method to set the focus on a particular widget. |
|----|----|
| Q2 | Invoking `redraw()` will allow the widget to redraw itself. |
| Q3 | The `Combo` can have a `SelectionListener` associated with it. |
| Q4 | The `widgetDefaultSelected()` is what is called when the default value is used, typically an empty value. |

## Pop quiz – using SWT

| Q1 | Use the `Tray` and `TrayItem` widgets. |
|----|----|
| Q2 | The `SWT.NO_TRIM` style means don't draw the edges of the window, or the close/maximize/minimize buttons. |
| Q3 | Use `setAlpha()` to control a widget's transparency, including `Shell`. |
| Q4 | Use `setRegion()` with a path describing the shape. |
| Q5 | A group allows you to group things together with a standard item. |
| Q6 | Most `Composite` use a null `LayoutManager` by default; it's only `Shell` and `Dialog` that have a non-default value. |
| Q7 | Use a `ScrolledComposite`. |

# Chapter 3, Creating JFace Viewers

## Pop quiz – understanding JFace

| | |
|---|---|
| Q1 | `getImage()` for showing an `Image` for an entry, and `getText()` for showing a text value of an entry. |
| Q2 | The `hasChildren()` method is used to determine whether or not an element is shown with an expandable element, and `getChildren()` is used to calculate a list of children. |
| Q3 | An `ImageRegistry` is used to share images between plug-ins or different views in plug-ins, with a means of clearing up the resources when the view is disposed. |
| Q4 | Entries can be styled with an `IStyledLabelProvider`. |

## Pop quiz – understanding sorting and filters

| | |
|---|---|
| Q1 | Specifying a `ViewerComparator` can allow elements to be sorted in a different order other than the default one. |
| Q2 | The `select()` method is used to filter elements, which is originally derived from the Smalltalk terminology. |
| Q3 | Multiple filters can be combined by setting an array of filters, or by writing a filter to combine two or more filters together. |

## Pop quiz – understanding properties

| | |
|---|---|
| Q1 | Add a `DoubleClickListener` to the view. |
| Q2 | The `Dialog` subclasses are used to create a dialog with custom content. |
| Q3 | Property descriptors are used to represent keys for properties on a particular object. |
| Q4 | Properties are displayed on a Properties view by having an object that is adaptable (either directly through the `IAdaptable` interface, or indirectly via the `IAdapterManager`) such that it returns a property source instance, which will return the property descriptors. |

## Pop quiz – understanding tables

| Q1 | To get the headers shown, get the `Table` from the `Viewer`, and use it to call the `setHeaderVisible(true)` method. |
| --- | --- |
| Q2 | `TableViewerColumns` are used to set properties on individual columns and to bind the label provider for the columns. |
| Q3 | Synchronization is achieved by registering the site as a selection provider (so that the selection events are sent to the workbench) and to listen for incoming selection events and adjusting the view as necessary. Care must be taken to avoid recursive selection calls in this case. |

# Chapter 4, Interacting with the User

## Pop quiz – understanding menus

| Q1 | `Action` are the old way of attaching executable content to menu items. A command is an abstract representation of the effect, which does not need to have a UI component. `Action` should not be used as they have been depreciated for some time and may be removed from a future version of the platform. |
| --- | --- |
| Q2 | A command can be associated with a handler to provide a menu item. Handlers are indirection mechanisms that allow the same menu (for example, copy) to take on different commands based on which context they are in. It is also possible to have a default command ID associated with a menu to avoid this indirection. |
| Q3 | The M1 key is an alias for *Cmd* on OS X, and for *Ctrl* on other platforms. When defining standard commands such as copy (M1 + C) it has the expected behavior on both platforms (*Cmd* + C for OS X and *Ctrl* + C for others). |
| Q4 | Keystrokes are bound to commands via a binding, which lists the key(s) necessary to invoke and the associated command/handler. |
| Q5 | A menu's `locationURI` is where it will contribute the entry to the UI. These are specified either as relative to an existing menu's contribution, or to its generic `additions` entry. It is also possible to specify custom ones, which are associated with custom code. |
| Q6 | A pop-up menu is created by using the special `locationURI popup:org.eclipse.ui.popup.any.` Note that the `objectContribution` is not as flexible and may be removed from the platform in future. |

## Pop quiz – understanding jobs

| Q1 | The `syncExec()` method will block and wait for the job to complete before continuing the code. The `asyncExec()` method will continue to run after posting the job but before it completes. |
|----|----|
| Q2 | The `Display` class runs jobs on the SWT UI thread, but the `UISynchronize` instance can be used to run jobs on non-SWT UI threads as well. For E4 applications, the `UISynchronize` is preferred. |
| Q3 | The `UIJob` will always run on the UI thread of the runtime, and direct access of widgets will not run into a thread error. Care should be taken to minimize the amount of time spent in the UI thread so as not to block Eclipse. The job will run on a non-UI thread, and so it does not have access to acquire or modify UI threaded objects. |
| Q4 | The `Status.OK_STATUS` singleton is used to indicate success in general. Although it is possible to instantiate a `Status` object with an `OK` code, doing so only increases the garbage collection as the `Status` result is typically discarded after execution. |
| Q5 | The `CommandService` can be obtained via the general `PlatformUI.getWorkbench().getService()` call, which takes a class and returns an instance of that class. The same technique can be used to acquire a `UISynchronize` instance. |
| Q6 | An icon can be displayed by setting a property on the job with the name `IProgressConstants2.ICON_NAME`. |
| Q7 | `SubMonitor` are generally easier to use at the start of a method, to ensure that the monitor being passed in is correctly partitioned as appropriate for the task in hand. The `SubProgressMonitor` should generally not be used. |
| Q8 | The cancellation should be checked as frequently as possible so that as soon as the user chooses to cancel the `Job`, the `Job` is aborted. |

## Pop quiz – understanding errors

| Q1 | An informational dialog is shown with `MessageDialog.openInformation()` (and also `.openWarning()` and `.openError()` as well). There is also a `MessageDialog.openConfirmation()` call, which returns the value of a yes/no answer to the user. |
|----|----|
| Q2 | The `StatusManager` is an Eclipse 3.x class, which is tightly coupled to the UI. The `StatusReporter` provides the same basic intent, but without a UI association. |
| Q3 | The status reporting is asynchronous by default; although a `BLOCK` option exists to make it synchronous. |
| Q4 | To combine the results of many things into one report, use a `MultiStatus` object. |

# Chapter 5, Storing Preferences and Settings

## Pop quiz – understanding preferences

| Q1 | The default style is FLAT but this can be overridden to provide GRID which provides a better layout for preference pages. |
|---|---|
| Q2 | There are many subclasses of FieldEditor, which include editors for Boolean, Color, Combo, Font, List, RadioGroup, Scale, String, Integer, Directory, and File. |
| Q3 | To provide searching in a preference page, keywords must be registered via the extension point. |
| Q4 | Don't use IMemento for anything. Use anything else including IEclipsePreferences or DialogSettings. |
| Q5 | The MessageDialogWithToggle class provides the "Do not show this message again" support. |

# Chapter 6, Working with Resources

## Pop quiz – understanding resources, builders, and markers

| Q1 | If an editor complains of a missing document provider, install an instance of TextFileDocumentProvider with the setDocumentProvider() method on the editor. |
|---|---|
| Q2 | An IResourceProxy is used by a builder to provide a wrapper around an IResource, but one which doesn't require the construction of an IResource image. |
| Q3 | An IPath is a generic file component that is used to navigate files in folders and projects. |
| Q4 | A nature is a flavor of a project, which enables certain behaviors. It is installed with an update to the project descriptor for the given project. |
| Q5 | Markers are generally created by a builder though they can be created by any plug-in on a resource. There is a specific function on resource which can be used to create a marker of a specific type. |

# Chapter 7, Understanding the Eclipse 4 Model

## Pop quiz – understanding E4

| | |
|---|---|
| Q1 | The application model is stored in the e4xmi file, and provides a way of representing the entire state of the application's UI. It is also persisted on save and then reloaded at startup, so positions of parts and their visibility is persisted. The model is also accessible at runtime via the various M classes such as MApplication and MPart, and can be queried and mutated at runtime. |
| Q2 | Parts are a more generic form of views and editors. Unlike Eclipse 3.x, not everything needs to fit into a View or Editor category; they are all just Parts which contain UI components underneath, and can be organized appropriately. |
| Q3 | Although extension points aren't used for things like commands, keybindings, or views, they are still used to define other extensions to Eclipse such as builders, marker types, and language parsers. The only thing that the Eclipse 4 model moves out of the extension points are the UI-related concepts. Even then, in the Eclipse 4 IDE the backward compatibility mode ensures that all the UI-related extension points are still rendered. For developing IDE plugins, the Eclipse 3.x APIs are likely to be around for the next couple of Eclipse releases. |
| Q4 | The Eclipse 4 parts can be styled with CSS, and the underlying renderer applies the styles on the fly, including if the CSS styles change. This allows theme managers to apply different color combinations in Eclipse 4 in ways which are not possible in Eclipse 3. |
| Q5 | The Eclipse 4 contexts are essentially a series of HashMaps that contain values (objects) associated with keys. Parts can dynamically obtain content from their context, which include all of the injectable services as well as dynamically changing content such as the current selection. A context is implicit in every Part, and inherits up the containment chain, terminating with the OSGi runtime. |

| Q6 | There are several annotations used by Eclipse 4, including: |
|----|----|
| | ◆ `@Inject` (used to provide a general "insert-value-here" instruction to Eclipse) |
| | ◆ `@Optional` (meaning it can be null) |
| | ◆ `@Named` (to pull out a specific named value from the context) |
| | ◆ `@PostConstruct` (called just after the object is created) |
| | ◆ `@PreDestroy` (called just before the object is destroyed) |
| | ◆ `@Preference` (to pull out a specific preference value or the preference store) |
| | ◆ `@EventTopic` and `@UIEventTopic` (for receiving events via the event admin service and on the UI thread respectively) |
| | ◆ `@Persist` and `@PersistState` (for saving data and viewing data) |
| | ◆ `@Execute` and `@CanExecute` (for showing what method to execute, and a `boolean` conditional which has a `boolean` return to indicate if it can run) |
| | ◆ `@Creatable` (to indicate that the object can be instantiated) |
| | ◆ `@GroupUpdate` (to indicate that updates can be deferred). |
| Q7 | Preferences are accessed with the `@Preference` annotation which can inject a value into a field. If updates are needed it should be set as a method parameter, which will be called when the preference value is changed. |
| Q8 | Messages are sent via the `EventBroker`, which is accessible from the injection context. This can have `sendEvent()` or `postEvent()` to send data. On the receiving side, using the `@UIEventTopic` or `@EventTopic` annotations is the easiest way to receive values. As with preferences, if it's set up as a method parameter then the changes will be notified. |
| Q9 | Selection can be accessed using the value from the context with a method injection or value injection using `@Named(IServiceConstants.ACTIVE_SELECTION)`. |

# Chapter 8, Creating Features, Update Sites, Applications, and Products

## Pop quiz – understanding features, applications, and products

| Q1 | The keyword `qualifier` is replaced with a timestamp when plug-ins or features are built. |
| --- | --- |
| Q2 | The files are `artifacts.jar` and `content.jar` as well as one file per feature/plug-in built. |
| Q3 | The older `site.xml` can be used, or a `category.xml` file which is essentially equivalent. |
| Q4 | If a feature requires another, then it must be present in the Eclipse instance in order to install. If a feature includes another, then a copy of that included feature is included in the update site when built. |
| Q5 | An application is a standalone application which can be run in any Eclipse instance when it is installed. A product affects the Eclipse instance as a whole, replacing the launcher, icons, and default application launched. |
| Q6 | An application is a class that implements `IApplication` and has a `start()` method. It is referenced in the `plugin.xml` file and can be invoked by `id` with `-application` on the command line. |

# Chapter 9, Automated Testing of Plug-ins

## Pop quiz – understanding SWTBot

| Q1 | The `JUnit Runner` that is required is `SWTBotJunit4ClassRunner`, which is set up with an annotation `@RunWith(SWTBotJunit4ClassRunner.class)`. |
| --- | --- |
| Q2 | Views are set up by driving the menu to perform the equivalent of navigating to **Window \| Show View \| Other** and driving the value of the dialog. |
| Q3 | To get the text value of a dialog, use `textWithLabel()` to find the text field next to the associated label, and then get or set the text from that. |
| Q4 | A `Matcher` is used to encode a specific condition, such as a view or window with a particular title. It can be handed over to the SWTBot runner to execute in the UI thread and return a value when it is done. |
| Q5 | To get values from the UI, use a `StringResult` (or other equivalent types) and pass that to the `UIThreadRunnable`'s `syncExec()`. It will execute the code, return the value, and then pass that to the calling thread. |
| Q6 | Use the bot's `waitUntil()` or `waitWhile()` methods, which block execution of the test until a certain condition occurs. |

# Chapter 10, Automated Builds with Tycho

## Pop quiz – understanding automated builds and update sites

| | |
|---|---|
| Q1 | The `GroupId`, `ArtifactId`, and `Version` are a set of co-ordinates (collectively known as GAV) that Maven uses to identify dependencies and plugins. The group is a means of associating multiple artifacts together, and the artifact is the individual component name. In OSGi and Eclipse builds, the group is typically the first few segments of the bundle name, and the artifact is the bundle name. The version follows the same syntax as the bundle's version, except that `.qualifier` is replaced with `-SNAPSHOT`. |
| Q2 | The four types are `pom` (used for the parent), `eclipse-plugin` (for plug-ins), `eclipse-feature`, (for features) and `eclipse-repository` (for update sites and products) |
| Q3 | Version numbers can be updated with `mvn org.eclipse.tycho:tycho-versions-plugin:set-version -DnewVersion=version.number`. Note that while `mvn version:set` exists, it will not update the plug-in versions, if chosen. |
| Q4 | JAR files are signed to ensure that the contents of the JAR file have not been modified after creation. Eclipse looks at these JAR files at run-time to ensure that they are not modified, and warns if they are unsigned or if the signatures are invalid. The standard JDK tool, jarsigner is used to sign and verify JAR files; the JDK tool, keytool is used to manipulate keypairs. |
| Q5 | A simple HTTP server can be launched using the command `python -m SimpleHTTPServer`. In Python 3.0, the command is `python3 -m http.server`. |
| Q6 | Eclipse features are typically published in the Eclipse Marketplace at `http://marketplace.eclipse.org`. This includes both open source and commercial plug-ins. |

# Index

## Symbols

.class files  163
@Execute annotation  110
.java source files  163

## A

AbstractUIPlugin  144
actions
  about  111
  creating  109
addColumnTo() method  103
addDoubleClickListener() method  92
addSelectionListener() method  59, 107
automated tests
  JUnit, using for  265
  running  300-302

## B

BooleanFieldEditor  153
bot  270
breakpoint
  about 25
  method breakpoints  25
builder
  building  168-170
builds
  enabling, for plug-ins  305

## C

Central repository  283

## clock.ui plug-in
  creating  36
Clock View
  custom view, drawing  38-40
  second hand, animating  42, 43
  second hand, drawing  41, 42
  UI thread, running  43, 44
ClockWidget
  creating  45, 46
  hours hand, drawing  50
  layouts, using  47-49
  minute hand, drawing  50
  updating  60
collapseAll() method  90
collapseToLevel() method  91
ColorFieldEditor  153
ColorRegistry  81
Combo  57
ComboFieldEditor  148
command parameters
  passing  224, 226
commands
  about  221
  binding, to keys  114, 115
  contributing, to pop-up menus  121-123
  creating  109
  creating, for menu bar  111-113
  menu, wiring to  221-224
Common Build Infrastructure  286
compare() method  88
compilers  168
Composite  49
computeSize() method  46

conditional breakpoints
about 26
setting 26-28
ConsoleViewer 76
ContentViewers
TableViewer 76
TreeViewer 76
context
modifying 115-117
using 206
values, calculating on demands 215, 216
context menus
about 110
adding 110, 111
createContents() method 150
createCustomArea() method 93
createFieldEditors() method 146, 147, 153
createPartControl() method 38, 58, 77, 82, 84, 88, 89, 92, 97, 103, 158
customArea() method 93
custom injectable classes
creating 232
service, creating 232, 233
subtypes, injecting 233, 234

**D**

debugging, Eclipse plug-in
about 18, 20
step filters, using 23
Declarative Services (DS) 299
DelegatingStyledCellLabelProvider 84, 85
DetailedProgressViewer 76
DialogSettings
about 157
using 159, 160
direct menu
creating 226-229
Direct MenuItem 228
DirectoryFieldEditor 153
dispose method 106
dispose() method 50
double-click listener
adding, to tree view 92

**E**

E4 application
creating 190-194
parts, creating 195-199
theme manager, using 205
UI, styling with CSS 200-205
E4 tooling
installing 188, 189
Eclipse
about 7, 163
feature, creating 238
headless application, creating 254-257
JUnit case, writing 266, 267
launching 15, 17
plug-ins, grouping with features 237
product, creating 259-262
Eclipse 4 model
about 187
working with 188
Eclipse Classic
download link 7
Eclipse plug-in
about 7
breakpoint types, using 25
building, Maven used 283
building, with Tycho 286-288
code, updating in debugger 22
conditional breakpoints, using 26
creating 11-13
debugging 18-21
debugging, step filters used 23
exceptional breakpoints, using 28
key files 13
running 15
signing 307-309
Eclipse SDK
download link 7
setting up 8-10
editor
creating 164-166
epf (Eclipse Preference File) 143
error markers 182, 183
errors
reporting 137-140

events
  dealing with 212-214
**exceptional breakpoints**
  about 28
  exceptions, catching 29, 30
  Expressions view 32
  Variables view 31
**execute() method 31**
**expandAll() method 90**
**expandToLevel() method 91**
**expressions**
  reusing 120, 121

## F

**feature**
  about 292
  branding 250-253
  building 292, 293
  creating 238-240
  depending, on other features 249, 250
  exporting 240-242
  installing 242-244
  update site, categorising 244-248
**FieldEditorPreferencePage 145**
**field editors**
  BooleanFieldEditor 153
  ColorFieldEditor 153
  DirectoryFieldEditor 153
  FileFieldEditor 153
  PathEditor 153
  RadioGroupFieldEditor 153
  ScaleFieldEditor 153
**FileFieldEditor 153**
**filtering, JFace 89**
**FontRegistry 81**

## G

**getAdapter() method 99**
**getChildren() method 79**
**getEditableValue() method 96**
**getElements() method 78**
**getFieldEditorParent() method 146**
**getFirstElement() method 95**
**getFont() method 85**

**getImage() method 81**
**getPropertyDescriptors() method 96**
**getPropertyValue() method 96**
**getSelection() method 94**
**getStateLocation() method 145**
**getStyledText() method 84**
**getSystemColor() method 50**
**graphics context (GC) 40**

## H

**Handled MenuItem 228**
**handlers**
  about 221
  creating 109
  creating, for menu bar 111-113
  menu, wiring to command 221-224
**hasChildren() method 78**
**headless application**
  creating 254-257
**hookContextMenu() method 110**
**HTML 188**

## I

**IDoubleClickListener interface 92**
**IEclipsePreferences**
  about 156
  using 156
**ImageRegistry 81**
**IMementos 157**
**incremental builds**
  implementing 174, 175
**installation, E4 tooling 188-190**
**installation, Maven 284, 285**
**IntegerFieldEditor 147**
**IPreferenceStore 144**
**IPropertySource interface 95**
**IPropertySupport interface 99**
**isOdd() method 266**
**isPropertySet() method 96**
**IStructuredSelection class 94, 95**
**IStyledLabelProvider interface**
  adding, to TimeZoneLabelProvider 84
**isValid() method 148**
**ITreeSelection 92, 94**

## J

jarsigner tool  306
Java
  URL  8
JavaFX  188
java.util.Date()  32
JFace
  about  75
  festures  75
  filtering  89
  resource registries  81
  sorting  86
JFaceRegistry  82
job properties
  setting  133-136
jobs  42, 124
JUnit
  about  265
  using, for automated testing  265
JUnit case
  writing, in Eclipse  266, 267
Juno (4.2)
  URL  188

## K

Kepler (4.3)
  URL  188
keybindings
  creating  226-229
key files, Eclipse plug-ins
  build.properties  14
  META-INF/MANIFEST.MF  13
  plugin.xml file  14
keys
  commands, binding to  114, 115
keystore  306
keytool program  306

## L

LocalResourceManager  82
logging
  adding  206, 207
LogService  206

## M

MANIFEST.MF file  37
markers
  using  182
marker type
  registering  184, 185
markup language example
  about  164
  builder, building  168-170
  deletion, handling  175-177
  editor, creating  164-166
  files, iterating through resources  170-172
  incremental builds, implementing  174, 175
  markup parser, writing  166, 167
  resources, creating  173, 174
markup parser
  writing  166, 167
Maven
  about  283
  installing  284, 285
  used, for building Eclipse plug-ins  283
maven quickstart plugin  285
memento
  adding, for Time Zone View  158
menu
  wiring, to command  221-224
menu items
  disabling  118-120
  enabling  118-120
MessageDialogWithToggle  160
method breakpoints  25
minimark  164

## N

nature
  creating  178-181
  using  178
New Class wizard
  dividing  280
NullPointerException  30
null progress monitors
  using  131-133

## O

openInformation() method 31
operations
  running, in background 125, 126
OSGi 187
OSGi services
  about 206
  dealing with, events 212-214
  logging, adding 206, 207
  selection service, obtaining 209-211
  window, obtaining 208, 209

## P

paintControl() method 40, 41, 45, 51, 58
parent project
  creating 289-291
parts
  about 195
  creating 195-199
PathEditor 153
performApply() method 150
performOk() method 150
plug-in. *See* Eclipse plug-in
Plug-in Development Environment (PDE) 8
plug-ins development 7
plug-in test
  writing 267, 268
plug-in wizard
  MANIFEST.MF 37
  plugin.xml file 38
plugin.xml file 38, 109
POJOs (Plain Old Java Objects) 188
pom.xml file 283
pop-menus
  command, contributing to 121-123
pop-up menu
  about 229
  creating 229-231
preferences
  about 143
  error messages, creating 147
  field editors, using 153, 154
  grid, using 150
  IEclipsePreferences, using 156, 157
  keywords, adding 154

list, selecting from 148
  preference page, creating 145, 146
  preferences page, placing 151
  using 217, 218
  value, persisting 144
  warning, creating 147
product
  about 295
  building 295-299
  creating 259, 261
  creating, based on features 263
progress
  about 124
  reporting, for tasks 127, 128
progress monitor
  dealing with cancellations 128, 129
project
  about 170
  version number, modifying 303-305
public static method 68

## R

RadioGroupFieldEditor 153
removeSelectionListener() method 107
resource management, SWT
  about 50
  colorful option, adding 51
  leak, plugging 54-56
  leak, searching 52, 54
resource registries
  ColorRegistry 81
  FontRegistry 81
  ImageRegistry 81
resources
  about 163
  creating 173, 174
  files, iterating through 170-172
  folders, iterating through 170-172
  using 163
reusable widget
  creating 45
reveal() method 91, 107

## S

saveState() method 158
selectionChanged() method 105

selectionListener  106
select() method  89
self-signed certificate
  creating  305, 306
semantic versioning  304
services
  using  206
setFocus() method  38
  using  58
setOffset() method  59
setSelection() method  107
setValue() method  144
sorting, JFace
  about  87
  view-specific sorting  87
SourceViewer  76
step filtering
  setting up  23, 24
submonitors
  using  131-133
subprogress monitors
  using  130, 131
subtasks
  about  129
  using  130, 131
SWT
  about  35
  resources, managing  50
  reusable widget, creating  45
  user interaction  56
  view, creating  36
SWTBot
  about  265, 268, 270
  installing  268
  used, for user interface testing  268
  welcome screen, hiding  273
  working with  273
  working with menus  271, 272
SWTBot runtime errors
  avoiding  274
SWTBot test
  writing  269-271
SWT rendering tool  188
SWT tools update site
  referenec link  56
SWT widgets
  about  60

groups and tab folders  66-71
items, adding to tray  60, 61
modal window, creating  64
shell effects  64, 65
user, responding to  62, 63
syncExec() method  43

T

TableTreeViewer
  creating  100
  selection, syncing  104-106
  time zones, viewing in tables  100
TableViewer
  about  76
  creating  76-79
  images, adding for regions  86
  images, using  81-83
  label providers, styling  84, 85
target platform  289
test case
  about  265
  writing, in Eclipse  266
testOdd() method  266
testPlatform() method  267
test suites  265
TextViewer  76
theme manager
  using  205
TimeZoneDisplayNameColumn  103
TimeZoneIDColumn class  103
TimeZoneLabelProvider  81
time zones
  displaying, in tables  100-103
Time Zone Table View  100
Time Zone View
  memento, adding  158, 159
TimeZoneViewerComparator  88
toolbars
  using  124
tools bridge
  using  234
toString() method  78, 87
TreeViewer
  about  76
  double-click listener, adding  92-95
  items, filtering  89, 91

items, sorting  87, 88
properties, displaying  95-99
**Tycho**
about  283, 286
plug-in, building  286-288
**tycho-surefire-plugin  302**

# U

**UI**
conditions, using  278, 279
interacting with  277
values, obtaining from  277, 278
**UI, for E4 application**
interacting with  219, 220
styling, with CSS  200-205
**UI job**
using  126
**update site**
about  293
building  293, 294
serving  309
signing  305
**user interactions, SWT**
about  56
focus, switching  57
input, responding to  58, 59
**user interface testing**
SWTBot used  268

**user preference  143**

# V

**values**
obtaining, from UI  277, 278
**view**
creating  36, 37
custom view, drawing  38
displaying  275
interrogating  276
working with  274
**viewByTitle() method  275**
**ViewerFilter class  89**
**viewers**
ContentViewers  76
**view menu**
about  229
creating  229-232
using  124

# W

**warning markers  182**
**window  208**
**workspace**
about  163
using  163

## Thank you for buying
## Eclipse 4 Plug-in Development by Example Beginner's Guide

## About Packt Publishing

Packt, pronounced 'packed', published its first book "*Mastering phpMyAdmin for Effective MySQL Management*" in April 2004 and subsequently continued to specialize in publishing highly focused books on specific technologies and solutions.

Our books and publications share the experiences of your fellow IT professionals in adapting and customizing today's systems, applications, and frameworks. Our solution based books give you the knowledge and power to customize the software and technologies you're using to get the job done. Packt books are more specific and less general than the IT books you have seen in the past. Our unique business model allows us to bring you more focused information, giving you more of what you need to know, and less of what you don't.

Packt is a modern, yet unique publishing company, which focuses on producing quality, cutting-edge books for communities of developers, administrators, and newbies alike. For more information, please visit our website: www.packtpub.com.

## About Packt Open Source

In 2010, Packt launched two new brands, Packt Open Source and Packt Enterprise, in order to continue its focus on specialization. This book is part of the Packt Open Source brand, home to books published on software built around Open Source licences, and offering information to anybody from advanced developers to budding web designers. The Open Source brand also runs Packt's Open Source Royalty Scheme, by which Packt gives a royalty to each Open Source project about whose software a book is sold.

## Writing for Packt

We welcome all inquiries from people who are interested in authoring. Book proposals should be sent to author@packtpub.com. If your book idea is still at an early stage and you would like to discuss it first before writing a formal book proposal, contact us; one of our commissioning editors will get in touch with you.

We're not just looking for published authors; if you have strong technical skills but no writing experience, our experienced editors can help you develop a writing career, or simply get some additional reward for your expertise.

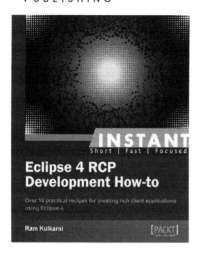

## Instant Eclipse 4 RCP Development How-to [Instant]

ISBN: 978-1-78216-952-9          Paperback: 68 pages

Over 10 practical recipes for creating rich client applications using Eclipse 4

1. Learn something new in an Instant! A short, fast, focused guide delivering immediate results

2. Produce rich client standalone applications using Eclipse 4

3. Create an application user interface using an application model

4. Customize and package your applications for multiple target platforms

## Java EE Development with Eclipse

ISBN: 978-1-78216-096-0          Paperback: 426 pages

Develop Java EE applications with Eclipse and commonly used technologies and frameworks

1. Each chapter includes an end-to-end sample application

2. Develop applications with some of the commonly used technologies using the project facets in Eclipse 3.7

3. Clear explanations enriched with the necessary screenshots

Please check **www.PacktPub.com** for information on our titles

PUBLISHING

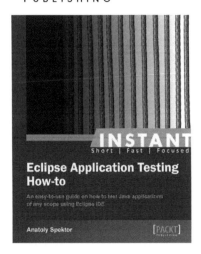

## Instant Eclipse Application Testing How-to [Instant]

ISBN: 978-1-78216-324-4          Paperback: 62 pages

An easy-to-use guide on how to test Java applications of any scope using Eclipse IDE

1. Learn something new in an Instant! A short, fast, focused guide delivering immediate results

2. Learn how to install Eclipse and Java for any platform

3. Get to grips with how to efficiently navigate in the Eclipse environment using shortcuts

4. Create your own Java sample app and learn how to test and debug it using a rich set of Eclipse debugging tools

## Getting Started with Eclipse Juno

ISBN: 978-1-78216-094-6          Paperback: 277 pages

A friendly and engaging tutorial on Eclipse Juno IDE that will help you to get up to speed with Eclipse

1. Learn subjects ranging from basic Java development to web app development, version control, and GUI programming

2. Discover how to use Eclipse to develop, test, and debug basic desktop Java applications proficiently

3. Integrate JUnit 4, the most widely used unit testing framework, into Eclipse

4. Get to grips with how Eclipse can be used to develop web-based Java applications that employ Java Servlets and JavaServer Pages

Please check **www.PacktPub.com** for information on our titles